ONE MAN'S WEST

By DAVID LAVENDER

Line Drawings by WILLIAM ARTHUR SMITH

UNIVERSITY OF NEBRASK

Lincoln and London

To BROOKIE
Who appears in these pages
under her given name
Martha

Library of Congress Cataloging in Publication Data

Lavender, David Sievert, 1910–
    One man's West.
    Reprint of the ed. published by Doubleday, Garden
City, N.Y.
    1. Lavender, David Sievert, 1910–   2. Ranch
life—Colorado.   3. Cowboys—Colorado—Biography.
4. Colorado—Biography. I. Title.
[F781.L3 1977]   978.8 [B]   76–45450
ISBN 0–8032–0908–8
ISBN 0–8032–5855–0 pbk.

The Bison Book edition is reproduced from the third (1964) edition, published by Doubleday & Company, Inc., by arrangement with the author.

Manufactured in the United States of America

CONTENTS

A NOTE TO THE THIRD EDITION

THIS BOOK, PUBLISHED FIRST IN 1943, WAS written in part out of a craving to stake out a familiar refuge amid universal and, to the writer, unexpected disasters. From that standpoint the account is unabashedly nostalgic, a deliberate searching backwards.

When a second edition was published in 1956, the author was still young enough that although he had originally concentrated on a region's past, he nevertheless wanted to appear abreast of its present. Accordingly he adapted a few sentences in the body of the text to keep them from sounding anachronistic and added a chapter about the countryside's zany rush for uranium, as it appeared to him to be.

This second edition was promptly dated. The uranium fever cooled. Other focuses of energy developed. Paved roads and monstrous, slat-sided trucks did away with the slow foot migrations of livestock, once so characteristic a part of the country's rhythms. A new national park embraced the canyoned desolation of Al Scorup's cattle ranch. Tourism, with its goat-like jeeps, its dude ranches, resort hotels, and ski tows, corroded the stubborn individualism of the lonely mountain towns.

The changes in the author were equally pronounced. For one thing, twenty years of historical research finally persuaded him to be more careful about embalming in print those easy evaluations and folk-tale "facts" that once had seemed to him as incontrovertible as sunrises. The itchings caused by these altered judgments and adjusted data clamor, now that a third edition looms, for more bits of "updating," more trivial "correcting." I have resisted. After all, my predecessor of 1943 was not writing history. He was not writing autobiography either, although some persons persist in calling it that. Rather, he was using the first-person pronoun to help bring immediacy to a people and a land that suddenly had become, to him, worth holding onto. Because he was not far removed from them in 1943 he still retained, it seems to me now, some of that unpremeditated vividness of impression which is a more viable part of youth than is a honed carefulness.

Within that frame of reference, revisions twenty-one years afterwards, however small or timely or even exact they might be appear irrelevant. My editorial tamperings with my predecessor's copy end, therefore, with the additions that were made in 1956, when the rush of change across the mountains still seemed more a matter of wonder than an irrevocable canceling of the past.

Ojai, California   DAVID LAVENDER
November 6, 1964

Part One

THE MOUNTAINS

1 WINTER TRAIL

CAME A DAY WHEN I WANTED TO
get married and needed a stake. To my youthful optimism, geared
as it was to the "thirty-a-month-and-found" wages paid cowboys,
the vast affluence of five dollars a day in the gold mines seemed to
offer the quickest solution.

I got on with the company which was leasing the workings of
the old Camp Bird mine above Ouray, Colorado, quite simply.
My stepfather, a cattle rancher in near-by San Miguel and Montrose counties, knew the superintendent. I myself knew no miners
and nothing about mining.

On a bitter-cold January day I landed in Ouray. It was a
gloomy little town, with down-at-the-heel brick buildings lining
the main street, an astonishing rococo hotel, and rows of widely
spaced, once-handsome frame houses radiating out from the
remnants of the business district. Over it all hung the ineffable
sadness of departed wealth. Its setting, however, is superlative;
I think no town in America can boast of finer.

The village lies in the bottom of an enormous rock amphi-
theater. The best way to see it is to stretch out flat on your back.
There is only one direction in Ouray—up. The sheer water-
courses, the scars cut by snowslides, the vaulting ridges—each
soaring line lifts your eye irresistibly to the crenelated peaks that

3

ring you round. Everywhere are bold smears of color. Bluish lime-stone low down, red and orange stratas of sandstone above them, and higher still the grays, browns, and intermediate shades of granite, porphyry and rhyolite. Threading all this are occasional streaks of bright yellow dirt.

Up these brilliant flanks crawl the forests, close-crowded wher-ever they can find a foothold. The best places are risky enough. Scarcely a stand of timber can be seen that hasn't been mauled by avalanches. In winter the aspens tremble bare and silvery; the pines are green, and the higher spruce appear almost black against the dazzling snow. You look at all this and the village seems to shrink and shrink until it is a toy town, and you no longer notice its patheticness.

There was only one way to get to the Camp Bird—ride horse-back nine miles, climbing in that distance some four thousand feet. I went to the livery stable and rented a weary, winter-shaggy bay pony. As I jogged out of the barn I noticed, on a hill back of the dingy, narrow-gauge railroad siding, a flock of mountain sheep feeding on hay the Forest Service had scattered out for them.

The wagon road settles right down to business. The first thing it presents is a little wooden bridge you could almost jump across. This bridge spans a chasm about a hundred feet deep, full of thunder and mist occasioned by Canyon Creek as it rushes out of the mountains to join the other streams around Ouray and form the Uncompahgre River. Canyon Creek should be a beautiful cascade but isn't. It has been fouled by milltailings to a thick, slate-gray sludge.

No matter how many times a horse has crossed this bridge, he always shies playfully at the hollow sound his hoofs make on the wooden planks. Mine added an extra flourish by way of a skid in the icy ruts, and all at once I found myself suspended by the saddle horn, so to speak, above that uninviting gulch. While I was busy reviewing my past the horse paused reflectively at the brink, seemed to decide that killing me wasn't worth the effort, and ambled on as though nothing had happened. Never again, kick and swear as I might, was I able to lift him out of a phlegmatic walk.

For six miles or so the road struggles up a massive, timber-filled, rock-ribbed gorge, sometimes skirting the bank of the stream, sometimes soaring far above it, hanging over breathless drops or huddled against black cliffs. All along the way the growth on the hillside shows the cruel cuts left by avalanches. I seem to be mentioning these marks rather frequently, but they are frequently in the mind of anyone who travels through the San Juan Mountains during winter. The least you can expect from snowslides in the course of a season is that they will uproot a certain number of power poles, flatten a few buildings, demolish bridges or block roads—accomplishing a good deal of this in spite of misses, for the concussion they create is terrifically capable of reaching beyond the avalanche itself. Every now and then they catch a man or two, a pack train or an ore wagon.

The slides generally run the same courses. They are known and named, and roads or trails avoid the danger spots wherever possible. It is not always possible, however. As I crept along on my charger I could see ahead of me, where the canyon narrowed, one of the most infamous runs of all. It is known as the Water Hole Slide and is not only forceful but treacherous as well. According to legend, it once attacked a pack train of twenty-six mules and three men. It roared down the canyon side, picked off the lead rider and the first five animals. The other two men and twenty-one mules escaped—temporarily. As if angered at botching the job, the slide continued a short distance *up* the opposite slope, carried by its momentum, then paused, rounded a knob of rock, and plunged back down. This time it made its victory a hundred per cent complete.

It occurred to me that I ought to put the spot behind me with dispatch. I belabored my horse as well as I could, considering that

I was wearing heavy, spurless overshoes—kicking his ribs with my padded heels was something like beating a drum with a pompon, and the bridle reins were too short to be effective. By this time the wretched animal was groaning in a most frightful manner and seemed scarcely able to place one foot in front of the other. Indeed, I had been alarmed about his condition until I noticed how he brightened when he spied one of the wisps of hay that here and there had fallen from the freight sleighs preceding us. He would put on a short spurt for these, devour them, and then sink back into somnambulism.

I deemed it only fair that he should put on at least one spurt for my sake. The slide course was right above us, and no time was to be wasted. I worked enormously, legs flying and elbows flapping. Had I expended equal energy afoot, I would have gotten across in seconds. But the horse took minutes—hours, it seemed. I know I bruised him sorely, but he quickened his creep not one jot. And of course he was right. An avalanche is like lightning; it strikes when it strikes, and growing excited about it doesn't alter matters a bit. We passed through without so much as a breath of wind to mar our stately progress. As a matter of fact, the Water Hole ran only once that winter and then harmlessly at night. Also, slides are not apt to occur until spring, when the heavy falls of snow which come after January are beginning to settle under the warming weather. That January, however, I did not know all this, and I sweat just as much as if eternity itself had hung over me by a thread.

Above the Water Hole the canyon rounds out into a magnificent basin walled by enormous cliffs and eternally green with sighing spruce. Squarely in the middle of it sit the mill buildings of the old Camp Bird. Through all these years they have been kept neat and fresh. Like most gold mills, they were constructed high on one end and slope steeply downward, so that the ore which entered the top would not have to be lifted as it went through the reduction process. There were two mills at the Camp

Bird, huge wooden structures painted dark red. Sprinkled among the trees around them are the white, gabled, green-roofed houses used by the early officials—regular mansions, some of them. The sight of this red-and-white settlement dreaming against its lovely backdrop of snow and forest and cliff is completely romantic. When my wife first saw it, a year or two later, she exclaimed, "Why, it looks like Santa Claus's town!"

In the old days others, too, must have thought that Santa Claus was around. Tom Walsh, who discovered the Camp Bird in 1896, took something like $2,500,000 out of it, then sold it for another $5,100,000 and some stock to the Camp Bird, Ltd., an English concern. Walsh then turned to mining high society. He was decorated by kings, consorted with presidents, and when he died left his daughter, Evalyn Walsh McLean, enough pocket change to buy, among other things, the Hope diamond with which she so thoroughly insulted the Russians by touring the Moscow night clubs with it in 1934. Meanwhile the Camp Bird, Ltd. reaped nicely in its turn—until 1916, when Santa Claus all at once moved on to a new stand. Reluctantly the company shut down.

The same situation prevailed at many of the large gold properties of Colorado. The mines finished working out the best ore bodies about the time that labor and material costs began an upward spiral during the early decades of the century. They could not raise the retail price of their commodity to meet these factors, for the value of gold is fixed by law. So they languished, as gold mines do during periods of national prosperity.

Then along came the depression of the '30s. Down went production costs again. Meanwhile, more efficient methods of ore reduction had been developed, and it was possible to work ground the early companies had ignored. Men began to paw over the old bones. The lease company for whom I was about to work reopened the Camp Bird. But not in its former glory. Those beautiful basin mills stayed silent. Ore had originally been brought down to them from the mine three miles farther up the mountain via an aerial tramway, but this had fallen into ruin and would have cost an enormous sum to rebuild. Accordingly, the lease company constructed a new little mill right at the mouth of the mine tunnels, 11,300 feet above sea level. When I hove in sight of the basin the old town was a ghost town. No one remained but a representative of the Camp Bird, Ltd., two or three watchmen, and a couple of packers who handled freight to the mine.

A new stir was sweeping the countryside, however. President Roosevelt, seeking paper profits, had suddenly pegged the price of gold from $20.67 per ounce to nearly $36. He later "histed" the value of silver, which in western Colorado usually occurs in conjunction with gold.

Whatever this may have been as economic sleight of hand, it was certainly a shot in the arm to the pick-and-shovel boys. The rush to the hills took on almost the color of a stampede. A pale color, however. Civic virtue had long since raised her head; the unrestrained boisterousness of the frontier days had to lower its voice and hide in the back room.

Back rooms remind me of a story which illustrates the severe strain that Prohibition placed on the ingenuity of the local residents. One summer shortly before Repeal a couple of cowboys decided to fetch from Ouray the wherewithal to relieve a monotonous stretch of fence building. Unfortunately a cloudburst interfered by piling slides of mud and brush across their road. Nothing dismayed—the storm was soon over and the sun shining again—the pair left their automobile and walked on to town, entered a cigar store, and made their order.

"To take out?" the tobacconist inquired.

"We're sure not going to set here and *look* at it!"

"I'm sorry, boys. I can't do it."

Anger, disbelief, and bewilderment. "Sa-ay, what are you trying to hand us?"

The merchant explained. The town was full of enforcement officers bent on damming the flow of liquor over the mountains to

Silverton, where an annual celebration known as Sheepman's Day was in progress. Of all the dispensaries in town this one alone had escaped the general roundup, and that only by the narrowest of margins. The bartender knew the cowboys and sympathized with them. He was even willing to risk serving them in his back room. But to all suggestions of smuggling a bottle outside into those dangerous streets he returned a flat and final no.

The situation demanded thought. The cowboys went outside, brows knit. After a time they reappeared, sauntered into the back room, and ordered a bottle. As soon as the saloonkeeper disappeared they opened an alley window and received from a grocer's boy, just then passing, a large watermelon. From the rind of this they pried a triangular plug and revealed a cavity which they had previously scooped out of the meat with a long-handled spoon. They poured the whisky into this, recapped the melon, and, at an all's clear signal from the grocer's boy, handed it back through the window. They next returned the empty bottle to the barkeep. He was somewhat astonished by this evidence of speed and capacity, but as he detected no suspicious bulges on their persons, he allowed them to depart. They collected their "water"-melon and hied themselves out of town.

The afternoon was hot and the melon was heavy. They reached the first of the mud slides barring the road, climbed laboriously to its top, and sat down to rest. Obviously the melon needed lightening. Now this pair had lived robust, outdoor lives; their constitutions had withstood all manner of assaults. However, Prohibition corn whisky mixed with warm watermelon juice produced results beyond anything either had experienced. The next morning when a road crew arrived to clear away the slide they found our heroes mingled with the mud and rocks, dead to the world. The cause of the trouble was a mystery. No lethal weapons were visible—nothing but a watermelon which one of the sleepers clutched lovingly to his bosom.

On arriving at the old mill in the basin, I discovered that the superintendent had come down from the mine and was in the office talking over royalties or weather or something that took an interminable time with the representative of the Camp Bird, Ltd. I waited for him out on the loading platform of the freight house. The sun was brilliant but ineffectual. My teeth rattled and my joints grew so stiff that I could scarcely control my pacing back and forth on the littered dock, redolent with its odors of hay, mules, old leather, and crated foodstuffs. Every now and then I stumbled up to my horse and hugged him close, not because I was overcome by my regard for him, but because he was faintly warm.

About this time I heard a bell tinkling in the trees. A horse snuffed, and out of the timber above the old mill came a pack train, a rider in front and sixteen mules strung out single file behind, the halter of each tied by a short rope to the packsaddle of his predecessor. The tiniest mule of all brought up the rear, and it was to his neck that the bell was attached. If any of the string got loose and dropped back the packer would know it by the sound—or lack of sound—from the bell. You would think he could discover this by simply glancing from time to time over his shoulder. But often the snow falls so thickly that it is impossible to see the length of sixteen mules, and then that silvery *jing-a-ling* is the only system of communication between the two ends of the train.

Up to the dock they swung, brisk and businesslike. The packer dismounted. He looked almost as round as a ball, due to his heavy sheepskin coat and woolly Angora chaps. His eyes were invisible behind dark snow glasses. To keep his ears warm he wore a blue bandanna tied over his head, like a European peasant woman, and on top of this was jammed a wide-brimmed black hat, sparkling with frost rime. As further protection against the weather he had grown a thick, short beard, and out of this his nose stuck red as a cherry and adorned with a glittering pendant of moisture

that danced and jiggled as he moved but never fell. Taken altogether, he was an extraordinary sight, and I had a moment of
wondering whether he, or any of the rest of this fantastic place,
was actually real.

"Howdy!" he said with great cheerfulness.

"Howdy," I replied.

The conversation then languished. He fell to unpacking the
mules. Each was loaded with four or five smallish canvas sacks
closed at the top with twisted wire—two sacks in a cradle of ropes
on each side of the packsaddle and, in the case of the larger mules,
another one in the forks. The packer grunted as he heaved them
onto the dock, and when I lifted one I discovered why. They
weighed eighty or ninety pounds apiece and were full of a gritty,
dark gray sand called concentrates. Only the coarser particles of
free gold could be extracted from the ore by the lease company's
mill. The finest stuff and the various gold, silver, lead, and zinc
compounds were sent through a complicated "floatation" process
that got rid of as much waste material as possible. The richly
laden sand which remained was then sacked and sent to a smelter
of final reduction. But it certainly did not look rich—dingy,
smelly, and with no apparent luster whatsoever.

The pack train now at the dock and another one which I could
hear coming through the trees made two trips a day from the old
mill to the mine three miles up the mountain for this unattractive
product. On the upward journey they carried lumber, steel, machinery, food, coal, hay, chemicals, dynamite, wire—anything
that a gang of men engaged in tearing the guts out of a mountain
might conceivably need.

On the six-mile trip from Ouray to the basin mill the goods
were transported in freight sleighs. A dismal trip it was, too, as I
discovered on a haul or two I made with them, the runners complaining with the cold and the tug chains jangling as the six big
draft horses set their shoulders into the collars. The horses could
pull only a short distance up those steep grades at a time. Then

they had to stop and rest. You couldn't keep warm up on the high seat, your hands full of stiff leather reins and your whole body exposed to every frigid blast that screamed through the canyon. The freighters devised various kinds of portable heat units to carry with them: rocks well baked in an oven and placed at the start in straw at their feet, candles burning in old kerosene tins, lanterns lighted under lap robes, and so on. When these things failed the men would halt their teams, get out and build a fire beside the road. There was one waspish individual, however, the oldest of the lot, who would have none of this, no hot rocks, no candles, no comfort of any sort. When his fellow teamsters dismounted he refused to leave his seat. Stubbornly he sat there above them, blue with cold and shaking so he could not roll even a cigarette for solace. Each and every trip, as the rosy glow of warmth began to steal over his comrades, he would thunder down his invariable contempt:

"Why don't you stand up and freeze like *men?*"

The mule packers had no choice but to freeze like men. True, their journey was only half as long as the freighters', and their mules moved more briskly than sleds. But they could carry no hot rocks; their animals would not stand by while they built a fire. Yet only once or twice that winter, during the most fiendish of the timber-line blizzards, did they fail to make their twice-daily trip. Again and again I have seen them stagger into the mine boardinghouse, frosted white as snowmen, their clothes frozen so hard they had to walk stiff-legged, crackling like fresh wrapping paper at every move. They'd gulp down a cup of coffee, thaw out their garments, and then plunge back again.

Nothing stumped them. If some piece of freight came along which they couldn't get on one mule's back—and it had to be singularly heavy and ill-shaped to occasion this—they would sling it on poles hung between two mules. Unusually recalcitrant pieces of machinery were lashed to a flat sled and pulled up the narrow, twisting trail by a whole string of mules in tandem. In ingenuity, brawn, daring, and plain brute courage, in all the tricks of dealing with evil nature and rebellious livestock, the mountain packers have no peers. Their race is fading from the earth; perhaps their spirit has been inherited by the newer race of truck drivers. But somehow it seems nice to know that in isolated spots throughout the mining district a few of them are still on the job with the same old color and skill and incredible profanity.

While I was marveling at the first packer the second one hove up to the dock. From all one could see of him, down to the very drop on his nose, he was an exact twin of his companion. He said "Howdy" to me just as the other had done and flew to unloading his string with the same swift precision. The maze of pack ropes fell apart as if by magic at their touch; the air was literally full of flying sacks. As fast as one mule was unloaded the packer would cry at his horse, "Hup, Jake!" or, "Hup, Boston!"—I can't imagine why a horse should be named Boston—and the riderless animal would move forward the precise number of steps needed to bring the next mule into position. Jake and Boston also knew when the last mule was unpacked. Without a word being spoken to them they led their strings around the freight house, down a side road to a barn temptingly full of hay, past it and into the proper corral, a different one for each group. I half expected to see them unsaddle and curry the mules as well.

The packers sat down on the pile of sacks, dug out their pipes, fired up, and regarded me with mild curiosity. I felt I should say something.

"Much snow up above?" I asked. For some reason this seemed a desirable piece of information.

"Why, I don't know," one of them replied. "I quit noticin' after the first twelve inches. Ten feet or twenty feet, it's all the same. You can't see nothin' but the top of it, nohow."

His companion nodded and spit, sealing the observation. Silence reigned.

I made another effort. "Cold, isn't it?"

They considered the matter. Then the first one—apparently he was the spokesman—drawled, "I wouldn't say so. Now when it gets so that a man rides along whistlin' to himself and the whistle don't make any noise on account of freezin' solid and fallin' to the ground as fast as it comes out, then it *is* cold. You'll notice it in the spring," he said. "The woods sound like a steam calliope loose and the stops tied down—all them frozen whistles thawin' out an' poppin' off. It spooks the mules considerable the first few days. For a fact," he said, solemn as an owl.

I was unutterably chagrined, recognizing the time-hallowed method of welcoming greenhorns. Now I had been born in Telluride, just across the divide, and had been brought up on a ranch not more than sixty miles away as the crow flies, and, although I knew little about mining, I most certainly did not consider myself a greenhorn. I groped for some of the tall yarns with which we greeted tenderfeet to the ranch, but they would not come. I had been fairly caught, and all I could manage was a feeble smile.

Further embarrassment was warded off by the appearance of the superintendent. The packers said "Howdy" to him and disappeared toward the corrals to care for their stock. The superintendent and I boarded our horses and headed for the mine. He was a tall, stooped man, so extremely thin and pale that I felt he had no business up here in these rigorous climes. I was wasting my sympathy, however. Sixteen hours a day, every day of the week, he was in and out of all the impossible corners of that mine, wrestling kinks out of the mill, bent over a drafting board, or riding back and forth over that dangerous trail. If ever his patience was taxed or his composure ruffled by the continual crises which confronted him, I never detected it.

From the old mill, situated at about 9500 feet elevation, the trail has to climb to 11,300 feet in three miles. It is a single-file horse trail, full of dizzy switchbacks. In wintertime the continual passage of the mules keeps a narrow ribbon of snow packed hard and firm, but to either side of this path is a soft, almost bottomless white morass. If my memory serves me right, it snowed thirty-three feet the winter I was at the mine. Of course this didn't all stay "on the level" at once, but it was quite deep enough—toward spring we were able to step out of the window of our third-floor room at the boardinghouse onto drifts that had banked against the rear side of the building—and in places where the wind piled it up the snow reached depths of fifty or more feet. Obviously a blaze placed low down on a tree trunk was soon covered and of no help in locating the trail during a blizzard. So the packers marked their route by tying rags to the tips of branches which at the time were within arm's reach. When the snow melted off in the summer the rags were left suspended halfway up the tree. I have seen tourists marveling at these bits of colored cloth fluttering high overhead, wondering how on earth they ever got there and why. Well, the mystery is hereby laid bare. I suppose I shouldn't do it. The stories the packers tell about jays carefully placing the rags so they can find their way home after a hard night have infinitely more flavor.

We rounded a gaunt shoulder of rock, and the mine was in front of us. Desolation personified. Looming over everything was the boardinghouse, a tremendous three-story structure of tongue-and-groove boards, painted a dirty yellow. It had been built during the heyday of the Camp Bird to house three hundred workers; now forty-odd men and two women were living in one corner of it, their occupancy fiercely contested by hordes of rats. A dozen snow-powdered spruce stood in front of the storm doors. To the left the rusty mill grumbled and clanked with its endless labors. Back of the workings was another cluster of trees. Then blankness. Up to the peaks, 13,000 feet high, the snow rolled in dead-white waves, broken here and there by dead-gray cliffs.

We dismounted. The horses we simply turned loose. They were self-returning taxis, such as are used throughout the mining districts, and would go straight home. As I tied the bridle reins

over the saddle horn the wind moaned and the snow blew with a
dry whisper over the crusted surface of the drifts. Suddenly I
loved that horse. He was an unabashed shirker, devoid of ambition, character, or intelligence. But in all that bleak waste he was
the only familiar thing.

He had no intention of staying familiar. Away he went for
home at a keen trot. I felt as though my last link with the world
had gone with him.

II   BOARDING AT TIMBER LINE

AT THE MINE I FOUND I LACKED A few necessities and was told that I could obtain them from a store located on the second floor of the boardinghouse. This store was run by a mill hand named Hughie and had, I am sure, no counterpart on the face of the earth.

Hughie offered for sale such items as chewing gum, candy bars, magazines, tobacco in all its forms, woolen trousers, overalls, carbide lamps and lanterns, helmets, stacks upon stacks of gloves, Mackinaws, yellow slickers, long underwear, rubber boots, picture frames, soap, hairbrushes, cosmetics and trash jewelry (to send to your sweetheart), wrist watches, writing paper, pens, pencils, various colored inks and postage stamps. All this and more— enough to supply forty men for a year—was jammed into a room twelve feet by ten, which also contained Hughie's bed, chest of drawers, and bookkeeping desk. Bales of stuff hung from the ceiling by ropes, was strung out on the walls, heaped in corners, stowed under, on, and in the furniture, and piled in tottering mountains about the floor.

In the midst of this confusion stood Hughie, suffused with gentle pride. His head was round, his nose so flat that it was scarcely a nose at all but merely a slight swelling punctured by two holes. A mill hand can't keep clean, no matter how hard he tries, and Hughie's efforts were open to suspicion. Rock dust and gray concentrates were visible in his hairy ears and in wrinkles of his neck. His apparel exuded the odors of the pine oil and sulphur fumes among which he worked. His teeth were encased in snuff.

The instant I appeared he thrust his face into mine, whispered one of the coarse jokes of which he had an inexhaustible supply, then threw back his head and laughed like a hyena. I suppose he considered this as part of his sales technique—putting the customer at ease. It was an invariable pattern whenever a purchaser entered his room.

Suddenly his laugh ended as though cut off by a knife. He fixed his eyes upon me and declared, as if the notion had just struck him like a bolt of lightning, that I probably wanted something.

I named my order. Hughie stood motionless, lost in thought. Then all at once his face lighted and his forefinger shot up like a beacon to returning memory.

"Ah!" he cried. "I know right where it is!"

He dived into one of those chaotic piles, scattering goods left and right like a dog digging for a bone. Some uncanny instinct guided him straight to the desired object. He rose, kicked the stuff he had scattered back into a heap, and handed me my purchase with a smile of utter triumph. The price he named was as breathless as his search—the original retail cost, plus freight, plus his own rampant fancies which, I soon learned, varied spasmodically from week to week. The only things he sold at face value were stamps, and he was compelled to this by law. He always looked sad when asked for them, and these alone he had trouble finding.

I feel constrained to add that the above picture of Hughie is not altogether fair. He was an excellent mill hand; he was completely loyal and completely cheerful. His interminable conversation at times drove us almost to distraction, but it was never mean conversation or devoted to personalities. He bustled mightily and, unlike most bustlers, he accomplished mightily.

I made my purchases and retreated, somewhat shaken, to my

room on the third floor. Because of the problem of heating, the boardinghouse quarters were piled on top of one another in one end of the building and partitioned off from the rest of the cold, echoing structure by plank walls. The kitchen and dining room, all in one big chamber, and the room where the cook and her daughter slept were on the lowest floor. The two stories above held the workers' quarters, smallish rooms opening off a wide hall and each occupied by two men. In the center of each hall was a huge coal stove around which all social life revolved. During the bitterest storms you could not, by any effort, fire the stove hot enough to make the surrounding rooms bearable.

The third floor was considered by its occupants to be more "tony" than the second floor. In the first place, Hughie's store was down there. In addition, the second floor also held the Swedes, Finns, and Slavs, most of them foreign-born and speaking the strangest sorts of English. Up on our floor we had a couple of Irishmen, some Cornishmen—Cornish miners are called "cousin jacks"—a Frenchman, two Norwegians (one of whom was my roommate), and a scattering of native Americans. We also had the superintendent, the foreman of the mine, and the foreman of the mill. These officials lived in rooms by themselves for need of office space but otherwise shared every item of living on a par with the men. We had one drawback. We got along very well together. Down on the second floor rough-and-tumble fights broke out on one or two occasions. They lasted only as long as it took the superintendent to race downstairs, hurl himself bodily on the participants, and tear them apart. Try as we might we were never able to beat him down and so missed seeing the fun.

This segregation of the Swedes, Finns, and Slavs prevailed only in respect to sleeping quarters and was not strict even there—two or three Americans lived with them by preference. At the table and in the mine or mill the men fraternized without racial distinction. The Americans, in an inoffensive way, considered themselves to be the best miners but weren't. The Swedes were,

almost without exception. The ones at the Camp Bird were in
their early twenties, were all handsome, and a couple of them
had a delicious, dry sense of humor, made all the more irresistible
by the musical, singsong inflections with which they delivered it.

The most difficult and dangerous work in the mine—slabbing
off the sides of old stopes, removing pillars, and so forth—was
often let on contract, and the Swedes invariably got the call. They
worked like fiends on these jobs, took desperate chances without
batting an eye, and earned, sometimes, triple the wages that the
rest of us did. While I was there one broken arm caused by a
timbering mishap was the only casualty among them.

The Slavs, mostly Russians, were the strong-arm boys and took
care of the bulk of the mucking—ore shoveling in the gas-filled
stopes and tunnels. They were broad-faced, stupid, unimaginative, husky the way an ox is husky, and generally good-natured.
The Finns—in all this I am, of course, describing only the handful
of each race we had at the mine and no inference is intended or
would be reasonable about nationalities as a whole—appeared
to be of two classes: "Black" Finns and regular Finns. I never
learned just what constituted the difference; it was one of those
things that are spoken of glibly but never satisfactorily defined.
To me all the Finns seemed equally ornery. When censured for
a slip they were quite capable of—and frequently did—telling the
foreman to go to hell. They were surly under authority, quarrelsome, snappish of speech, when they bothered to speak at all, and
first-rate workers if the mood so moved them.

In this connection it was interesting to note the reaction of the
different types toward a breakdown in a machine with which they
happened to be working. The Finns generally consigned it to the
devil, left it where it was, and walked out of the mine; the Russians generally sat down beside it and waited for someone to come
along and fix it; most of the others tried to repair it well enough
to finish out the shift and often succeeded with such ingenuity
that additional mending wasn't necessary at all.

Trouble between the men was rare and in the main limited to personal feuds about trivial matters. Cabin fever, it is sometimes called, and results from too close confinement in one another's company. It would roar up in a sudden white-hot flare and then, except in the case of the one or two fights previously mentioned, die almost as quickly as it came, without violence. At first this struck me as surprising. Mining, by its nature, is violent work, and I had arrived at the Camp Bird with queer notions about a man's trade reflecting itself in his character. But most of these differences were fuse sputterings without dynamite attached. Had the explosion come, however, I imagine it could have been pretty terrible, and this probably accounted for the superintendent's swift activity at the first sign of friction.

Of "labor" trouble there was none whatsoever. The only union organizer to appear on the scene while I was there was immediately given the bum's rush by the men themselves. Some of the workers did have union cards, but this was a matter of great unconcern to them and everyone else. Of course this was during the depression; jobs were hard to get and carefully nursed when found. Paradoxically, the mine also had difficulty obtaining men, for, with WPA to fall back on, the average miner would not come up to that dreary, isolated place. So it boiled down to a Jack-Sprat-and-wife sort of situation: the men being satisfied with work they might not have looked at during better times, and the superintendent content with men he might not have hired in a different place. Another factor making for stability was the few "boomers" we drew—that is, floaters who work in one mine until they have a couple of months' wages in their pocket and then drift on. Of course we got some, but in the main our population was permanent; we grew to know each other and our bosses, our likes and our dislikes, and acted accordingly.

Even so, it is surprising that there was not more complaint about living conditions. In some respects they were appalling.

There wasn't a shower or bathtub on the place. You came out

of the mine caked with mud, took off your filthy outer garments, and hung them in the change room on the lower floor of the boardinghouse. Theoretically this room received some heat from the kitchen; actually the clothes were often frozen stiff when you came to put them on again. Running water was limited to a single washbasin on each floor. The pipes were equipped with electric thawers, but most of the time they availed to pass only the tiniest of trickles. If you managed to reach the basins ahead of the rush you *might* get a little hot water. If you wanted a bath you lugged up a tin washtub from the kitchen, but since both the water and the rooms were apt to be frigid, only the most finicky steeled themselves to the ordeal. In an unused room outside the partitioned part of each floor was a urinal—a foot long, three-inch pipe fixed in a hole bored through the wall and trailing, outside, a ten-foot icicle of astonishing color. The other toilet facilities were on the typical country lines, except that ours, which was reached via a snowshed, was built out over a forty-foot cliff. The blizzards that whipped through the basin swirled up underneath this structure and packed the openings tight with snow. You beat them clear with a club provided for the purpose and then exposed yourself to the blasts. Very little time was idled away in this spot.

There were compensations, however. We had a radio on each floor. Food was always set out in the kitchen at night for snacks. The superintendent had a number of books he was glad to lend, though he was hardly swamped by the demand. The favorite diversion, outside of yarning and smoking, was cardplaying. And what card games! I received an indescribable shock the first time I walked into the boardinghouse and saw four grimy, bull-necked, ham-handed sons of toil hunched over a table, playing—so help me—bridge! Of course dice, poker, blackjack, and seven-up were also popular, especially right after payday.

Liquor was absolutely taboo. You could, if you liked, come up from town so paralyzed you had to be helped to bed, but that ended it. No eye openers, no little snifters before dinner. At high altitudes an insidiously small amount of alcohol will make most men roaring drunk in no time at all. Besides, the average miner has no judgment in the matter; a full bottle is an affront to be wiped out as soon as possible. He delights in taking it underground with him, as a preventative against chills, and thereby becomes a menace to himself and his fellows. This last, of course, was the reason for the ruthless prohibition. Sensible drinkers probably existed among the men, but it would have been favoritism to draw the line on that basis, and so no one was permitted any liquor at all.

Whether or not this was the cause of turning such a surprising percentage of them into bridge players, I can't say. But something did. When the truest of the addicts got together for a tournament between the second and third floors, the only thing that could break up the game was a rat hunt. The barns and the unused portion of the boardinghouse swarmed with rodents. We couldn't do anything with them there; they had too many runways. But frequently they would invade our living quarters. Someone would spot one. A war whoop would ring out. We'd grab brooms, boots, sticks, butcher knives, and chunks of coal—whoever has not backed a Rocky Mountain pack rat into a corner has only a pale idea of what ferocity can be. Up and down the halls the mad chase raged, in and out of rooms, furniture crashing, missiles flying, oaths ringing, and rats squealing. It is a continual wonder to me that the hunters didn't injure themselves more often than they did their quarry.

Another stampede broke out each time the dinner gong rang. The vast old building shook with the rush, and the bottleneck created by the door into the dining room was a dangerous thing. Yet I have been assured by good authority that our approaches to the laden board were models of decorum. For instance, when the old Tomboy mine (five or six miles across Imogene Pass from the Camp Bird and linked to it by tunnels) was running full blast, the dining-room crew had to carry on its preparations behind massive doors held shut by an iron drop bar. As the crucial moment of mealtime arrived three husky flunkies set their shoulders against the mob surging outside the panels. Another slipped the bar. Then all four jumped for their lives. Once—and I have this from an eyewitness—a dog belonging to one of the flunkies happened to be in front of the doors when they burst open. It was trampled to death in the rush. We weren't quite so impetuous; I think a very nimble dog could have gotten out of our way. Still, at the table you had to be quick when reaching for the meat platter, else you were liable to have your hand stabbed by a fork.

We ate at two long tables covered with oilcloth and lined with wooden benches. By unspoken rule you always occupied the same seat. Conversation was limited. All energies were devoted to consuming the greatest amount of food in the least amount of time. When I think of the withering speed with which those dishes, so laboriously prepared over so many hours, melted away, my sympathies go out to the cook. The producer of radio programs who sighs over the short life of his offerings has no true appreciation of the really transitory nature of human effort.

The food was excellent, due to the heroic efforts of the cook, and always fresh, due to the heroic efforts of the packers. It was prepared at one end of the room on a monstrous black coal range longer than a double bed and almost as wide. I used to eye it daily, wondering how it was transported over the trail, but all the information I ever got was a shrug and a "Why, they just brung it up." Just, indeed!

Over this stove the cook and her daughter toiled for hours that put our most grueling stint in the mine to shame. They were up at five o'clock in the morning frying mountains of eggs and forests of bacon, stirring up barrels of mush (on which we used condensed milk and even got to like its taste), acres of potatoes, and oceans of coffee. During their spare moments they filled lunch

boxes which the day shift took into the mine. Breakfast over, they
started on the big meals of the day. They baked all the bread,
peeled the potatoes which we ate three times a day, prepared
vegetables, stews, roasts, steaks, and on Sundays fried chicken.
Twice every day forty men had pie *and* cake to go with various
fruits and puddings. In spare moments there were lunch boxes to
ready for the night shift, dishes to be washed, and pots to be
scoured. The two women generally got to bed about nine o'clock,
and you can figure for yourself how often they sat down and
rested during their sixteen-hour stretch. For this the cook received
$125 a month and her daughter $100—by their own statement
the best pay they had ever obtained. They loved the job.

And they were loved wholeheartedly. When you felt you
couldn't endure your fellow workers another minute you went
down to the kitchen. It was a delightful spot—warm and sparkling clean and full of delicious smells. The two women were
always cheerful—I can't imagine how they managed to keep
themselves so, but they did—and always made you feel welcome.
In humble attempt to show appreciation we would help a little
with the dishes, mop the floor, pack coal for the stove, or lug out
the garbage and throw it over the cliff.

The cook was pretty, for all that she had a grown daughter.
Black-haired and blue-eyed—Irish, I think. And the daughter
had all this, plus youth. Our conversation with them was strictly
of the "joshing" variety, interspersed with periods of silence when
we just sat on the bench with one knee cupped in our hands and
watched them moving about their work. Neatly moving they
were, too, or at least so they seemed to our starved eyes. Yet if
anyone made a pass at them I know nothing of it. They were—
well, two women in a world of men, and the esteem they evoked
probably sounds—and was—absurdly sentimental. God knows it
was the only sentiment we could find to indulge in, and so for the
food and cheer and goodness they gave us we made them our
angels, though whether or not they really were angels away from

the mine I wouldn't attempt to say. And when they would slip us—pretending it was very much on the sly—a hot hunk of apple pie or a heel of bread still smoking from the oven, their halos were complete.

III UNDERGROUND

IMMEDIATELY AFTER BREAKFAST
the day shift went into the change room, where the blue jeans
and jumpers we wore over our woolen clothes hung on nails
driven into the walls. There followed the matutinal cacophony of
the miner: a great clearing of throats, fits of coughing, grunts,
groans, and snorts. Meanwhile, we beat our pants on the floor.
The damp garments had frozen during the night and had to be
limbered up before they could be donned. Then on went knee-
length rubber boots and off we marched, single file, humped up
like turtles with our hands thrust deep in our pockets, lunch boxes
under one arm, and our after-breakfast cigarettes hanging out of
the corners of our mouths.

The first part of the journey led through room after room in
the uninhabited section of the boardinghouse. These rooms were
filled with endless crates of foodstuffs, with piles of kindling wood,
and mountain upon mountain of coal for the stoves. At length
we came to a room containing several spools of black fuse and a
shelfful of small bright red boxes. Lettered in white on each box
was, 100 BLASTING CAPS. DANGEROUS. The drillers cut off several six-foot lengths of fuse. To each length they crimped one of
those detonator caps, a shiny copper cartridge about two inches
long and quite capable, if jarred sharply or touched with an open

flame, of blowing off a hand or nose or ear. The finished product the men wound in a coil and hung over one shoulder.

On we trudged through a snowshed into a barn jammed to the roof with massive timbers for bracing the rock in the tunnels and with bales of hay for the mules that pulled the ore trains over the rusty tracks in the mine. Here we filled our double-compartment carbide lamps, putting icy water which we dipped from a barrel into the top compartment and little gray pellets of calcium carbide in the lower one. Water dripping through an adjustable valve onto the carbide produced acetylene gas. It hissed out of the lamp's jet and ignited with a pop when we sparked the flint wheels with our thumbs. The pointed yellow flame was our only weapon against the utter blackness into which we were about to plunge. Sometimes the gas jets clogged. To clean them we had needlelike slivers of steel called reamers, which we carried in tiny metal tubes buttoned in our shirt pockets. We were careful of the reamers; life itself might depend on producing light in a hurry.

Already the sub-zero weather had chilled us through. With stiff fingers we hooked our lamps to the metal frames on the front of our cloth caps, put a tobacco can full of extra carbide in a hip pocket, and hurried on, still single file, still almost without conversation. Inside the mine the air was warmer. During winter the temperature stayed a constant forty-two degrees. In summer it dropped to forty degrees, for the many surface openings lost their covers of snow, and drafts stirred back and forth through the hollowed mountain.

The tunnel bored straight into the side of the hill for a half mile. There it intersected the vein and branched both ways, like a *T*. The geologic structure might be pictured something like this:

Consider the mountain as a cake. Slice into the cake at an angle not quite perpendicular with a bent, jagged knife. This thin, uneven gash is the vein, a fissure in the crust of the earth piercing to unexplored depths. It is not empty. Ages past, a non-metallic filling called gangue squeezed into it. There are all kinds of gangue with fancy scientific names; the most familiar one is quartz. Of itself quartz is worthless, but it may contain metal. For eons cold water from the surface has drained into the fissure; hot water from below has bubbled upward, transplanting minerals either by erosion or in hydrothermal solution. These minerals were changed by chemical action; they were squeezed and pressed; they were precipitated sometimes in thin streaks through the gangue or dumped into pockets like raisins.

A quarter of an ounce of gold dusted throughout a ton of quartz, in specks too infinitesimal to be seen by the naked eye, is enough to be profitable. In go the miners. But they don't mine those tiny flakes of metal. That would be impossible. They mine quartz and leave to the millman the intricate job of mangling the gangue into fit shape for extracting the gold.

Still, though he almost never sees the yellow mineral he is after, the gold miner has a feeling for his craft possessed by no other worker. He used to insist on payment in gold, believing he was retaining in different form what was in essence his very own. Moreover, his product was complete; it called for no bartering, no haggling. The miner did not serve as middleman for anyone or anything. This was dignity.

Today the enigma of economics prevents payment in kind; it puts the good things the miner has won from the earth back into the earth at Fort Knox, Kentucky, and he doesn't like it. Something of the directness, the simplicity has disappeared. You can't mine paper; a pay check isn't the same as seeing your own gold in your own hand. Even so, the pride persists. The miner goes to his wet, lonesome, sunless trade with his head up; he calls himself a quartz man, a hard-rock stiff, and considers himself superior to the grubs who toil in softer, easier mediums.

We met the Camp Bird vein which had produced millions upon millions of dollars for its owners and destroyers deep in the bowels of the earth. The original workers, starting at the surface, had followed it down and down until the cost of lifting ore back to the top became so great that it was cheaper to drive a horizontal haulage tunnel in from the side of the hill. One such tunnel had been driven, then another still farther down, and another and another. Now the vertical depth of the mine was better than twice the height of the Empire State Building. And the vertical part was inconsequential. Horizontal drifts branched out for miles. (A drift is a tunnel which follows a vein, as distinguished from a crosscut which drives into it from an angle.) Raises went up; shafts and winzes went down, connecting a maze of sublevels. Where ore was encountered in profitable quantities the vein material was removed in great blocks, leaving behind cavities (called stopes) hundreds of feet deep, hundreds of feet long.

Once I had occasion to climb through one of these hollow old stopes, my only guide the speck of light on my head. An ancient ladder clung to the rough walls. I moved slowly, afraid of rotten rungs. Mica crystals winked balefully. Beneath my heels was a pit of blackness. Above, all I could see was a short stretch of the ladder, shiny wet, disappearing into more blackness. Over my shoulder I could discern the opposite wall of the vein, ten feet or so away. It was like being in the jaws of a vise. If the rock wearied, if it slipped, I would be squashed into a jelly that not even the most skillful millman could distill.

A dislodged pebble fell, *clink, clink, clink . . . clink.* Then silence. I couldn't tell whether it had landed on the bottom or had dropped so far that I could no longer hear it. Winded, I had to stop and rest, clinging with one arm hooked about a rung, the feeble center of a feeble little pool of radiance. Somewhere water dripped—*ploomp, ploomp, ploomp*—and the sound gave back an echo until the whole cavern seemed to sigh.

Nothing can convey the impression of that overwhelming darkness. It was not just the absence of sunlight, for the sun had never touched this spot. The top of a mountain, the middle of a desert have their stars, wind, dawn, their feel of space. Here was nothingness. Eternity passes our comprehension, but in that forgotten pit I think I had a flash of what it might be like. . . . Then as I climbed higher I heard the faint rat-tat-tat of a drill machine. Above me and off in a side tunnel, men were working. I scrambled on; the sense of mystery fell away, and my pit became what it properly was—a hole in the ground. Even so, I climbed out of it a little wiser than I had been. I doubt me now if there is any such thing as complete self-sufficiency. Wherever we go, whatever we do, we travel with the inbred knowledge that somewhere others of our kind are waiting. Were it not so, we would lack the courage to travel at all, and hell is a place where man is alone.

By no means all of the vein material had been mined out by the Camp Bird's original operators. Throughout the mine's extent were immense blocks that had scarcely been scratched in the day of twenty-dollar gold. Now, encouraged by thirty-five-dollar gold the lease company was gouging away at a few of these forgotten bodies. When we walked in through the three-level crosscut and met the vein we swung left. The whole character of our surroundings changed. The tunnel was no longer straight but undulated along the uneven path of the vein. In the crosscut the rock had been a dull gray andesite, speckled with drab shades of green and brown. Here it took on life: sparkling white quartz, glittering mica and bright pyrites, red stains of iron, and the purple-green-blue flashes made by the peacock ores of copper.

We walked along the vein for another half mile, our boots sloshing in the water and the long, lamp-cast shadows of our legs scissoring along the wall. Finally we came to a room hewn out of solid rock. It was about thirty feet high and of indeterminate width, for half of it was filled with two massive bins. The car tracks ran under the mouths of these bins. Beyond the tracks and fenced off by guardrails, a square black hole yawned in the floor. A cable ran out of this hole, over a sheave wheel in the top of the room, and back down to a drum about as big as a medium-sized barrel. This was the tugger hoist, powered by a compressed-air donkey engine. Behind the engine was a wooden seat.

My new roommate nodded toward it. "There's your baby," he said.

Since then I have seen the huge lifts which whir skips up and down the thousand-foot shafts at Cripple Creek and in California; I have watched the hoist operators on their raised platforms, absolute masters of their polished levers, gauges, and dials, and of their obedient grease monkeys, and I realize now that I bore no more relationship to them than a barge captain does to an admiral. Still, I had to be called something for the sake of the bookkeeper, and so I was listed as a hoistman. And if my engine was not large, or my station magnificent, at least it was peculiar.

My roommate was my tutor. He spent about a day and a half showing me the routine, and I spent heaven knows how long convincing myself that the machine wasn't going to fly apart in my face the next minute. The hoist was designed to keep supplies flowing to the miners on four level, a hundred and fifty feet below us, and to a pair of Swedes who were sinking the shaft another hundred and fifty feet below that. All told, the elevator functioned to a depth of three hundred feet and had to move everything from men and timber to dynamite and ore.

The vehicle which did this job was a steel bucket four feet deep and three feet in diameter, hanging on the end of the cable. The bucket slid down greased wooden rails—the shaft wasn't quite perpendicular but followed the tilt of the vein at approximately a seventy-five-degree angle—and was kept from spinning around and around by two short steel arms that stuck out on either side and rested (occasionally) against the guide rails. When men were to be lowered the bucket was stopped with its top flush with the floor level. One miner got inside it; two more stood on the slippery rim, clutching the cable. Then down we dropped them into the maw of the earth. There were no gauges to show the position of the bucket; we judged this by the amount of cable paid out from the drum. After a little experience we were able to guess its every location within three or four inches.

The men disposed of, I lowered their material. First fifty or so pieces of drill steel freshly sharpened in the blacksmith shop outside. Then dynamite, three fifty-pound boxes to a load. At first I was scared to death of the stuff and treated it as gingerly as a person might treat—well, dynamite. I practically tiptoed when carrying a box and bent myself into all manner of ungainly squats so I could set it down without a jar. Meanwhile, the other men slung it around regardless, and none of them got blown up for his lack of pains. Familiarity soon bred a similar contempt in me, which was a great help both physically and mentally, for I had to handle tons and tons of it. Fresh dynamite, I learned, is not very touchy; in fact, it generally has to be exploded with another explosive—the detonator caps full of mercury fulminate, which the blasters crimped onto their fuse ends every morning. Deteriorating dynamite, however, can be wicked.

The mouth of the shaft was surrounded by a wooden floor. Water dripped on this and mixed with the mud to form a slime. Footing was uncertain to say the least, and working around the edges of that three-hundred-foot grave kept me in a dither that no amount of familiarity could alleviate. Fear is a wonderful skin preserver. In certain respects a greenhorn is safer in a mine than a veteran, for the tenderfoot is imaginative. He sees danger in the shadows, hears it in every creak of a timber, every thundering explosion. The veteran—pooh, he knows all about those things and they don't bother him. Perhaps they should. It is a fact that most mine accidents happen to the oldest hands.

There is, for example, the case of the hoistman who worked on the opposite shift from me. He had been on the job for a couple of years; he carried a mental map of every square inch of the hoist room. But that didn't keep his feet from slipping one fine day. *Whoosh!*—down the shaft he went.

God's peculiar grace was with him. He bounced around from timber to timber for about twenty feet and then chanced to hang up on a spar. There he was found unconscious—no one knows how much later—with his ribs bashed in, a leg broken, and his skull fractured. Salvaging him was a grisly business, fraught with considerable difficulty. Any complacency I might have developed was well chilled by this incident. I stayed scared and I stayed healthy.

The hoist was powered by compressed air sucked in from out-side the mine, where the temperature was below zero. The air rushed into the machine at a pressure of more than a hundred pounds per square inch, did its business, and escaped with an un-earthly scream. The moisture in it, chilled still more by its swift expansion, condensed in a thick gray fog. After an hour's rapid hoisting the machine—and operator—would be sheathed in a white, brittle layer of hoarfrost.

When hoisting ore, however, we jumped around like fleas on hot rocks, too busy to think about being cold. Down below us on four level were huge bins kept full of freshly mined rock bound for the mills. Moving this was our main job, and we could lift half a ton of it a trip. Speed was our goal. We'd drop the bucket two hundred and ten feet (the depth of the bins added sixty feet to the distance between the levels). A man working the semi-automatic loader on the four-level bins would fill the skip, signal us with the bell to take it away. Up we'd haul it, engine bellow-ing and fog swirling until we could see scarcely three feet in front of us. As the bucket emerged from the shaft we'd leap from our chair, seize a rope overhead, and slam a trap door shut, so that stray rocks wouldn't fall back into the shaft and brain somebody down below. Then we'd scoot the bucket into mechanical trips, dump it into the hoist-room bins ready for the ore train, jerk open the trap door, kick the engine out of gear, and let the vehicle fall like a plummet back down the shaft for another load. By whipping ourselves into a frenzy of effort we could—and did—make forty round trips an hour, less than two minutes each, involving I don't know how many separate split-second actions.

Why we went at it so hard, except for the sake of bragging to each other how fast we were, I don't know. Two or three hours of such hoisting took all the vinegar out of us. It would also empty the bins down below, and then there was nothing left but to sink back, cold and limp, into the painful process of doing nothing at all. Man is a strange animal. He will work himself to death just so he can find time to bore himself stupid.

Exhausting though the hoisting was to us, the loader had it worse. He was jammed into the scaffolding between the shaft and the ore chute, utterly alone. Suddenly the bucket would rush down out of the darkness, ready to peel off his skull or his toes if he was an inch out of position. He'd trip the gate, letting rock clang into the steel skip, pry out any boulders that stuck in the chute jaw with a crowbar, and then jump clear so we wouldn't hoist him along with the muck. Between trips, while he was sweating there in the dark and dust and the sharp, coppery smell of powdered rock, a trammer might dump a fresh load of ore into the wooden bins over his head with a crash that sounded as though it were bringing the whole world down on top of him. Or a stone might fall out of the ascending bucket and bounce down the shaft, *bang . . . bang . . . BANG!* He'd jam his nose into a corner then, his arms locked over his head, and hope to God the thing fell straight instead of caroming off onto his dome.

My loader was a round-faced, round-bellied Slav with an unpronounceable name. We called him Pete. Pete often came up to eat lunch with me. For many days he never spoke but gulped his food in silence, punctuated by broad grins to let me know his intentions were honorable. Then away he'd go with only a shy smile as he disappeared from sight. One lunch time, however, I saw that he had something on his mind. He squirmed, opened his mouth a time or two, and at length managed to ask if I could write "writing." I confessed I could.

And so, at Pete's dictation, I undertook his wooing for him. It seemed he was enamored of a Russian lady in the near-by mining camp of Ophir, though you could never have guessed it from his singularly dull and passionless letters. I was pardonably curious about her and once I asked him if she was pretty.

"Yah!" he said. "Lak a mule!"

I divined that he meant her strength and not her appearance was mulish, the latter being a minor consideration. She was already married to a man whom she supported by taking in washing and sawing cordwood for most of Ophir. These virtues so impressed Pete that he was determined to transfer them to himself. He furnished her with funds for a divorce, and one summer day off he went. In a week he was back.

"Married?" I asked him.

"Yah!" he said. He didn't seem very happy about it and wrote no more letters. Neither did he go down the hill to see his new wife all the time I was there. He didn't say why, and I didn't press him, but I think perhaps she had disappointed him by refusing to saw wood for his support. . . .

Occasionally we had mechanical difficulties with the hoist, one of them so stupendous in its devastation that it was almost magnificent. This happened to my roommate, when he was filling in for the hoistman who had fallen down the shaft. He was lifting ore, had the trap door closed and the bucket almost to the dump trips. Suddenly the hoist gears broke. Down went the massive steel bucket, loaded with half a ton of rock. It splintered the two-inch lagging of the trap door to smithereens, plunged on. The Swede at the loader heard it coming and scrambled for his life.

From side to side of the shaft it slammed, tearing out great chunks of timbering as it went. Into the bottom it roared with a crash that brought men running from all over the mine. By sheerest chance the workers in the shaft had a few minutes before climbed the manway ladder to four level to cut some timbers they needed. My roommate didn't know this. He raced down the ladder to do what he could for the remains. Since I had often had nightmares of this very thing happening to me, I could well imagine his feelings when he discovered that nothing was hurt which couldn't be repaired—though the repairing took several days.

Fortunately I had no such accident. But I did have my troubles. I hadn't been at the mine very long when the braking system on the hoist went out of kilter. I set the bucket down on the trap door and with utterly no idea of what to do started delving into the machine's innards. To reach them I had to unwind a lot of the greasy cable. I got it snarled all over the place. I smeared myself with oil and mud. I lost my temper—and at that moment someone down below rang for the bucket.

There is a wire that runs the length of the shaft. It is attached to a gong by the hoistman's ear, and by jerking the wire so many times for such and such a purpose, the miners can let the hoist operator know what they want him to do with the bucket. It is amazing the amount of expression they can put into the bell. The instant it clanged at me this particular time I knew the ringer was in as foul a mood as I.

I couldn't heed him, so I ignored him. Pretty soon the bell was saying all manner of evil words. Completely exasperated, I went to the manway and screeched down the story of my difficulties. There was no chance of my being understood, for the echoes in the shaft distorted sound out of shape.

Whoever was down below yelled back. "Gliggity-glig-blug-blug-wump!" he said.

"Aw, go to hell!" I bawled and went back to digging my mechanical grave, hoping that my sentiments, if not my words, were plain.

They were. The bell chattered in a perfect frenzy. By way of rebuttal I seized the wire and yanked it out of my tormentor's hand.

Silence fell. I finished tearing my machine asunder, and then with a mortification that defies description I discovered I could not put it back together again.

While I was sitting there among the greasy ruins of my career a new hand rang the bell, very gently now. *Bong, bong, bong . . . bong.* Three-one. If the bucket had been down below the signal would have meant that a man was coming up. Since the bucket wasn't there, I could only surmise that a man was coming up without it.

Sure enough, a few minutes later Tommy Rice's ugly Cornish face appeared through the manway hole. He was perhaps fifty years old, brown and wrinkled as a withered apple. One of his upper front teeth was gone, and two of his lower ones were made out of gold. His left leg had been shattered in an explosion, and he walked with a strange hitching, half-hopping gait. Something had also happened to his vocal cords; he talked in a husky whisper that cracked every now and then into a shrill falsetto. He was only five feet tall and thin as a splinter, but none of these infirmities prevented his being one of the best hands in the place and straw boss of our shift. Like most miners, he chewed snuff perpetually. I don't know how so big a heart as his came to be in so odd a body.

He eyed my chaos. "Good gracious," he whispered, or words to that effect. Then he picked up a wrench and went to work. While he repaired the damage he taught me the whole mystery of the machine. Not by tone or gesture did he imply that I was anywhere near the fool I really was. I loved that man.

Certain other difficulties arose that I tried to handle myself. The most annoying was a drip of water that fell from the roof and landed square on the back of my neck when I sat in the hoist chair. Either it didn't strike the other operators in just that position, or else they had more forbearance than I. Anyhow, they did nothing about it, and I brooded alone, wondering how I could reach the thirty-foot ceiling, find the leak, and plug it.

I couldn't. So finally I set up a couple of posts, persuaded the
trammer to haul me in a sheet of corrugated roofing iron, and
erected a shelter. It was a very flimsy affair, for it never occurred
to me that it would have to withstand more than a few drops of
water. But more of that later.

Things against which I could devise no shelter were the empty
hours that set in when there was no hoisting to do. Some of
the time I filled trying to make a pet of a mouse who lived in
the false bottom of the toolbox. I saw him scuttling along the
base of the wall one day (if there is such a thing as "day" in a
mine) and thought I was having visions. But he was real; he was
alive, and he was hungry. He subsisted on mule droppings and
bits of food spilled from our lunch boxes. I was finally able to win
his trust to such an extent that he would snatch a morsel of bread
from my fingers. But I was never able to touch him, and I never
figured out what prompted him to come here, a full mile inside
the mountain. It was a journey none of our myriad rats ever
undertook.

Considering his small size, the mouse did a great deal to
alleviate the terrible silence. For one thing, I could talk to him
without feeling that my brain had softened, as would have been
the case had I talked to myself. Still, the companionship of even
a sociable rodent is limited.

Now and then there were brief visitors. The foreman or
superintendent might drop by, and three or four times each shift
(unless he was hauling in another part of the mine) the trammer
would come in from the mill for a load of ore. Two brothers,
native Americans with truly native drawl and pungency of speech,
did the tramming on the two shifts. They drove a little train of
four cars whose engine was a mule with a carbide lamp on his
harness to serve as headlight.

Hank Green, broad, loose-jointed, and unbelievably strong,
drove an enormous yellow mule named Buck. Every time Buck
hove into the hoist room he waggled his long ears at me in a most

friendly manner, as though to say, "Howdy, old soak!"—or maybe, "What about the apple core?" For, like everyone else in the mine, I saved tidbits out of my lunch box for him. He was our mascot, gentle and responsive, the one thing on which we could lavish affections that had no other outlet. He played up to us in great style: stamping his feet in pretending petulance when we overlooked him, butting us with his muzzle for food or a scratching. He had more friends than anyone else on the mountain.

Not so his associate, a compact brown mare called Jen. Jen was brisk and businesslike. She knew she was expected to pull only four cars; if a fifth was hitched on she would look at it with a haughty glare and refuse to budge until it was uncoupled. Sometimes Buck, busy fooling around, failed to spot his cars properly under the ore chutes. Not so Jen. Prim and precise, she wrought with efficiency, ignoring everyone but her driver, and so we retaliated by ignoring her in favor of Buck. I can't say she seemed to give a damn. She was a painfully self-contained animal. Since then I have seen trim, neat businesswomen so much like Jen that their very facial expressions were similar. Sometimes I wonder what goes on in their minds.

We also had a Peck's bad boy. He was a jet-black mule named Cooney. He had temper tantrums. Occasionally he would run away with a string of cars and often, for no reason at all, he would reach out and bite a man. The sight of a brandished stick sent him into a fury. One summer the superintendent, trying to head him in the pasture behind the mill, picked up a chunk of wood and threw it at him. Enraged by this *lèse-majesté,* Cooney laid back his ears, opened wide his mouth, and charged. He chased the super all over the hill and finally treed him up a power pole, where he kept him for a full half-hour, to the secret delight of the workers who ambled out to make a few halfhearted attempts at rescue.

Came a day when Cooney paid for his sins. He was being used

for tramming up on two level. This was three hundred feet above the main three-level haulage tunnel, and since there was no mule-way inside the mine, he had to be led up a steep, rocky trail on the surface. The trail was just his meat; frequently he would catch his master off balance, break loose, and run away. To avoid the continual battle of leading him back and forth to the barn, he was penned inside the mouth of the two-level tunnel. At first this wasn't bad; he could look out through the bars, see sunlight, and bray at the other stock. But suddenly an early blizzard swooped down, covering the mouth of the tunnel and blocking the trail. Rescue was impossible.

It was very dark inside that hole and very lonesome. No amount of braying would bring an answer, no tantrum break those soft chains of snow and blackness. Cooney settled down to half a year of meditation.

At least he wasn't hungry. Deep inside the mine a raise connected three and two levels. It was fitted with a tiny lift. Each day one of us would load it with hay and grain, send the provender up to two, then climb the three-hundred-foot ladder and feed it to the mule. Cooney was always waiting. When we emerged into his cavern he whickered with pathetic joy. As long as we were there he followed us around like a dog, begging for a word, a pat, any gesture of companionship to which he could cling during his solitude.

Sometimes there was work for him to do. No fits of rebellion now; he was a new mule. And when the chore was done he drooped visibly, knowing that more hours of loneliness stretched ahead. We would leave a carbide lamp burning for him on a post and go back down the manway. The last thing that met our ears was a low, heartbreaking bray, the saddest sound I have ever heard.

Next summer the snow melted away from the tunnel mouth and, after a cautious interval at the exit to get his eyes used to the light, Cooney was allowed to escape. Back and forth across the basin he raced, kicking his heels and shaking his head. Then down on the warm earth to roll and roll before he leaped up again to run some more, as though he had to pack a lifetime of sun and air into those few minutes before darkness closed down again. We all expected, when his first spasm of joy passed, that he would resume his old ways. But he must have searched his soul during those black months and taken a vow. An uplifted stick would still make him bare his yellow teeth, but otherwise he became a model citizen.

When hoisting was very slack and the miners on four level particularly busy, I was sent down the ladder to help them. The air was foul there. Each shift blasted at three-thirty, morning and afternoon, and the following shift came on at seven-thirty. In the interim blower fans were hard at work, but they never sufficed to clear out all the blue, stinking powder gases.

Into this reek came the workers. First they pried down with crowbars—"barring down," they called it—the shattered rock left on walls and ceiling by the previous explosion. In spite of this, someone every now and then got rapped on the skull by a stone that had been overlooked. Then the muckers went to work on the debris—by hand, for there were no fancy mucking machines at the Camp Bird then. They sprayed the pile with water and let air from an air hose play over it. Still the gagging stench of powder smoke clung to the ore as they shoveled it into a car and then pushed the car to the bins.

The mouth of the bins was covered with a grizzly, a crisscross of heavy iron bars. Rocks too large to pass through the spaces between the bars (and hence too large to pass through the loader chute into the hoist bucket) had to be broken up with an eight-pound sledge. It is said that the qualifications for a successful mucker are a size-forty shirt and a number-two hat. There is some justice to the claim.

Meanwhile, the machinemen were setting up their pneumatic hammers. Roughly, drilling consists in punching holes into the rock. Actually, it is a very technical process. The drill runner must know the varying nature of every kind of stone, the proper angles, the number and depth of holes for a given surface, in order that he can get maximum breakage from each charge of dynamite.

First he drills "cut" holes around the center of the face, angling them in the outline of a pyramid with an apex not quite reached inside the rock. Above them he punches "back" or top holes, then side holes, and finally the "lifters" at the bottom. The cut holes will be fired first, blowing out a wedge of rock. Seconds later the surrounding holes blast in rotation, breaking the rock sideways into the center core. If it were not done this way, if the rock did not have this empty core into which to expand, it would not break, and the force of the explosion would go cannonlike out of the mouths of the holes, to no avail.

A good machineman can drill about fifteen holes five feet deep, or a total of seventy-five feet, in a shift. This doesn't give him much time for admiring the scenery. He stops only to change dull steel for sharp or to adjust his machine. Jets of air and water forced through the hollow steel clean out the cuttings and reduce the deadly rock dust which shreds your lungs, producing silicosis, the grim reaper of the mines.

In a narrow tunnel one man works alone; on a broader face two or more drill side by side. The demoniac tattoo of the machines fills the narrow confines until it shakes your very bones. Compressed air fogs about you, shutting you off alone in a world of crashing noise and terrible power. It is no wonder that the machineman is looked up to by the muckers as king of the trade and that his skill and stamina—mental stamina to stand that unholy racket—command higher wages than any other job in a mine. He is a proud man and a touchy one. He often thinks he knows more than he does, and when he is being introduced to a new-type hammer which he doesn't like because he is ignorant of it, or when he is asked to change his procedure to meet circumstances he hasn't experienced before, he must be handled by the foreman with kid gloves that would melt an opera star. Particularly was this true of the Camp Bird's sullen, surly Finns, who could drill like fiends and weren't going to be told a damn thing by any damn man.

After the mucker had cleaned out the debris in came the timbermen, laying track and building stulls, burying whole forests inside the earth. Their neatest work was done in the stopes. These are excavations from which ore is removed. Many highly technical processes may be used, but at the Camp Bird the engineers stuck mainly to "shrinkage stoping." A pillar or solid block of ore was left in the roof. A battery of funnellike chutes was cut up through this and sub-drifts run horizontally both ways from the tops of the chutes. Miners then worked up from the sub-drifts, blasting down the ore from the roof into the chutes. Each shift stood on the muck pile left by its predecessor. Inasmuch as broken rock occupies some 60 per cent more space than when solid, the working gap had to be kept clear by drawing off ore through the chutes each day and dumping it in the bins. And so the stopers grubbed their way up and up and up until they met the level above. Stoping can't go down very handily, because each day's blast would bury the next day's working ground. Getting rid of such muck is partly why shaft sinking is the most expensive operation in a mine.

They were weird places, those stopes. We entered them through a narrow manway drilled up through a vertical pillar left intact at each end of the stope and connected with it by short side tunnels. The floor was a rough, uneven pile of boulders. Strung out along the cavern's length were the drillers, hunched like gnomes in the yellow gloom of their lamps. The noise was a shattering crescendo. The quivering steel pointed upward. Mud from the water jets dripped in the operators' faces. Once in a while one of them would shut off the water, preferring to breathe dust. This was strictly against mine regulations and, if persisted in, meant suicide. But sometimes death from silicosis in the uncertain future seemed preferable to present discomfort.

Punching holes into a ceiling weakened by scores of previous blasts has its dangers. Once a huge thick slab of stone, the full width of the vein and twenty feet long, caved down into the stope. It fell between shifts, and no one was hurt. But it might just as well have fallen when two or three men were underneath it. Things like this breed into a miner his strange mixture of fatalism and superstition. It also builds strong currents between the men. They work in isolated little groups, side by side in noise and peril and hardship. Either you are cemented to your fellow with an uncommon bond of friendship, or you get to hate his guts so intensely that you will not so much as look in his direction outside the mine.

The drilling finished, the dynamite was prepared for blasting. This I occasionally helped do, without ever being impressed by its desirability as a means of livelihood. We opened one end of the yellowish paraffin-saturated paper that covered the eight-inch-long cartridges. With a wooden skewer we punched a hole in the powder, inserted blasting cap with fuse attached, then refolded the waterproof paper and tied it tight. A stick of powder so prepared was called a primer and was a deadly thing, for the blasting caps are very sensitive to fire, friction, or jar. If a cap explodes the dynamite explodes, and if you are anywhere around —well, you suddenly aren't around any more. This, however, was a mere possibility. What was very real was the splitting headache that handling nitroglycerin (as distinguished from nitro-starch) dynamites gave some of the men, myself included. I suppose it is a form of allergy; I am not up on the physiology of it, but I can certainly speak for the effects.

The drill holes were then blown clean with compressed air. In went two or three sticks of unprimed dynamite, pushed into place with a wooden tamping pole. Next came the primer, whose explosion would detonate the whole load, and on top of the primer a few more cartridges were rammed. The hole was then "stemmed" with clay, wet sand, or some other binding material. All this was done with great care, for any stick of powder that failed to explode constituted a grave threat to the next shift. Many a grisly tale the miners tell about a machineman driving his drill steel into a live cartridge, or a mucker detonating one with his pick.

Tools were cleared away and mucking boards laid down, so that the debris falling on their smooth surface would be easier to shovel up than if it piled on the rough floor of the tunnel. The fuses were strung out in orderly array. The various holes in each "round" (as a series of holes in a face is called) were fired in sequence, the timing being determined by the length of the fuse. We used a gutta-percha fuse that burned approximately one foot in forty seconds. This was a rough average only, and plenty of leeway was allowed. The fuse was cut two thirds through, bent backward, like an elbow, and fired with a carbide lamp. From there on it was left strictly to its own devices.

All this work required, in addition to the machines for which each user was personally responsible, a great variety of tools and spare parts for repairs. These were kept in a toolbox in the hoist room. Whenever anything was taken the hoist operator made a note of it. Most of the men obliged my ignorance by naming the various collars, bolts, sleeves, gadgets, and what not that they requisitioned. But one drillman exasperated me beyond endurance.

He was a monkey-faced Black Finn named Herman, so short in stature that he was almost a dwarf. Quite in accord with his nasty character, I thought, were his clothes. He wore black boots —the rest of us wore red or white ones—a black slicker, and, instead of the usual cap or helmet, an enormous black rain hat. He smoked the tiniest pipe I have ever seen, with a J-shaped stem and a bowl that couldn't have held enough tobacco for more than four or five puffs. I don't know how he lighted it without burning his nose. He stayed to himself, never joined any of the card games, never spoke more than two or three grunted words at a time to anyone.

When he took a tool he hid it out of sight under his slicker and slunk away without a word. I reasoned with him. "Herman, what did you take? I've got to keep a report of this stuff." No answer. I pleaded; I threatened; I cajoled. He'd just smile an incredibly monstrous smile around that obnoxious pipe. I considered violence, but I never quite got around to it—I was secretly afraid of the little villain, the way you might be afraid of a snake—and as things turned out I didn't need to. Herman was building up to his own downfall.

One day he was put to running a raise a short distance down the drift from the hoist room. Because of a bend in the tunnel the room was safe enough from flying rock, but I was afraid the noise of his explosions might drown out my bell signals. When the two boys who were sinking the shaft spit (lighted) their fuses there was no time for fooling around. They stood in the bottom of a three-hundred-foot well, right on top of a hundred or more sticks of dynamite, and if I didn't get them out with the bucket they'd never get out.

To add to the difficulties, the cable had developed a bad habit of jumping off the drum when it wound up near the end of the spool. I had a pry bar rigged up so I could snap it back into place without trouble, but it took fast manipulation, and I didn't like the idea of doing it with Herman's blast going off in my ear.

I went back to his raise. "Herman," I said, "don't shoot until I've got the boys up out of the shaft."

He just looked at me.

Shooting time rolled around. The boys in the stopes and the four-level drift spit their fuses and came up to sit around under the little tin roof I had built. Their explosions rumbled out, far away and muffled, yet somehow thrilling me, as they always did. The concussion set our lamp flames jiggling, drove its force through the rock to tickle the soles of our feet.

Suddenly the bell clanged. Three-four—"Starting to spit in the shaft. Get ready to take us away!" I gripped my levers. Every day I did this, and every day I was nervous. Herman flitted by like a black wraith, headed outside. No one noticed him, for he never stopped to talk to us.

The bell clanged again, one sharp ring. Lift! I started the air, watching the cable.

BAM! With an indescribable roar Herman's first explosion rent the silence. The concussion screamed into the hoist room, blew out every one of our lights.

At that very moment the cable jumped off the drum. Futilely I jabbed at it with my pry bar. I couldn't see. I missed. The cable snarled on the axle, froze. The bucket stopped, a deathtrap hung over those relentless fuses in the shaft bottom. I clawed blindly, trying to free the cable. It was no use. I was responsible for saving those men in the shaft and I was helpless. I believe no fear for one's own life can be more devastating.

BAM! Herman's second blast jumped through the dark. The flimsy tin roof I had built over the hoist gave way. Down it fell with a clatter on our heads. A post toppled. Two men jumped up, collided, fell. I tripped over my seat. We were all in a heap on the floor, tangled with the wreckage. *BAM . . . BAM . . . BAM . . .* And then it was over. We lay still, listening for some sound in the shaft and too deafened to hear it.

And then the explosions began below. *K-thonk, K-thonk, K-thonk*—the weird, knocking boom of disintegrating rock— followed by a deathly silence.

The tin creaked as someone wriggled out from underneath it. A man began to swear, a low, flat string of triple-jointed oaths, terrible in their utter lack of passion. I found my lamp, spun the flint wheel. The acetylene flared, and the yellow light rolled over us. We gaped at each other, ludicrous in our disarray and yet not knowing how ludicrous we really were.

Suddenly the bell went *jiggety-jig-jig-jig*. I flew to the hoist, unsnarled the cable. Soon we had the shaft workers out, scared pasty but intact. The bucket had lifted them barely within reach of the manway ladder. When the hoist stalled they had swung out and climbed to safety by the skin of their teeth.

They didn't beat Herman up, as I expected they would. They didn't even cuss him out. But the disapproval of the entire mine was let to lie upon him in a massive weight, in gesture, in look, in little words and crooked grins that hurt. He had broken faith. He had been untrue to the code of the miner which says you must remember your fellow, no matter what, no matter how.

Herman stayed on. The stuff of his nature that enabled him to stand that icy contempt passed my understanding. But now he would answer you eagerly—almost pathetically—when spoken to. The trouble was, no one would speak to him.

IV A BATH FOR EASTER

THE DAYS DRAGGED ON. AS SPRING drew near, the snow piled over the tops of the snowsheds. The lower windows of the rooming house were boarded to keep them from caving in under the drifts; thick frost on the upper windows passed only a thin gray radiance. The day shift went into the mine in darkness, emerged in darkness.

Things were a little better when we were working nights—the shifts changed every two weeks. We came out of the mine about four o'clock in the morning, chased the rats from the kitchen, fried eggs, made coffee, ate three or four pieces of pie, went to bed, and slept until lunch time. On good afternoons—and there were many—we could venture outside, blink at the sky like owls, and return somewhat refreshed to our smoking and yarning around the stove.

One clear, cold day the packer brought us our first sign of spring. It was a migrating mallard duck he had found in a snowdrift beside the trail. Something had half paralyzed its right side. It couldn't fly and it was lame—if you can imagine a duck's being lame. For a time it supplanted even Buck, the mule, in our affections. We kept a galvanized tub for it in the kitchen where the water wouldn't freeze, and before long it was tame, quacking through the halls, in and out of every room. The only man who didn't like it was big Bull Sulenz. That was because the duck, not housebroken, persisted in making a nest in his laundry box.

The weather turned bad again. For twenty-seven straight days it stormed. The duck began to fail. On a bitter-cold Thursday before Easter it died.

That night we sat huddled around the hall stove. Outside the wind was threatening to tear the building from the ground and hurl it down the canyon. In gasping lulls between each fresh roar we could hear the *slap-slap* of the hard, granulated snow beating against the board walls.

Christmas Tree John, the blacksmith, rubbed his hand over his shiny pate. Though fairly young, he hadn't a hair on his head. His hooked nose and brilliant blue eyes were predatory. He'd got his name because once in a saloon, during a holiday brawl, he'd beaten a man nearly to death with a club he'd whittled from the Christmas tree on the bar. We called him Christmas Tree; he didn't seem to mind the association with his past, though he'd spent a couple of years in prison for his escapade—assault with a deadly weapon. He was a Finn, very ornery but more social than the others we had. It was his theory that our duck had developed a fatal attack of miner's consumption.

French Elic had a different idea. "Zut!" he said. "Ze Bool take a bath in his water. Poor leetle fellair, no wonder he die."

Everyone guffawed except Bull Sulenz. He hated to be laughed at. I thought he was going to swing on Elic, but slowly his fist uncurled and he slumped in his chair, staring at the floor. An ugly tension, the kind that gets a bunch of men after they've been shut up too long together, settled on us.

Suddenly little Tom Rice stood up with an oath. "I'm going to town Saturday," he whispered. "Warm bath, warm drink, warm girl. Damn this cold!"

"It's tough weather to tackle the trail," someone muttered.

Tom just grunted and spit on the stove.

We straggled off to our rooms, and I guess we were all thinking the same thoughts. To get my mind off mine, I put on a couple of sweaters and climbed into bed to do some reading. I'd no more than started when Boxcar Kelley, an Irish timberman, came in. A red-faced, red-haired monster of a man, his bulk almost filled the doorway. He asked to see my Montgomery Ward catalogue. He couldn't read, but I thought he wanted to look at the pictures.

I told him where it was. He didn't get it. He fumbled around for a while and then said that what he really wanted was a letter written for him. "It's to a—it's to a—a gorl!" he stammered.

Apparently my fame as an amatory amanuensis was spreading. I climbed out of bed, fetched pen and paper. "Fire away," I said.

He had a terrible time getting it out. He shifted from foot to foot, stared at his knuckles, and swore in agony. At last he jerked a few words loose. It seemed he wanted a date on long-change day, when we went from day to night shift. We would stop work at four o'clock Saturday afternoon and wouldn't have to report again until seven-thirty Sunday evening. Like Tom, Boxcar was going to utilize his twenty-seven hours of freedom by going to town.

He managed about four lines of dictation. Then, "O Christ!" he roared. "That's all!"

I signed it, "Affectionately yours, Boxcar."

He grabbed me by the shoulder. "Don't tell nobody! She's a nice gorl!" Whether he wanted the romance kept secret or whether he dreaded the damning exposure that he was writing to a nice girl—of all things—I don't know.

The next day, Friday, Pete and I finished our ore loading early. He came up to the hoist room to wait with me while I pulled the men out of the shaft.

"Long change tomorrow," I remarked.

"Yah." Pete nodded. He took an apple from his lunch box and munched it, eyes dreamy. "I tink I go to town wit' Tom."

"In this storm? Remember Hansel. He tried to cross the pass to Telluride in that Christmas blizzard and froze to death."

"Poof!" Pete was scornful. "Dat because he sit down. Keep move. Den de blood, he move, too, an' you no freeze. Anyhow, storm better. Snowslide no run den. Beside, for five month I haven't one bath. I get one for Easter. Wow! Won't dat be fine?"

"Why don't you bring up the tub from the kitchen?"

Pete gave me a withering look. "I said bath."

The bell sounded a signal. I dropped the bucket and pulled up the men.

"Who's got some snouse?" Tom Rice asked as he stepped from the hoist. Several boxes were offered. He took a pinch of snuff from one and pushed it into a ball under his upper lip while he counted the explosions thundering in the stopes.

"Nary a miss. Good enough," he whispered in his cracked voice. Then he grinned. "Who's going to town tomorrow?"

It developed that over half our shift was. For months the dubious glamour of Ouray had been insufficient to compensate for the stormy rigors of the trail. But it was different now. Easter, with its promise of spring, fell the day after tomorrow. It was still winter here in the ice-sheathed lap of Imogene Basin, but Herrin, the stableman in Ouray who brought up the mail, had told us that in the valley our snows were rain. The ground, he said, was bare and the grass showed fresh green on the southern slopes. Storm or no storm, we were going to see these things for ourselves.

When we reached the mouth of the tunnel Tom opened the storm doors and looked out. Snow was still falling, but gently now in great, lazy flakes.

"The wind's died," he whispered. "If this fresh fall don't start sliding we won't have a bad trip down." To me he added: "Why not call that long-legged mailman an' have him bring up nags for whoever wants 'em?"

After dinner I checked up and telephoned Herrin that we

would rent seven of his horses at the close of the shift on Saturday. Herrin had started life as a Montana cowpuncher and had a poor opinion of miners in general. But he still considered me a ranch hand, temporarily strayed, and we got along fine. I often acted as go-between for the miners and him.

"Okay," he said, "but you tell them dumb honyaks to be careful. The trail's in bad shape. The crust is strong where the packers' mules have kept it tromped down, but on the side there's ten feet o' new snow. If a horse puts one foot over the edge of the trail he'll sink to his ears. It'll cost thirty bucks a head for any that slide into the canyon."

Saturday afternoon we blasted early. The foreman let us beat tally time so we could get a good start. Tom, the first one outside, peered through the storm doors.

"Clear as a bell!" he stated.

He went on out. His voice cracked into a shrill trumpet call. "It's warm!" he yelled. "My God, it's warm!"

We tumbled into the open, shouting and pushing one another into the drifts. We could not stay long, however. The glare of the sun, smashing back from the white sweep of the basin, tore at our winter-weakened eyes. We raced upstairs to get dark glasses, our best boots and breeches. Just as we started for the horses which the mailman had left hitched to the rack by the mill the telephone rang. I answered it to hear Herrin's voice.

"Listen!" he said. "This chinook has loosened the snow. It'll have slid the trail full in places. Take shovels to dig through. And watch out! The big avalanches are ready to run!"

We climbed on our indifferent horses, feeling envious of the Swedes who flashed ahead of us into the timber on their skis. It was a faultless day, the world all asparkle. An easy wind blew snow lacings from the mountaintops. Our trail zigzagged down the slope away from the cliffs, avoiding, where possible, the danger of avalanches. Although the heat of the sun had pene-

trated deep into the fluffy mass of new snow and left it moist and
sticky, the going was not bad at first. But presently the way cut
across a steep, exposed hill. Here miniature snowslides had piled
across our path. We had to dismount and dig.

Higher up, little balls of snow were breaking loose and leaping
down the slope, gathering size as they went, until they looked like
huge cinnamon rolls, big as wagon wheels. We had to duck them
as they thudded softly past.

Tom shook his head. "Bad sign, them balls. Means the snow is
ready to slip."

We shoveled in desperate earnestness. At last we cleared a path
and pushed on to a near-by stand of timber. Suddenly a loud
cra-ack tore through the stillness. We looked back.

"She's broke!" Bull Sulenz cried.

Down the slope we'd just quit pounded the avalanche. A
cloud of powdered snow rose hundreds of feet above it. Through
the reverberations we could hear the air popping like a giant
whip as it rushed in to fill the vacuum left by the slide. A wall of
air surged ahead, booming like thunder from cliff to cliff. Over
the lip of the canyon it poured like a monstrous cataract of sugar,
foamed into the bottom, and almost languidly came to rest. We
rode on in silence. Through the stiff branches of the trees the
white wrinkled faces of the cliffs looked aged and tired.

Half a mile farther on we reached the old Camp Bird mills.
As we dismounted to stretch our legs the watchman came out to
say howdy. "Better wait till the sun goes down an' it freezes," he
cautioned. "Icicles are fallin' from the cliffs in the lower gorge.
The packers aren't goin' through again until they can get rifles
an' shoot the 'cicles down."

"Icicles—zut!" French Elic shrugged. "We dodged zat slide.
One leetle piece ice, we dance right around heem."

"You'll dance, all right," the watchman said.

"Ve vill," agreed Christmas Tree John, hatless and grinning
like a satyr, "but ve'll do it at the Idle Hour. Come on, boys!"

Below the old mill the canyon narrowed to a yawning slit. The road crawled under beetling precipices. Beneath was a long white drop to the frozen stream. Overhead tremendous blue-white icicles reached sharp fingers down the rock.

Suddenly Boxcar Kelley, in the lead, jerked his horse back on its haunches. "Look!"

A dagger of ice had broken loose. It jabbed downward, drove its point into the road, shivered, and broke into a thousand pieces.

Christmas Tree John put his hand on the top of his bald head. "One hit—good night!"

"Shall we make a run for it?" Tom asked.

"Shure!" Boxcar affirmed. "We want to be in town when the noight begins."

We spurred to a gallop. Another icicle fell. We didn't see it but heard it hit an abutment of the cliff overhead and explode into fragments. A crystal shower buzzed down, stinging our humped shoulders. But no more full-sized icicles fell onto the trail until after we were safely past.

"Wow!" Pete said. "I get dat bath after all!"

The snow at the lower elevations was melting fast, the sodden surface of the ground almost bare. The horses seemed to catch our eagerness and broke into a run without urging. Laughing and yelling, we slithered down the miry hill into town.

We all got beds at the Miner's Friend. There was no running water in the rooms, and the only bath was at the end of the hall. We drew lots to determine the order in which we should possess the cheerful tub.

"First! First!" rejoiced Pete, peeling off his clothes where he stood.

We grouped around the door and listened to the hot water gurgling into the tub. We heard Pete get in. There was a tremendous splashing that gradually subsided into soft ripples. A blissful sigh came bubbling out to us as he slid full length into the limpid depths.

"He will be zere all night," moaned Elic, "and I am last. *Le bon Dieu* is not kind."

We followed him outside to get a drink while waiting our turn.

Baths finished, most of the men went exactly where you think they went and purchased a fleeting touch of gentleness they could get in no other way. The rest of us went to a movie. It was a Western thriller, very bad, and we enjoyed it so enormously that we sat through it twice. A little thing is enough, sometimes, to help you forget.

My movie companions stayed in town on various affairs. When I reached the stable Sunday afternoon, where the crew was to meet for the ride back to the mine, only Tom Rice was in sight.

"Where is everybody?" I asked him.

"Well," said Tom, "Boxcar got married, sudden-like. Said he's going to the desert for a honeymoon. Christmas Tree John and French Elic got in a fight with some cowpunchers at the Idle Hour. They threw Elic out of a bedroom window in his underwear. He's in the hospital. John's in jail again. The others'll be staggering along pretty soon. Let's go ahead. We don't want to have to herd a bunch of drunks up the hill."

The cloudless glory of yesterday was muffled in a dull pall of mist. As we rode higher, scuds of snow swirled in our faces. Tom kept smiling to himself at some recollection and singing over and over in his tuneless whisper:

> " 'Mother, Mother!' the child in terror said,
> 'A dirty mucker is in the drillman's bed!' "

It was freezing, so we passed the icicles in the gorge without mishap. But when we reached the avalanche-wrecked trail above the old mill we had to dismount and pick our way through the debris with care. I was stumble-footed with weariness. When I got back on my horse I let my body hit him as if I were loading on a sack of grain. He stepped to the side, off the trail, to brace himself. The snow was bottomless there. In an instant he was floundering in a panic.

Before I could jump off and give him his head he upset on the forty-five-degree slope, pinning me underneath. Like a living toboggan, we scooted for the canyon bottom, the horse smack on top of me. The soft snow kept me from being hurt, but I couldn't kick loose. I couldn't yell or breathe or see. My brain was full of a roaring noise, and the rest of me was palsied with fear. All I knew was that we were zipping headlong toward a forty-foot drop into the creek bed.

The horse did what I couldn't. He rolled over and I slipped free. I spit out a great gob of snow, clawed my way to the surface, and blinked my eyes clear. The horse had stopped a few feet farther on, flat on his back, his feet waving feebly in the air. I bulled my way down to him through the clinging drifts. After considerable labor I mashed out a trench around him and by pulling now on his tail, now on his legs, now on his head, I got him over on his side. He struggled the rest of the way to his feet under his own power.

He was trapped, however. The snow, except where we had tramped out a hole with our floundering, was almost level with his back. I took off his bridle and adjusted the saddle on his back, hoping it would help keep him warm while I summoned assistance. Then I left him. Never in my life have I felt like such a heel.

I very nearly didn't make it back to the trail. The snow was up to my armpits and the slope was steep. I lunged ahead against the soft mass and nothing happened. I tried lying flat on the surface to distribute my weight and wiggled like a worm. That didn't work. It was the most desolate feeling of helplessness; I wanted to sit down and bawl. Then Tom managed to throw a small log within reach, and I was able to get some purchase on that. How long it took me to go fifteen or twenty feet I don't know. But at last I was able to grasp Tom's rope, and the rest was fairly simple.

I looked back at the horse. "What's Herrin going to say about this?" I wondered. I was wringing wet with perspiration; my knees were limp as grass.

"He'll say thirty bucks," Tom grumbled, "and you deserve it. It's going to be hell getting that critter out of there. I thought you were supposed to know something about horses. . . . Well, let's go."

He started up the trail, with me walking behind and clinging to his pony's tail for a tow on the steeper grades. It was almost dark when we reached the mill, rumbling mournfully in its cavern of snow. Fearfully I cranked the wall telephone, rang Herrin, and told him what had happened.

He laughed fit to kill. "You!" The receiver rattled with his delight. "An old cowpoke pulling a bonehead like that! Ha, ha, ha, ha!"

Ears burning, I said, "I'd help you dig him out, but there's no one else to run the hoist and——"

"Oh, I'll get him tonight. Ha, ha, ha, ha!"

"About paying——"

"Forget it!" he said. And off he went into another gale. I think he must have had to lean against the wall to keep from falling down in his mirth.

Sure enough, he rescued the horse. He rode to the point where the trail crossed the canyon, then snowshoed along the creek until he reached the trapped animal. He carried with him a shovel and two large pieces of canvas. He dug the horse clear, then spread a canvas on the snow. The pony could stand on this without sinking. As it moved forward from one canvas to the other Herrin would pick up the rear one and respread it in front. It took him all night to maneuver the horse to safety. If one of the foreign-born miners had been responsible—Herrin always grimly anticipated the worst from them—he would never have gotten over it.

But he didn't speak a word of censure to me, beyond joshing me unmercifully every time he saw me. It doesn't make sense, I grant, but, at that, man's prejudices have been responsible for stranger antics in higher places.

After the phone call I joined Tom in the kitchen. The cook had hot soup and pie waiting for us. As she dished it out she asked, "Anything happen?"

Tom considered. Avalanches, icicles, brawls, snow-sledding horses—none of them was worth a mention.

"Why," he said with a superior smile, "we had a bath."

V   SUMMER PASTORAL

IT WASN'T LONG BEFORE OUR WHOLE basin had a bath. The stubborn clouds broke apart, trailed away in long, wiggly wisps, and the full flush of the spring sun poured through. Melting snow water leaped over every cliff, chuckled in every draw. Every tree, every rock sang with the bright drip-drip-drip. The drifts shrank away from the open slopes; moist, dark spots of earth appeared, joined hands, and grew like magic. Almost overnight, it seemed, the basin turned green. I cannot tell you how *green* it was. The dead-white blanket was gone and our world was alive again.

At best I had scant affection for my hoist. Now, with soft winds blowing and cloud puffs fat in a fathomless sky, the strange compulsion that kept the miners going contentedly back to their dark holes was to me incomprehensible. I applied for a transfer outside, and one June morning I was assigned to the rock pile.

Everyone thought this a great joke. I soon discovered why.

The rock pile was a huge mound of boulders by the side of the mill. All winter it had been growing, a sort of wart on the orderly face of the reduction process. This is how it happened. The trammer brought his ore cars out of the mine into the top of the mill and dumped the load down a sloping grizzly onto the steel floor by the crusher machine. The crusher man then shoveled the ore

61

into a pair of crunching steel jaws that chewed it into pebbles for the mill.

Theoretically the ore reached the crusher in easily handled pieces. This happy state was fairly well realized on three level, where the muck had to be hoisted, but in other parts of the mine, where it was simply dumped into chutes for the trammer, theory paled before reality. Rock breaking is no fun; any object which a strong man could possibly roll into the chutes was considered "small." Often the trammer appeared at the crusher with boulders far too massive to fit the machine's hungry jaws. The crusher man thereupon consigned all miners to the infernal regions and with a twelve-pound double jack set about reducing the chunk to workable sizes.

Near the crusher man's elbow was a door which opened into thin air high in the side of the mill building. He was supposed to throw out through this door any piece of waste (non-metallic) rock which escaped the sorters in the mine. The crusher men had a strictly unofficial fair-practices code about this. It decreed that the difference between waste and ore was approximately twelve minutes. If a boulder, however metallic, could not be broken in that much hammering time it became waste. The worker took a quick look around to see that no boss was near by and hastily rolled the hateful lump through the door onto the rock pile.

By the time summer made outdoor work possible the rock pile had swelled to mountainous proportions and had to be hauled away to make room for next winter's discard. The supers pretended not to see the metallic boulders scattered here and there among the waste, for lugging them back to the top of the mill and breaking them in pieces would cost more than they were worth. Everything was loaded indiscriminately into a rickety car, pushed out onto an equally rickety trestle, and dumped into one of the numerous gullies surrounding the mill.

It was beyond my physique to boost the heavier boulders into the car; I had to break them into lighter pieces with a sledge hammer. Now these were specially selected rocks, collected here because the crusher men had not been able to dent them. I used to beat on those things until I was blue in the face; I knocked off their corners until they were practically round, but some of them I could not crack.

This gave vast pleasure to the crusher men, who would have been humiliated had I succeeded where they had failed. Wreathed in smiles, they stood above me in the waste doorway, leaning on their shovels and calling down witticisms as I swung my futile hammer. One of them was particularly obnoxious. He was at least sixty years old, a massive, bull-chested Hercules with a fine, rugged head topped by tight gray curls. With his huge work-warped hands, tree-trunk legs, and twinkling eyes, he looked like the very spirit of Happy Toil. His name was Jim Short, and he was far and away the strongest man at the Camp Bird.

I brooded darkly over his sallies; after all, his surreptitious boulder rolling on black winter nights was in part responsible for my predicament. Then one day I remembered how Tom Sawyer had succeeded in getting his fence whitewashed. Perhaps a similar approach would serve me.

The next morning I picked out a medium-sized boulder and, making sure he was watching, beat on it in a frenzy. Winded at last, and having accomplished nothing, I sank down to rest, mopping my steaming brow.

"Where's your poosh?" said Jim gleefully from above. "Can't you put that little rock in the car without marceling it all morning?"

"This rock?" said I. "Ha! I'd sure admire to see the man who could lift it all in one piece."

"Why, I could," said he, not boasting, but stating a plain fact.

I knew a dare would reveal my strategy, and he'd back off with a whoop of delight at discovering so obvious a trick. I had to make him think that he really oughtn't tackle the boulder. Dubiously I said, "It's pretty big. You might strain your back."

"What?" cried Jim, dumfounded that anyone could entertain such a notion about *his* back. Down he rushed. He wrapped his great arms around that rock; he heaved upward and cast it into the car with a clang that echoed from the peaks.

"There!" he said, brushing his hands together.

"Golly!" I breathed in hushed and reverent tones.

"Aw, 'tain't nothing," he said modestly. His chest was expanded, his biceps corded. His eyes roamed about, hunting prey worthy of his power. They fell on the biggest boulder in the pile. He grappled with it. I thought he would die of apoplexy. His eyes started out of his head; the veins in his temples swelled and throbbed; his face turned positively black. But he made it.

"Golly!" I breathed, and this time I meant it.

From then on I saved my largest, hardest rocks for Jim. He never tumbled. Like most strong men, he had a childish pride in his strength, and he went on lifting three-hundred-pound rocks in return for my not altogether synthetic admiration. Considering his gray locks, this perhaps sounds like a low trick to have played on him. But age had left Jim with energy to spare. He said it was because he neither drank nor smoked. Vices, he called such practices, since they weren't "natural." Other things he seemed to find natural indeed, his sixty years notwithstanding. Once or twice a week, after a hard day's labor on the crusher, he walked nine miles to town, spent the night in licentious pursuits, and the next morning *walked* back up the hill in time for work. There's no telling how many "two bucks a throw" my rock lifting saved him that summer. Perhaps not as many as I think. He was an extraordinarily vital old goat.

Jim was also blossom gatherer of the place. He rambled far and wide on the steep hills, plucking the exquisite blooms that spread in a sea of color above timber line. He had a predilection for columbine, the gorgeous five-petaled, blue-and-white state flower of Colorado. But he liked his beauty en masse. He jammed his bouquets together until he had a solid column of stems larger than even his great hand could span, then lashed them firmly with string. "Heft that!" he'd say proudly. "I'll bet it weighs four pounds!"

Using old coffee and lard cans for vases, he put the flowers all over the boardinghouse. Other armfuls he carried to town with him as good-will offerings to the dazzled chippies. Still others he wrapped in wet moss and brown paper and mailed to friends throughout the Western states. I actually feared that his exuberant reaping might denude the slopes, but he was a thoughtful botanist. He never disturbed the roots and in every patch he left more than he picked for seed. He had been at it for years, and the ranks upon ranks of blossoms that stretched from our doorstep as far as the eye could see betrayed no marks of his activities. It takes a caravan of Sunday motorists from a city to kill a wild-flower patch.

Summertime was vacation time. We worked seven days a week —without overtime pay—and no one seemed worried by this outrageous breach of union standards. The men hoarded up the Sundays they should have had off and took them all in a lump. This gave them a chance for a real vacation and gave me a chance at any number of jobs. I was continually taken off the rock pile to fill in some gap in the mill, and so by various haphazard steps I followed the ore from the time it entered the reduction works to the time it left.

To any untrained eye the mill looked like a hopeless clutter, its racket-making machines packed as close together as possible, since every foot of roof space was a liability in that country of heavy snows. The building was constructed in tiers, following the slope of the hill, so that the water-borne ore could carry itself ever downward. The air was a maze of stairways, ladders, pipes, conveyor belts, wires, stanchions, braces, runways, troughs, and what not. You had to walk with care to keep from being brained on a low obstruction or from falling down a hole. There was only

one color—gray. Gray rock dust, gray mud, gray concentrates—
they crusted every single thing. Now and then you'd see a man
sweeping the floor and the machines, probing his broom into
every nook and cranny. The rubbish he collected he carefully put
back into the mill flow, for each seemingly worthless pile of dirt
in the place carried its infinitesimal particles of gold and silver.

A grimier group of humans than the millworkers was never
seen. Their clothes were saturated with rock dust, oil, and slime;
their faces were streaked, their hair matted, and they reeked of
the odoriferous chemicals among which they worked. At a casual
glance they seemed to spend most of their time scurrying about
in aimless fashion, like a dog exploring a stubble field. They
weren't much on theory, and a formula would have floored them.
But, like most skilled workmen, they could poke and pry, sniff,
squint, feel and taste, and tell almost as well as a laboratory ana-
lyst how their product was coming along. It is the sort of ability
that is achieved only through long experience, and mostly I
watched them openmouthed, without the faintest idea of what
they were doing.

The mill's multitudinous activities were designed to separate
so far as possible the valuable minerals—silver and gold—from
worthless impurities and gangue. The crusher started the process
and passed the pebbles along with a stream of water to the ball
mill. This was a huge, hollow steel cylinder, perhaps eight feet
tall and somewhat longer. It was loaded with hundreds of iron
balls and rotated on its own axis with a deafening clatter. The
clanging, rolling, bounding, crushing balls gave the ore a thor-
ough trouncing and discharged it as a gray slime. Just in case
some of the ore got by without being ground fine enough, the
slime was screened and the coarse particles raked by an ungainly
contraption called a classifier back into the ball mill for another
shot.

There followed various contrivances—jigs, jerking tables, set-
tling tanks, thickeners, agitators, and so forth, all based on the

fact that gold and silver are heavier than most other substances and can be lured away from them by gravity separation. After the metal had been more or less freed from its worthless companions the remaining pulp was washed over electro-silvered copper plates set in tables on a gradual slope. These plates were regularly given a coating of mercury. Particles of gold and silver adhered to the plates, the mercury penetrating them and forming a pasty, silvery-colored amalgam.[1]

Amalgamation is satisfactory only for coarse gold and silver. About 40 per cent of the available total—fine particles as well as that mixed with the sulphides of lead, zinc, copper, and iron also present in the Camp Bird ore—skipped over the plates scotfree. This loss has been bothering men during untold ages of gold recovery by the mercury method (Pliny described amalgamation in his *Natural History, circa* 75 A.D.), but it was not until the close of the last century that scientists discovered how to check it.

One method is the cyanide process. Fine particles of gold and silver are dissolved out of the pulp by a weak solution of deadly poisonous potassium or sodium cyanide, filtered and then reprecipitated as an unappetizing black goo on zinc shavings or zinc dust—all of which sounds simpler than it actually is.

Another method, often used in conjunction with cyanidation, is the flotation process—an outstanding example of the way in which man has learned to make inert materials do his work for him. At the Camp Bird we would add a small amount of aromatic pine oil—the only nice-smelling thing in the whole works —to the pulp. The liquid was then run into a series of cells, each equipped with an electric motor which whipped it into a froth. The "oiled" mineral in the pulp was less easily "wetted" by the water than the gangue. The gangue sank, in exact reverse of the

[1]Mercury-saturated corduroy cloth is gradually replacing copper plates. The ribs in the cloth act as riffles to catch the gold; it can then be washed out in a tub, much as you would launder an old pair of pants. It is called a "new" process, though actually it harks back to the days of the forty-niners, who used to put pieces of carpet on their sluice boxes.

gravity-separation principle. Meanwhile, the rising air bubbles
in the froth seized the tiny particles of heavy metal by the scruff
of the neck and lifted them to the surface, helped on their way
by the addition of another nasty chemical called xanthate. The
froth was very stiff, smelly, dark gray, and poisonous. It slopped
with its precious burden over the edge of the cell into a trough
and flowed to an iron drier shaped like an inverted cone, underneath which some hunky, such as myself, kept a fire burning.
Here the water was driven off—so, too, was a nauseating reek
of sulphur fumes—and the resultant warm, dark sand was shoveled into a pile on the floor.

This sand was known as concentrates. It contained, along with
a good deal of stubborn rock that refused to be kicked aside,
particles of gold, silver, lead, zinc, copper, and iron, the latter
four in such small, hard-to-get proportions as to be almost worthless. On achieving the concentrates, the mill had done all it could.
It had taken each day some one hundred tons of ore raw from
the mine, each ton containing a tiny fraction of 1 per cent of gold,
and had beaten it down to four or five tons of concentrates containing 20 per cent to 30 per cent gold. It was only by going
through this complex rigmarole that transportation to the smelter,
where the concentrates were reduced to their component parts,
became humanly or economically possible.

It kept one man humping—I know from arduous experience
—to wrap the concentrates for shipment. We funneled it into
canvas sacks about eighteen inches deep, laced them shut with
wire, and staggered with them to the loading platform, ready for
the packers' ill-tempered mules. We had to wear thick leather
aprons for the work—the sharp-edged grains cut like razor blades
—and at night our skins would be gray and sore from particles
that permeated our clothes. The sulphur fumes from the drier
were bad enough in summer, when I could leave doors and windows open; in winter, when the place was shut tight, the throat-
searing stench must have been all but overpowering.

Toward afternoon those eighty-pound sacks seemed to triple in weight. Fresh from my triumphs over Jim Short, I used to try to flatter Hughie, the storekeeping mill hand, into helping me. He'd pick up a shovel or a sack, as if about to comply. Then suddenly he'd give a great guffaw, beckon me to his side, and whisper one of his lewd jokes into my ear. After repeating the point two or three times to be sure I caught it he'd slap me a mighty clap on the back and roar, "Funny, ain't it? Almost as funny as if I'd be sackin' concentrates." Then away he'd go, leaving me to stew in my own trap.

Obviously a concern engaged in the manufacture of pocketable wealth presents its temptations. Down in Ouray, as in every mining town, there were fences glad to buy whatever amalgam, rich concentrate, or high-grade ore you could smuggle to them. Many a miner was glad to aid and abet.

Occasionally in some drift or stope the men would break into a veritable treasure chest, a pocket of ore assaying twenty-five or thirty thousand dollars a ton, as contrasted to the usual run of some eight dollars a ton. (There was rarely a whole ton of such fancy ore in any one pocket, however.) This, indeed, was picture rock, the kind you read about in storybooks—spangled and scabbed and encrusted with solid gold. A single selected piece might be worth a hundred dollars. Pebbles like that in your jeans or hidden under a sandwich in your lunch box added a nice flavor to your next night in town.

To prevent leaks either the mine foreman or the superintendent checked the workings every morning. On the rare occasions when picture rock appeared the regular shift was moved out. One or two men of proven honesty—whispering Tom Rice was one— took over the work. No common milling for this rich ore. It was hand-sorted, sacked, and sent direct to the mint.

In spite of these precautions a trickle of high-grade (a stealer of rich ore is called a high-grader) found its regular way via irregular channels down the mountain. The company knew it and accepted the fact with resignation. The trouble that would be occasioned by subjecting the men to the indignity of a daily search would cost more than the ordinary piece of high-grade was worth. This didn't mean, of course, that the officials went around with their eyes shut. Any miner caught red-handed was immediately turned over to the sheriff.

It was in the mill rather than the mine that the possibilities for theft were greatest. The sediment in the bottom of any machine was incredibly rich. This was particularly true of the ball mill, whose cylindrical interior was fortified against the terrific pounding it received by specially hardened steel plates called liners. Every so often we had to change these liners. We unbolted a trap door in the belly of the cylinder, crawled inside with huge wrenches, and stripped off the old liners. Underneath there was a mat of fine black sand that had sifted through the cracks. Carefully we scooped it out. The yield was perhaps a tubful. It looked as useless as the crust from an old kettle, yet that tubful was so charged with gold that it would keep a man in filet mignon for many a day. Any fence would pay well for even a tobacco pouch full of it, and the foreman kept a weather eye peeled when it was being handled.

And always there was the thin coating of amalgam on the copper plates, the easiest prey for a petty thief. A man with a scraper and a couple of unobserved minutes could in time collect himself a pretty penny, dab by little dab.

It was impossible for the bosses to watch the plates every minute. As a result the millworkers had to be trustworthy. A mine foreman might hire a hand after sizing him up with a thoughtful squint, but a mill foreman was more careful. He didn't depend on letters of recommendation, either. An astonishing grapevine connected gold properties all over the state; every superintendent knew the record of workers in other plants. Let a man get in a "scrape" (pun intended) at one place and he could rarely find employment at another. This, plus the fact that mill hands are not apt to be as fiddle-footed as hard-rock stiffs, lent a solidity to the reduction plant which the mine did not possess.

Still, there was no use tempting a man too far. The "stripping" of the amalgam plates was the private function of our mill boss, Hap Stone. He was a mechanical wizard, ruthless with himself. He thought he was equally ruthless with his men. He was always breathing dire fulminations—which he seldom carried out. Round-faced, sapphire-eyed, profane, and evil-minded, he could converse intelligently on only one subject—gold milling. Twice a year he started off on a two weeks' vacation and came back when about six days of it were gone. Since boyhood he had been surrounded by machines and he was contented nowhere else. He was destined soon to die among them, on the job as usual.

Each day Hap peeled the amalgam from the plates with a knife shaped something like a putty scraper. The precious stuff he stored in a safe in his littered office beside the bone-shaking ball mill until he'd collected enough for retorting. His retort was a cast-iron vessel with a conical bowl whitewashed inside, and he prepared it for work with all the ceremony of a religious ritual. When he placed amalgam in the bowl his lips moved as if he were uttering an incantation. He smeared the rim with lime paste to seal all cracks and clamped down the lid with a thumbscrew. Then he fired up the furnace under the retort and, giving way to the poisonous fumes of the vaporizing mercury, reluctantly left the room. Not until then would he answer a question or speak a word.

A small pipe led from the retort's lid to a condenser. The heated mercury passed out of the amalgam as a gas, condensed back to liquid in the water-cooled pipes, and was captured for further use. As a gas it was deadly and, as the miners said, "salivated" a person. The victim's gums grew black, swollen, and bloody. His teeth fell out, and his salivary glands poured forth quantities of fluid. Death, if it came, was generally an anticlimax.

The end product of retorting was an extremely heavy, drab yellow lump about the size of a cantaloupe. If you saw it lying in the street you would probably kick it aside with one foot. Yet it was compounded of gold and silver worth from five thousand dollars to ten thousand dollars, depending on its size and purity.

The superintendent himself saw to getting these lumps down the hill to the express office. I never knew on which 'of his many trips he carried bullion rolled up in his slicker and tied behind his saddle, and I don't think anyone else knew. He was never molested. In a way this was disappointing—not to him, but to my romantic imagination. In the old days some bold spirit would at least have tried to catch him with the goods. But now that the mere possession of gold is a criminal offense, a highwayman would be hard put to dispose of his ill-gotten gains. In the face of the government's gigantic national steal—metal men still consider the Federal confiscation of gold a steal, no matter by what justifiable terms the economists describe it—the former sweeping methods of bullion robbery have degenerated to petty thievery, with some miserable fence disposing of driblets of smuggled goods to the mint (the sole legal purchaser of gold today) under pretense that he has mined it himself from an old dump or falsely incorporated placer claim.

During summer we spent little time in our rooms. After supper we played catch—we couldn't organize ball teams since there was no flat spot on the boulder-strewn slopes large enough for a diamond—or we pitched horseshoes to the accompaniment of crude practical jokes. Most of the men were young and buoyant and enjoyed slapping each other around like so many bear cubs. During the winter's tension a scuffle was all too apt to end in serious battle, but now friendly wrestling matches in the fragrant bunch grass were spontaneous occurrences. Loafing around together out under the sky, we even discovered that some of our fellows were not nearly as unendurable as we had thought them to be.

The Slavs, the Finns, even most of the Swedes, were content to stick around the boardinghouse after shift, spending their leisure in pure idleness. But there was in the native Americans, millman and miner alike, a touch of the prospector, a dream that they might find a claim of their own someday. They got out and rambled the hillsides, scrutinizing outcrops, probing into old dumps, sampling gravel beds. They didn't fool themselves any. They knew perfectly well that the development of an ordinary block of ore requires such a vast outlay of capital that few companies dare undertake it without careful study. They knew that the chances of finding in that heavily prospected country a vein rich enough for them to develop alone were incalculably remote. But that didn't quell their curiosity.

Perhaps it was a hang-over of the old pioneering spirit. Perhaps it went even deeper, to the roots of what was meant when long ago it was written "all men are created free and equal." It doesn't cost anything to look, to dream, to try. We dare do the honest things our spirits bid us do, and no man tell us nay. It is not so everywhere else in this world.

When we were on graveyard shift (the mill ran three shifts a day to the mine's two) we could have a full quota of daylight for our explorations. We'd work from eleven at night to seven in the morning, eat "breakfast," and take off into the hills, not returning until suppertime. Then a little nap and back on the job. Sleep? We could make that up the next day. Or the next. Summer was short, and we wanted to utilize it to the full.

There was plenty to see. During the depression years, when employment was down and the price of gold was up, an unadvertised stampede took place back to the Colorado hills. It had little in common with the reckless get-rich-quick rushes of frontier days. It was not centered in one locality or fanned by exaggerated rumors of some sensational strike. Instead it was made up of an army of poor men who could not find jobs. Lonely men going by ones and twos to the streams and forests, sluicing old mine dumps and forgotten placer beds, salvaging the price of a meal from some workings that had been abandoned when gold was cheaper. Hope, armed with a rusty pick and a secondhand shovel.

Yet it was all like prospecting in this: the next shovelful would be IT.

Once, where lonely Ten Mile Creek boils down into the canyon of the Animas, I saw a splintered cable spanning the roily waters of the river. Along the cable bounced a cracked, rusty tramcar. In it was hunched a man. He was coming across for supplies which the narrow gauge railroad had left for him beside the track. As he tossed a sack of flour, a five-pound can of coffee, some lard, and dynamite into his conveyance he asked me over for dinner, promising fresh trout. We climbed into the swaying tramcar and by means of a rope pulley nailed to the tree on the opposite bank hauled ourselves over the river.

My host's name was Fred. He lived in a hollowed-out pile of brush, rock, and scrap iron that looked like a beaver hutch. As we fried the trout (out in the open lest we burn his house down) Fred told me he was the best prospector in Colorado. "Look at that fissure vein." He pointed with his knife. "Nobody else would of seen it. But I located it. Pay ore, too. A few more rounds an' I'll have it."

As far as I know, Fred is still there, still looking. But—the *next* round . . . They never stop believing.

They even laugh at their own faith. They have all chuckled over the hoary joke of the heaven-bound prospector stopped at the pearly gates by Saint Peter, who said, "You can't come in. I passed a bunch of miners last month, and now they're assaying their harps, digging up the golden streets, and stoping out the Elysian fields. It's driving the rest of the angels frantic."

"I'll make a bargain with ye, Pete," the prospector said. "If ye'll let me in I'll get rid of every mother's son of them hard-rock stiffs."

The terms were satisfactory, and the gates were opened. The prospector started a rumor that there was a big gold strike in the vortex of hell. In an instant the entire mining population cast aside their crowns and disappeared over the rim. As the last one passed from sight the old prospector suddenly grabbed up a pick and set out in pursuit.

"So long, Pete!" he called over his shoulder. "I'm goin' too!"

Our favorite walk was up Canyon Creek toward Yankee Boy Basin. Once this majestic, timber-filled, granite-studded gorge had teemed with life. Now fire-blackened mills and tottering houses stood forlornly in flower-spangled meadows. The ruins looked dead as a hammer. But if you peered closely you'd see a lone man feeding a sluice box beside an ancient boardinghouse where once hundreds had lived. Or a father and son running a dinky gasoline-powered placer machine in the shadow of a rusted battery of stamp crushers. A woman cooking for them in a patched cabin. They didn't make much money, but they got along and were thankful. Relief had not yet become a standard of living.

On a day late in August one of the Camp Bird trammers and I visited a man with patched trousers and boots laced with string who had contrived a mill out of a discarded boiler turned by water wheels. We looked over the samples of another unshaven, mud-spattered prospector who had found a stringer of quartz in an abandoned stope in the Ruby Trust and was already thinking of moving his wife up to share its development with him. We also learned that not all the effort and hope were honest, that trashiness is never very far away from greatness.

As we ambled along the creek we met the county sheriff astride an old white mare. After we'd swapped some small talk he asked us if we were in a hurry. We said no.

"Then I reckon I'll deputize you," he said. It seemed that a certain ne'er-do-well had stolen several hundred feet of belting from a freight house (don't ask me how on earth he managed it or why he picked on that unwieldy commodity) and was trying to peddle chunks of it at bargain rates to near-by prospectors. The sheriff had received a tip that the thief was living in one of a cluster of dilapidated houses we could see on the hillside, and he had come up to apprehend the man.

The sheriff wasn't armed. In fact, he seemed very casual about the whole thing, yet we knew he meant business. This apparent casualness, this yawning and scratching of beards with thumbnails, was a favorite mask to cover all sorts of emotions—sentiment, fear, anger, anything you didn't want your neighbor to see.

Having been "reckoned" in as deputies—there was no other ceremony—we followed the sheriff toward an obvious clue: the only house on the hill which had smoke coming from the chimney. The sheriff went straight to the door and knocked loudly, regardless of the fact that anyone so inclined could have taken position behind the shuttered windows and leisurely shot him down.

No answer. The sheriff rattled the knob. "Locked," he said and gazed thoughtfully about. His eyes fell on a four-by-four timber lying on the ground, a handy battering ram. We picked it up. The sheriff considerately took the front end, where he would be the first to meet whatever greeted us.

The door burst open at our first charge, and we tumbled inside. Not a soul was in sight. Yet someone had recently been there. A pot of coffee and a kettle of beans simmered on the stove. We searched the house and at length discovered our prey hiding under a brass bedstead. We had a terrible time extracting him; he clung with such resolution to the bed leg as we tugged on his feet that finally we had to jab him in the ribs with a broom handle to make him let go. The sheriff then stood him in a corner where he alternately glowered and sniveled. We ate his beans—he no longer needed them—and went our separate ways. So ended my career as an officer of the law. At least I suppose it ended, though we were never undeputized. We figured that on a wage basis of three dollars a day the county owed us thirty-seven and one half cents each for our effort. We never got it. Perhaps the treasurer figured that we had devoured our salary in beans.

The contact with the sheriff did this to me: it heightened the restlessness I had been feeling all summer. He was like the men I had known on the ranch, and nostalgia overwhelmed me. Not that I had any disdain for the miners; indeed, I had grown very fond of some of them. But they were of a different stamp from cowpunchers. Ranch work—the sun and wind and far horizons, the continual self-initiative demanded by a job where there might be no foreman to tell you what to do—lent a salty independence that was missing from the ordered routine of the mine. True, the average cowboy was apt to be lazy and opinionated; no hard-rock foreman would have put up with his stubborn ways. Still, the contrast between his free life and the dark caverns inside the earth was inevitable. I found myself thinking of it more and more. Besides, I was getting some money in my jeans. Nothing makes a person cockier, and I began to walk with a critical eye.

I had come to the Camp Bird with a goal of fifteen hundred dollars. So vast a fortune, I thought, would enable me to marry the girl patiently waiting back in New York State; we could then settle on the ranch and spin out the rest of our days in affluence. Love is often mistaken for good sense.

I was still two or three hundred dollars short of this rainbow vision when suddenly in September the first blizzard howled down on the peaks. It blew me right over those remaining dollars. I spent about a minute and a half remembering the previous winter, then packed my war bag and went down the hill as fast as I could go.

I took many a memory with me, and today they have their poignant reminders. Not long after I left the Camp Bird lease a fire gutted the old boardinghouse. No one was hurt, though some of the men got out with only their night clothes (underwear), and by dynamiting the snowsheds and barns, the mill was saved. But Hughie's store—Hughie's unparalleled store—disappeared in smoke.

The company built a new boardinghouse, a modern one with showers and a warm change room. Hughie re-established himself in a room with real shelves and cupboards and lockers. But it wasn't the same. The mountain seemed to know it and resent it. A snowslide roared down the slope and wiped the new building from the face of the earth. Hap Stone, the mill foreman, was killed beside one of his beloved machines. The cook was killed, and the blacksmith and four or five more with whom I'd sat and smoked and spit. Others were desperately hurt. Hughie, bankrupt by the second loss of all his stock, keeps store no more.

After that the company moved down to the old mills in the basin to work the mine from lower, safer levels. Now in the summertime you can drive a car to it. Your family can live with you in one of the little white frame houses of Santa Claus town; your children can go to the one-room schoolhouse under the spruce. But even this may be doomed by the war. Production costs are mounting, and the price of gold stays fixed. No one seems to want gold any longer. Priorities are denied the mines by a government that already has joined the rest of the world in scrapping a monetary-metal standard. Paper economy seems sufficient in these days of billion-dollar pen squiggles, and whether the future will have a place for the things men used to hold precious no one can say. But of this I am sure: whatever kind of money we use tomorrow, there will be pleasanter ways of getting it than digging.

VI HIGH-ALTITUDE ATHLETICS

LONG AGO DAVID SANG, "I WILL LIFT up mine eyes unto the hills."

Their majesty is inescapable, yet very few alpine dwellers ever climb. Mountaineering in many of its aspects entails a devilish amount of work, and those who wring livelihood from the high country already have enough of that.

To be sure, a valley rancher after forty years in the shadow of some crag may at last want to see what his domicile looks like from above. He inveigles his neighbors into a picnic; they slog up the easiest side of the peak, point out their fence lines to each other, and slog back down. Prospectors occasionally make an ascent while looking for outcroppings, and now and then a sheepherder will assuage boredom by heaping a mound of rocks on top of some pinnacle to show he has been there.

None of these ventures is mountaineering, however. None is undertaken with the idea that spiritual values or even plain fun might lie in them. This viewpoint is reserved for certain city dwellers who physically are by no means as well fitted for it as their country cousins. Nonetheless, climbers during the past half century or so have become an integral part of the mountain scene. Oblivious to the stares of the natives, they clump in growing numbers through the streets of the decaying mining towns, sounding like horses in their hobnail boots. Thousands of them have banded together in clubs which publish bulletins, conduct outings, and lobby vigorously in the legislatures for pet conservation bills. During any week of the summer and many weeks of the winter you are apt to find in some remote, hard-to-reach vale groups of from two to sixty ragged, sunburned people enjoying a side of the mountains that the early pioneers seldom saw. Today they are as real to the high country as the miners or sheepherders, and some of my happiest times were spent in the company of these strangers who my compatriots at the Camp Bird and elsewhere sincerely believed were a little "tetched."

My brother Dwight was first infected with the virus, for the mountains had always been a passion with him. We had been born in the mining town of Telluride, Colorado, where the canyon of the San Miguel heads in a U-shaped basin half a mile deep. The boys of the village scrambled about the bases of the bright-colored cliffs as boys elsewhere climb trees and barns. It was an aimless zeal, however, and the idea of focusing it on a peak top never occurred to us until we had theoretically reached the age of better judgment. And then Dwight met some members of the Colorado Mountain Club.

When it developed that the club was planning a week-end assault on Mount Wilson, near Telluride, there was no restraining him. The great day arrived; we threw a pack on an old horse—we were living on the ranch then—and made a two-day ride across the hills to town.

I shall never forget the look on the hotelkeeper's face when we entered the lobby and it dawned on him that we were there to join the mountaineers. He was an odd little man, very frail and very neat, with the thin, high-domed face of an aesthete. His soft eyes peering blandly through thick spectacles made him look as though he should have been on the lecture platform of some university rather than behind the counter of a moribund hostelry.

But behind it he had been since the glamour days of gold, when Telluride boasted twenty-six saloons and no church; when a quarter was the smallest coin in circulation and the conductor on the little narrow-gauge railway announced the town by bawling "To Hell You Ride." In those times champagne and caviar and terrapin had been staple items on the hotel menu; engineers' wives and mineowners' mistresses had come to its parties in Parisian gowns. Sudden death, sudden fortune, sudden poverty—all this the proprietor had seen and shared. Yet he looked at Dwight and me as though he could not believe his eyes.

"Are you going with this outfit?" he said, glancing at the climbers. We hung our heads and mumbled an admission. It was a painful moment.

As I recall it, nineteen people showed up for the trip, twelve men and seven women. Now Telluride was not as populous as it had been. The last of the great mines, the Smuggler-Union, had closed down a few years before. However, the town still remained the county seat; here and there a fresh green lawn showed that some stubborn settler was hanging on. A few fat-bellied, rusty-faced politicians wandered through the red sandstone courthouse; mountain ranchers occasionally stopped by to trade, and bewhiskered placer miners still hopefully poked about the dumps. But for the most part the stores were boarded up, and broken windows gaped in the abandoned houses. The arrival of nineteen people in a body could not escape note.

The astonished city fathers did their best. They gave us a banquet. A good one, too, with the ghosts of the hotel's old chefs rising nobly to the occasion. Instead of receiving the pieces of high-grade ore that in former days had been passed out to distinguished guests, we were treated to abundant samples of the town's last going industry—brewing. There were speeches. The beauties of the landscape were rhapsodically extolled by men whose axes and dredges and dynamite had done their best to destroy that beauty. The old phrase "Switzerland of America"—

every mountain sector of the West calls itself that—was trotted
out and dusted off by half-a-dozen willing throats.

Warmed by their own voices and their own beer, the hosts
began having a wonderful time. Then, just as the party was taking
on a faint blush of former celebrations, the climbers all stood up
and went to bed. They were leaving for the assault at four o'clock
the next morning and they wanted to leave fresh. Incomprehensibility worse confounded! If the dismayed city fathers needed
further evidence of idiocy, here it was.

Four o'clock the next morning was cheerless. Dawn had not
yet come, and no stars were visible in the sodden sky. However,
weather is one of the accepted hazards of climbing. We piled
into cars and away we went along the narrow, breath-taking dirt
road that skirts the vast upper gorges of the San Miguel. Eventually, after passing through the huddle of huts which is Ophir and
skidding wildly along the greasy branch road that leads to
Dunton, we reached a high, alpine vale known as the Dunton
Meadows. Here we left the cars and set out afoot. It was daylight
now, but Mount Wilson was not to be seen. Clouds lay on the
treetops.

I might as well admit now, before some gimlet-eyed purist
admits it for me, that this trip was not mountaineering as a
fortunate handful of alpinists are able to practice it. Very few
American mountains are comparable to the danger-bristling
giants of other lands. American climbers, self-conscious about this,
have taken to describing their peaks as "friendly," meaning that
they are not prone to repay a moment's carelessness with instant
annihilation. Still, danger is a relative term, and most mountains
present somewhere in their course the topographical feature of
rising rapidly in elevation. Longs Peak, above Estes Park, Colorado, has probably been climbed by more people than any other
mountain on earth (except those which can be surmounted via
automobile or funicular railway). Yet even Longs Peak presents
one absolutely unscalable section, plus others where you can kill

yourself without half trying, as several battered corpses testify. It does not pay to treat even a friendly mountain with contempt.

There are fifty-odd peaks in Colorado fourteen thousand feet or more in elevation, and most require only stout shoe leather and stout lungs for a successful ascent. Mount Wilson (14,250 feet) is not one of them.[1] In spots you have to scramble. Moreover, its rotten rock tends to sheer off in great gobs at a touch. All this worried our leaders. Nineteen people are far too many for a delicate climb. From an avid mountaineer's standpoint they are far too many for any ascent. Such herd affairs smack dismally of the strange community-picnic instinct so ingrained in Americans. But the picture has its other side. By pooling resources these club outings enable persons to climb who otherwise would lack the individual means and individual skill to get very far into the high country. And the trips can be a deal of fun, once you get into the spirit of things; certainly they present problems far beyond the ken of the small-group mountaineer.

Our leaders ran the gamut on that Wilson climb. Trail finding was the worst. At lower elevations we encountered mazes of timber falls and impenetrable thickets of underbrush. We struggled through what seemed miles of scree and talus, steep slopes of shattered slide rock that have fallen from the cliffs and roll backward under you with every step you take. Rain drenched us, and as we climbed higher we were presented with the odd spectacle of snow going straight up instead of down.

This phenomenon was occasioned by the wind whipping through the basin below. When it met the towering ridge along whose knife-edged summit we were worming our way it was deflected upward with its burden of sleet. The effect, as we crouched there in our lonely miasma of mist, was indescribably weird. It was also cold. I had no gloves, but for some reason I had slipped an extra pair of woolen socks in my pocket. I put

[1] Mount Wilson has since had its name changed to Mount Franklin Roosevelt, but it seems less confusing to use the name under which we climbed it.

these on my hands. The luxury was wonderful—until I noticed, though I tried hard not to, that one of the ladies of the party was also gloveless. I surrendered my socks. Never have I enjoyed so rich a feeling of chivalry or suffered so from frigid fingers.

The storm kept building up intense fields of electricity. When the load reached maturity in the womb of the cloud a thunderbolt was born. It ripped earthward along whatever projection offered the shortest route. A man standing on that bald ridge would serve very well as cosmic obstetrician—once. He would never live to do it again.

Fortunately lightning in the making is easy to detect. The crackling static skitters from rock to rock, zings around your hat-brim, and literally stands your hair on end. By snapping your arm overhead as if cracking a whip, you can, Jove-like, discharge tiny, tingling lightning bolts from your finger tips. The unearthly sizzling all about you is known to mountaineers as "frying eggs," and when you hear it, it is time to hunt a hole.

Again and again we flattened down in the lee of some pro-tecting crag. Suddenly we would feel the bolt go off. It caused no particular pain, and yet we were conscious of some terrific force tearing through our bodies. Instantly the report came, a crescendo of crackles rising to an ear-shattering *spl-i-i-t*. Hard on its heels rolled the typical crash of thunder, so overwhelming by proximity that it seemed the whole mountain must be shaken to pieces. Equally startling was the sharp, acrid smell—keen green, if I may take the descriptive liberty. This, I suppose, was ozone, produced by the electrified oxygen.

When we finally staggered onto the fog-shrouded summit it was 6:00 P.M. We had no desire to wolf out the night on the moun-taintop, yet we knew that fatalities might well repay any attempt by nineteen tired people to descend in pitch-darkness the exposed cliffs we had climbed. Brows knit, the board of strategy went into a huddle. It was decided to select a much longer but safer route to the sheltering timber some three thousand feet below. Westward, long snow slopes dropped into a basin—Killpacker Basin, some disgusted packer had named it long ago. After reaching its bottom, rounding its southern arm, and then doubling back through the spruce forests, we could, we hoped, regain our cars without breaking our necks.

With nineteen ice axes and the ability to use them, the descent of the snow fields could have been accomplished in minutes by a glissade. This is simply skiing without skis. You slide on your feet, crouching with the hip-high, T-headed, steel-pointed ax braced behind you, serving as both rudder and brake. There is nothing more exhilarating; on a thousand-foot run you can build up tremendous speed. Like skiing, the glissade is best done with swishing zigzags and swoops and as few cartwheels as possible. Just make sure there are no crevasses in the way.

On this Wilson trip, however, we had only two or three ice axes, which the leaders used for hacking out steps on icy pitches. So we had to creep downward like snails with the freezing night crowding hard on our heels. Suddenly one of the men flopped in the snow and refused to budge another inch. Nervously we cajoled him and in desperation even shook him up a bit. In the end we had to take him by the arms and drag him down the hill. He became violently ill, retching pitifully.

It was a thing which might have happened to any of us. Mountain sickness is no respecter of apparent physical condition. In extreme form it affects the brain, and by undermining the powers of judgment has played a tragic part in some of the Himalayan fatalities of recent years. At the lower elevations of American mountains the results are not so fantastic. Here headaches, listlessness, nausea, vomiting, cold hands, and cold feet are the main symptoms.

The trouble is apparently caused by insufficient oxygen in the blood stream. Aviators rising from sea level to fourteen thousand feet sometimes faint without artificial oxygen and compensation for pressure changes. A climber ascending on foot affords his body more time to adjust itself. Even so, before he rushes his peak he should spend a day or two conditioning himself in a high-altitude camp. He should also take salt. A short teaspoonful the night before an ascent and another at the start will help keep him healthy, for it seems that mountain sickness, like heat prostration, can be aggravated by loss of essential body salts through perspiration.

When we at last reached timber line on Mount Wilson we tried to bivouac, but the ground was a sea of mud, and the smoky, stuttering fire we managed to kindle was inadequate to cope with the mass miseries of nineteen exhausted souls. In despair we blundered on, clambering endlessly through deadfall and underbrush, falling into ravines, tripping on roots, wallowing knee deep in mountain bogs. Toward dawn we located the cars, returned to Telluride, and collapsed into bed. My first organized climb was over.

The next evening I came down to the hotel lobby, ravenous and creaking in every joint. The proprietor asked, with some maliciousness, I thought, "Well, did you like it?"

I considered. Fortunately God gave man a poor memory for physical discomfort. The active ingredients which made the hurt so brutal at the moment lose their keen edge in retrospect; we are able to look back on them with certain detachment and even make them subject matter of our dearest conversation pieces. Pleasure is different. Memory fondles it. It becomes a nostalgia, poignant and real and difficult to put into words. And so I remembered Mount Wilson. Not the cold and the cruel fatigue, but rather the multitude of tiny things which in their sum make up the elemental poetry of rock and ice and snow. The feel of granite under your fingers, the obedient flex of your muscles swinging you upward to the stance you must reach or fail, the taste of a cigarette when you hunker for a moment under a shelving rock. A flash of sunlight, a laugh, an incongruous patch of dwarf flowers at the base of an icy boulder.

"Yes," I said, "I liked it."

Not long after this my brother Dwight and his hulking, two-hundred-pound side-kick, Melvin Griffiths, the latter now soaring even higher as a member of the Army Air Corps, discovered the choice mountaineering possibilities of Blaine Basin in the western San Juans, between Telluride and Ouray. Spectacular, jagged spires ring the basin round, and its lonely depths are shadowed by the stupendous north face of Mount Sneffels.[2]

Dwight and Mel became so enamored of the spot that with incredible toil they packed up to timber line on their backs enough material to build a shelter cabin. Other enthusiasts occasionally helped them, and when the cabin was completed they were able to reach from it a multitude of pinnacles which for difficult rock problems need bow to few better advertised crags. Sometimes they tolerated me on their climbs, and here Dwight developed the superlative technique which later enabled him to make outstanding ascents in several parts of the Rockies. Had not infantile paralysis killed him when he was twenty-three years old, he would undoubtedly have become one of America's leading climbers. Many of us owe to him what small mountain skill we have, and to him is due our understanding of the things the high country can bring to man's spirit. Brother or no, once you have known a few climbers like him, the world becomes a better place to live in.

The top of the peak is not the mountaineer's main goal. If it were, he would select the easiest route of ascent and become not

[2]Sneffels' odd name was derived from a pair of early surveyors, a Dr. Endlich and an unnamed companion. The abyss below the north shoulder of the peak struck them as comparable to the great hole described by Jules Verne in *Journey to the Center of the Earth*. Pointing to the peak, Endlich exclaimed, "And there's Snaefell!" The doctor thus created a spelling debate long waged in local climbing circles. Snaefell, a mountain in Iceland, did serve as Verne's inspiration, but Verne used the spelling "Sneffels." His misspelling was eventually retained for the new peak, though why, in that unclassical part of Colorado, it has not degenerated to Mount Sniffles I cannot say.

a climber but a sort of goat-footed, barrel-lunged uphill hiker. This is not to gainsay the pleasures of walking above timber line. They are manifold, and many a person has enjoyed collecting summits as a philatelist collects stamps. But such is not the cragsman's way; he wants the toughest path he can find.

Right here he is faced with a decision that will make of his efforts either a rich, human experience or a shallow fraud. Mountaineering can be justified in many ways—exercise, health, scenery, accomplishment, the poetry of the great outdoors, and all that—but in its essence it is utterly elemental, the ancient conflict between man and the earth. In certain respects it is even a form of escape, enabling one briefly to reduce the bewildering fight of modern survival to clear, simple factors of muscle and rock. To danger, also, and to fear. To the primitive animal terror which sickens your belly and sweats your temples.

What are you going to do with this danger and this fear? It can be a salutory purge: to ache with your whole body for retreat and then to learn that you are still able to go ahead. But it can also degenerate into mere thrill chasing, a bristle of anger mixed with obstinacy and vanity, glorified under the vicious concept of "living dangerously." Goaded by such a philosophy, Nazi climbers before the war made incredible ascents in the Alps. They also suffered so many ghastly fatalities that mountaineers in other lands took to calling them the "suicide climbers." Success or death seemed their only alternatives, and for the first time in mountaineering's history the sport became a symbol of national superiority. Hitler and Mussolini actually awarded live victors with medals and dead ones with state funerals. At first honest mountaineers could not understand. They do now, and it is not nice.

This does not mean that the element of danger can be avoided, or even that the climber wants to avoid it. But it can be controlled and it is in this control that mountaineering takes on its happiest aspect. Not mere excitement, but initiative, quick decisions in the face of unexpected threats, perseverance, self-reliance, co-opera-tion—all reduced to bare essentials which anyone can understand and share.

In general, the climber is posed with two problems: first, how to keep from falling off the mountain; second, how to keep some-thing else from falling on him. In each effort it is handy to have a little specialized equipment and quite a little good judgment.

Neophyte mountaineers often suffer from lack of both. I re-member wryly being stranded one rainy evening at the top of a perpendicular slab. We could not get down without artificial help, for, as every small boy knows, it is easier to ascend a thing than to descend. In climbing you are working with your eyes conveniently near your future holds. But when you start down you find that your vision is badly placed in regard to your feet.

In such situations it is well to have a rope along. You can loop its middle about some convenient belay and toss both ends down the cliff—making sure, of course, that they reach the bottom, lest you find yourself quite literally at the end of your rope. You next straddle the doubled strands, face in toward the rock, pull the rope up the outside of one thigh, diagonally across your chest, over your shoulder, and down your back, thus cradling yourself in a kind of sling. Then you fall backward into space. This is rather alarming at first, but the friction of the rope soon checks you and you learn to let yourself down in long swoops, with your feet thrust against the cliff face to keep your body from spinning around and cracking your noggin against the rock. This is known as the *rappel* and, in photographs, is one of mountaineering's most spectacular stunts. By hauling on one of the doubled strands you can retrieve the rope for future reference.

On this particular trip we had no rope. A hundred or so feet of Manila hemp, half an inch in diameter, is heavy to lug around all day, and we had hopefully assumed without first taking the trouble to reconnoiter our route, that we wouldn't need to. It was too late now to hunt another path, so we improvised. We fastened our belts together and buckled them around a jutting rock. We then reluctantly removed our trousers, tested them for strength, and tied the leg ends together. By securing our weird chain to the loop of belts we were able to slide down it hand over hand to a narrow, insecure ledge. It wasn't much fun. It was less fun to leave our apparel hanging there for the entertainment of some future explorer and to walk trouserless eight miles through the rain-soaked underbrush to camp. But it did show us the wisdom of being more circumspect in our choice of route and equipment.

A mountain is not a static thing. It is continually falling apart due to weathering. All the geology books tell you so, but we needed a near tragedy to bring the fact home. It was on the east face of Longs Peak, a breathless precipice rising two thousand sheer feet above Chasm Lake in Rocky Mountain National Park. We got off to a late start, and the August sun was dangerously hot as we started across an ice *couloir* (a gully in a cliff face) known grandiosely as Mill's Glacier. Right while we were in the middle of the gulch a horrid cannonading shattered the silence. Our eyes flashed up the steep-walled couloir. It bent like an elbow a hundred yards above, and we could not see around the corner. But we knew what was coming. The sun had thawed loose the frost bindings of weathered rocks that had been frozen into the snow.

I don't know how many there were, nor how large. It seemed like a million, huge as houses, as they slammed around the bend and hurtled down on us, crashing deafeningly from wall to wall of the narrow trough. Teetering there in narrow steps we had hacked out of the ice, we had no chance to run. We flattened down. Luckily we were just beneath a spot where the ice bellied out somewhat. The boulders hit this hump and leaped over our heads, snarling with their speed and trailing that unforgettable coppery smell of shattered rock. Chips and small pebbles rattled about us. One—a tiny one—struck a man on the head, laid open a long gash, and knocked him limp as yesterday's gravy.

It could have been avoided. Any snow field with rock tracks across it, any gully with a pile of debris at its bottom, any icy couloir when the sun shines into it is a danger spot to be treated with care. Or with recklessness. Once a mountaineer learns his elements, the rest is a matter of choice.

In the early days of climbing rockwork consisted mainly of a grunt-and-groan process of muscling one's way from ledge to ledge. But many cliffs with their smooth flanks and tiny holds cannot be strong-armed that way. So cragsmen evolved a subtler approach known as balance climbing. This new maneuver is nothing more than an adaptation of a principle familiar to all bicyclists, namely, that it is easier to maintain an upright position while moving than while standing still. The balance climber holds his body as nearly vertical as possible. His hands, brushing the cliff face, are used more to sustain equilibrium than to hoist weight. He chooses his support in advance, learns to step where he is looking, and, instead of fumbling for a fulcrum, keeps moving. By skittering swiftly from hold to hold and using fractional wrinkles of rock that would never support him if he tried to remain motionless on them, he is able to negotiate short, hair-raising stretches in a manner which appears almost magical.

Of course it is still possible to fall. That is why the climber employs his rope, his belays, his pitons, and karabiners.

I suppose every mountaineer has ground his teeth over the question, "How do you get the rope up there so you can climb it?"—as if he were somehow able to charm the hemp skyward like a Hindu fakir. The rope gets there by being carried. And although convenient for descent, it is rarely employed as a direct aid to elevation. Its main function, like the eraser on a pencil, is to remedy mistakes. After all, we learn largely by experience, and we would never progress far in anything if our first slip was our last one.

The rope is also a visible sign of the intense teamwork which binds a climbing party together. For instance, your leader is plastered against a sheer cliff. His face is red with exertion; sweat glistens on his forehead. Previously he has stood on your shoulders —a *courte-échelle*—to reach a narrow crack. Into this he has jammed an elbow and knee and fought his way upward via a series of convulsions. Now he has left the crack, and his main support is the friction of his hip and hand pressed hard against the sloping stone.

Cautiously he reaches out, tests a new hold for solidity, rolls his weight forward. He is anchored somewhat. He has driven a short steel spike, a piton, into a crack in the rock and fixed his rope to it with a snap-ring karabiner, so that the cord has support out on the cliff face like a belt run through a loop in a pair of trousers. If he slips, this pivotal point will limit the arc of his fall —provided you have taken up a solid belay and can hold the rope fast the instant trouble develops.

You brace yourself, passing the rope around your shoulders or back, for you never in the world could stop a hurtling hundred and sixty pounds of man with your hands alone. And if you don't stop him and if the rope doesn't break, he will drag you off your perch; you will drag the fellow behind you, and suddenly the rope, instead of being a life line, becomes a suicide pact. Very carefully you pay it out, never letting it go slack and tangle on some projection, never pulling it so tight that it cramps the climber ahead. With this moral parachute tied about his waist, knowing that the chances of a fatal fall are reduced to a minimum, he is able to cross the ticklish spot. And when he reaches a solid stance he plays turnabout by guarding you while you come up—climbing the cliff and not the rope; weasling that way is mountaineering's prime form of cheating.

Neither of you could have managed alone, and you both know it. As in no other sport, you have put your lives in each other's care. You have achieved not singly but through the concerted effort of your own hearts and hands. From this comes a comrade-ship that is rare and true and completely selfless. If mountaineer-ing offered nothing more, its appeal would be unshakable.

Proficiency gained, there comes to the climber a mania which goads him to furies of effort, strands him in miserable bivouacs, ruins his feet, his clothes, and his digestion, but lifts his spirit to heights unknown by ordinary mortals—the desire to make a first ascent, to stand where no other creature has ever stood before.

This business of being first on any American peak is open to suspicion. Animals get around the crags more than you would think. Not only mountain sheep and goats. The grizzly bear, now extinct in Colorado, was an inveterate alpinist. Franklin Rhoda, who as reporter and member of the Hayden survey climbed extensively throughout Colorado in the middle 1870s, was con-tinually grumbling about bears:

> Claw marks on the rocks on either side of the summit [of Mount Sneffels, which Rhoda regarded as his greatest climb] showed that the grizzly had been before us. We gave up all hope of ever beating the bear climbing mountains. Several times before, when, after terribly difficult and dangerous climbs, we had secretly chuckled over having outwitted Bruin at last, some of the tribe had suddenly jumped up not far from us and taken to their heels over the loose rock. Mountain sheep we had beaten in fair com-petition, but the bear was one too many for us. . . . To show our utter disgust [on Hunchback Peak this time] we yelled and threw stones after the bear until he was lost to sight far down the mountainside. In our hate we even wished we might have been in a position whence we could have rolled rocks on him.

There is also the matter of Indians. They certainly used some of the peaks as lookout stations during Kit Carson's trapping days in Colorado, and at least one peak, Longs Peak, was the location of a fascinating enterprise, described in the report of

Oliver W. Toll on the visit of Arapaho Indians to Estes Park, 1913. An Indian named Griswold tells the story:

"Right on top there is a hole dug in oval shape. The top of it is big enough for a man to get down through, but below it widens out and is big enough for him to sit in. This was up there when he [Old Man Gun, an Arapaho brave] captured all those eagles, for it was an eagle trap. He had a stuffed coyote up there, and some tallow. Gun used to sit in this hole, so that he couldn't be seen, and put the coyote on the ground above him, and the tallow by it. The eagles would see the coyote from a great distance and would come to get it. When the eagles lit by the coyote Old Man Gun would grab the eagles by the feet, reaching up by the back of the coyote. Now, this man who used to trap those eagles had some kind of herb that he used, so that just as soon as he grabbed that eagle, the eagle had a fit and was helpless, and he would pull it in. This herb was on his hands, and if he touched you with it you would have a fit. This herb is something that no one else knows what it is. He would catch the wildest horses in the country with it. . . . Shep said that it was probably something like loco weed."

The reporter of the story adds, "Mr. W. N. Byers, the first white man to climb Longs Peak, had made several previous attempts and, after several failures, had prophesied that no living being would ever reach its summit unless they had wings to fly with. It is interesting to know that the Indians had climbed Longs Peak before the white men had ever seen it." [3]

Discounting Indians, bears, and the early fur trappers, who left no records, there is still the matter of local settlers. In determining the virginity of a summit the best you can do is rely on circumstantial evidence. Mountain dwellers, as we have seen, do not go out of their way to climb. If your peak lies far afield, in a region

[3]*Fourteen Thousand Feet,* by John L. J. Hart and Elinor Kingery, Colorado Mountain Club, 1931.

offering neither gold nor grazing grounds, the probabilities are high that it will never be vanquished save by mountaineers. All that remains is for you to be the first mountaineer to reach it.

There are such peaks, though their number is steadily diminishing, in the hinterlands of the Rockies and the Sierras. Most of them are not even named, for they are tucked shyly out of sight at the head of some forgotten valley or dwarfed behind the thick shoulders of a mightier neighbor. Getting at them is apt to be much harder than getting up them. If you are fortunate you can hire a mule packer to transport your gear, or perhaps a donkey which you can load yourself. Beware the burro, however. His innocently ridiculous face hides great guile. His favorite trick is to emit a death-rattle groan and collapse in the middle of the trail. Alarmed, you unpack so as to ease his last hours. He thereupon waggles his ears with a blissful sigh, and to your blasphemous chagrin comes the realization that you have been victimized. Repacking him gives his muscles, though not yours, a delicious rest.

Often the climber must be his own pack horse, fording rivers with the perishable part of his duffel balanced on his head like the water carriers of old Jerusalem, skirting morasses and hacking out trails through brush-clogged canyons. The ultimate camps are Spartan, to say the least. And yet their very inaccessibility gives them a grandeur no easier spot can match.

There was the time when three of us back-packed into the head of Titcomb gorge in the Wind River Mountains of Wyoming. We left timber line far behind, slogging along a stream milky with the floured rock discharged by the glaciers. The gorge was hung with a necklace of tiny sapphire lakes shimmering in cups of solid rock. Patches of moss were springy underfoot from snow just gone; dwarf blossoms of forget-me-not, primrose, king's-crown, and gentian, unable to exist in these rigorous climes as single plants, formed societies of solid color. Bibs of white circled the peaks. Rank after rank of them, tier after tier. Thumbs and fingers and fists all pointing skyward. A dazzling world of swift, sharp lines and crystal light.

At about twelve thousand feet elevation we reached the skirts of a glacier that swept down from the fine double-horned summit we wanted to climb. At the glacier's base we found a massive boulder, its bottom undercut to form a sort of cupboard four or five feet deep and three feet high. A made-to-order shelter, we thought, without stopping to wonder how it had been carved in that particular fashion.

While sunset crimsoned the snow fields we set up our little spirit stove, prepared powdered soup, tea, flinty salt-water biscuits, and dried fruit. We named the camp Little America and had absurd delight in hoisting a flag on top of our boulder—an old shirt hung to an ice ax. The stars winked on, ice-white clusters that spread a frosty phosphorescence across the tumbled rocks and snow. The wind threaded a thin obbligato through the lonely sonata of rushing water, and the huge, awed wonder of space and timelessness filled our throats.

Sitting in such a spot, hugging your knees, you can sense as a tangible thing the hurtling sweep of the earth on its orbit. The very vastness of the pattern stabs you to the heart. But it is not humility. Man would not aspire; he would not be laying his bold chains on every cosmic force he can reach were he only meek. The insignificance some persons profess to feel on seeing a natural wonder which more determined men, given motive, could sail over, tunnel under, or fly around is to me incomprehensible—a hang-over, perhaps, of the oriental fatalism that early tinged our religion. Why not a healthier pride—without arrogance—in being able to muster the courage to see and touch and share the fringes of creation, knowing that if we work well others can share still more? Man is small enough, God knows, without his making himself smaller.

We kicked the larger stones out of our bedroom and by virtue of that happy invention, the air mattress, enjoyed a comfortable night. The next day we climbed our mountains, gave them the unimaginative name of Twin Peaks, and came down again. Darkness and a downpour caught us as we reached our boulder. Soon we learned why the rock was shaped the way it was. Storm water had carved it. It drained a foot deep off the glacier into our cave. We had the choice either of squatting in it or going outside into an icy deluge such as must have started Noah building his boat. We alternated. It was a long night, and we did not enjoy it. Still, it was small price. We had made a first ascent. Climbers will understand that. Non-climbers never will.

Part Two

STOCK TRAILS

VII THE LONG WAIT

WE DIDN'T SETTLE DOWN ON THE ranch. Not for more than a year. Even then, in my most optimistic moods, I did not dare face a girl fresh from the East with Paradox Valley, winter headquarters of my stepfather's ranch.

I had precedent. My stepfather, who really knew Paradox, sent Mother to Denver during winters, but to us Denver seemed a long way off. Martha and I compromised on the county seat of Montrose, a mere hundred miles by vile roads from the valley. Consoling myself with the thought of occasional visits "home" when work was light and highways open, I went alone to wait out the long season of death which in happier climes is known as spring.

The valley runs roughly east and west, a flat-bottomed sink of red soil three to six miles wide and twenty-five or thirty miles long. The ends of the trough are open, but its north and south walls are vast cliffs of red sandstone half a thousand feet high and scalable in only one or two places by breakneck trails. Overlooking it from the Utah border to the west is the majestic triple-peaked rampart of the La Sal Mountains, an isolated massif that rears in solitary grandeur from the surrounding desert. Eastward, Paradox points like an arrow toward the rising sun and the highlands of the Rockies. It is this which makes it of value to stockmen. When snow buries the lush mountain pastures the ranchers have to move their herds to more open spots. Paradox is one of them.

As its name suggests, the valley is a geologic aberration. It has its river, the chocolate-hued Dolores, but instead of flowing along the valley from end to end, as a normal stream should, the river cuts *across* from south to north. It pierces the bastion wall in a titanic, crimson-cliffed canyon of singular beauty, spills sluggishly over the table-flat valley floor in a series of horseshoe coils, gathers itself, and plunges out the northern side in another echoing gorge. In passing it bisects the valley into two distinct entities—East Paradox and West Paradox, each playing its separate part in our scheme of stock raising.

Stock raising. Today that sounds like ancient history.

The war has given Paradox' once-simple economy a violent wrench, all because there exists in the gaunt sandstone mesas surrounding the valley a curious canary-yellow substance called carnotite. Years ago this stuff was important; uranium could be extracted from it and radium from uranium. Later the discovery of extensive deposits of pitchblende in Belgian Congo and the Arctic depressed the market; the Paradox mines and mills shut down. Until the war. Then manufacturers remembered that vanadium, essential to certain steel alloys, can also be extracted from carnotite.

Now the nearby mills are thundering again on a scale never dreamed by the old radium miners. Towns stand on once-desolate flats. Scores of crisp, efficient ore buyers swarm where formerly a chance cattle speculator might wander in and drive a long-winded bargain. Trucks snort about where we had only trails.

But there are some of us who cannot forget. . . .

The dreary month of April rolled around. The scant snow which winter had brought was gone. Under the pale, wind-streaked sky the air was raw and cold. Out in the scattered farm lands which dotted the few choice sections of West Paradox,

Mackinaw-clad plowmen—driving teams because the valley could not then afford tractors—were turning the red earth for spring planting. When summer came the cliffs would reflect the searing sunrays until the great trough simmered like an oven. Corn, wheat, and alfalfa would grow rich and tall wherever water could be brought to it through the irrigation ditches that tapped the thin streams of the La Sal Mountains. But in April there was no hay. Last summer's crop had been devoured. Gaunt wooden derricks stood useless in the empty stackyards. Cattle bawled hungrily on the feed lots.

As we had been doing for days now, a long, lazy, horse-faced cowboy named Mike Gaynor and I loaded hundred-pound sacks of "cotton cake" on pack horses and rode out to one of the fields. The cattle were clustered by the gate, waiting for us. They were range stock, white-faced Herefords and normally wild. But now they sniffed around us like dogs, so close we had to slap them aside as we opened the sack mouths. We doled the cake out to them like gold. It had been trucked over snow-choked roads from the railway at Montrose, and when it was gone there would be no more. We dribbled it on the ground in long ribbons, so all the animals could get at it.

They couldn't gulp it, though they tried. Cotton cake, a yellowish-gray stuff pressed out of cottonseed into lumps about the size and hardness of pebbles, takes chewing. It is pure, concentrated food. For bulk the animals had to eat brush. Up on the ditchbank we could see willow stubs, as big around as our thumbs, which they had gnawed like beavers, trying to fill the hollow places in their stomachs. It hadn't been enough for some of them. A couple of dead ones lay near by; we would have to get a team, drag them off, and dump them in an arroyo. We stood there shivering in the wind, watching the animals quarrel over the life-giving cake, hooking one another aside, grabbing a mouthful, and then running along the line as if they thought there might be tastier bits at the next place. The best of them looked none too good, their winter-roughened coats all woolly and their backbones sticking out like the ridgepole of an unguyed tent.

Mike Gaynor swore under his breath. Whether the creatures lived or died made no difference to him; he drew his wages just the same. But a cowboy feels far more than impersonal pity for a hungry animal.

He glared at the cold sky. "My God," he said, "won't the grass ever grow again?"

We went back to the gate. The farmer who owned the field and sold us its produce came rattling up in an old Bain wagon. He was transporting a plow, and before he opened his mouth we knew what he was going to say.

He spat a stream of tobacco juice, wiped his runny nose on the back of his hand, observed, "Spring gets later every day, don't it?" and added, "You gotta get these cattle out of here so I can plow."

"I don't know where to take them," I said. It was a stock reply, and I couldn't ask my stepfather, ill in a Los Angeles hospital, for a better one. Besides, the situation was familiar. It happened this way every year.

"Maybe," the farmer suggested, "you could shove them across the river into East Paradox."

I measured him. There was no animosity between us; it was simply a case of adjusting ourselves to what had to be. For ten days I had been stalling him, but now he looked as if he meant business. It was my turn to give in. "We'll try to do something," I promised.

Mike and I took our horses back to the barn, got in an old pickup truck, and went bouncing along the narrow dirt road toward the river to see what we could see. We didn't even consider turning the cattle onto the open range around the feed lots. The farmers of the section had first claim to it, and their herds had grubbed it out weeks ago. Nothing remained but inedible saltbrush, shiny green greasewood, drab sage, and spreading acres of canaigre, a low, broad-leafed, obscene-looking plant from whose roots early settlers had extracted a yellow dye for coloring their rag rugs.

East Paradox, uninhabited and desolate, was part of our winter range. Each fall we turned into it the steers and dry cows we thought were husky enough to fend for themselves without hay. Its low red hills were streaked with the grisly white marks of gypsum and crowned with runty groves of cedars and piñon pine. Dry tumbleweeds ("Roosian" thistles, as the cowboys pronounced it) went skittering along before the wind, to find graveyards in the arroyos and coves among the rocks. When snow softened their spines tumbleweed served as a fodder of sorts and kept many a cow from starving. Here and there were sparse stands of shadscale, grama, and curly buffalo grass.

It was a waterless country, with a gap of eighteen miles between the river and the next drink. The graze soon disappeared in the vicinity of water, and the cattle had to rustle far afield for a meal. Their existence sank into a series of three-day cycles. They spent one day hoofing it out into the desert, another day hunting up their sorry feed, and a third day coming back to wet it down. Their own stomachs, and not cowboys, did the driving.

Somehow they eked out a living until spring. By then the old grass was gone and the new had not yet started. Late in March we had rounded them up and driven them onto the tawny, tree-bristling mesas surrounding the valley. Here they might find a few pickings as they waited for the weather to open up, when they would start drifting on their own accord into the brushy foothills of the mountains.

Mike and I drove to East Paradox to see if enough new grass had started yet to hold our evicted herds. It never had before, but every year we followed the useless hope.

The wind whined with a sullen organ sound through the stiff sage. It caught up clouds of red sand and hurled them futilely at the encircling cliffs. We met a horseman and stopped to talk to him. His right ear was full of sand, so we knew he had ridden down from the upper end of the valley with that side of his face to the wind. When he stopped his horse humped up and turned its tail to the blowing dirt. Way out on the flats we saw three steers we had missed on the roundup drifting aimlessly before the gale. Nearer by, a few sheep had gathered around a tight clump of brush and thrust their heads into it. The branches helped filter the sand out of the air they breathed. They looked like gossip-mongers, whispering nose to nose at a tea party.

"Feed?" the rider said. "Not yet." He blew on his fingers and thrust them in his armpits. "Worst spring I ever seen."

"Ain't it, though?" we agreed, though each year was almost the same and only seemed tougher because of proximity.

We drove back to the river. Here was our ace in the hole, our last stand. Embracing both banks of the Dolores was a huge pasture, three thousand or so acres in size. Under the gnarled old cottonwoods and among the dense willows some of last year's grass remained. Here new grass would start first. When we could turn no place else with the cows and calves we had been nursing along in West Paradox we came to the river. We put it off as long as we could; at best the pasturage could last but a few weeks, and if it gave out before the foothills turned green we would be hard pressed indeed. Also, the place was dangerous. Quicksand traps lined the river. Each hour the herds stayed there meant dead cattle. But now we had no other choice.

We borrowed horses from a near-by farm and rode around the fence, splicing the barbwires where they were broken, stapling them to the fence posts where they sagged. How Mike hated the chore! He was forty years old; his father and grandfather had been cattlemen before him, and he remembered the days—or at least stories of the days—when a cowboy did no work that couldn't be done from horseback. He cramped his feet in high-heeled boots too small for them, and walking was a misery. Rather than lead his horse from fence post to fence post, he would mount, ride a dozen steps, and dismount again, to the tune of soulful tirades on the degeneracy of the times. I wish I could recapture them. For sheer fluency they had no equals.

Toward evening we finished patching the fence. The wind had died, but the air was still freighted with sand. It was gritty on our skins; it rasped between our teeth.

Mike heaved a long sigh. "It's Sunday," he said.

He had nothing religious in mind. There weren't any churches in Paradox. Once in a while a circuit preacher would come by and deliver a fire-and-brimstone sermon in the schoolhouse. Mike liked these; their influence was discernible for weeks afterward in his poetic profanity. But this wasn't the day for the sky pilot, and the only other religious function available was the evening service conducted by the valley Mormons. These held no appeal for Mike. They were conducted by local laymen, earnest but unspectacular. (Once I asked a Mormon why they had no paid ministers. He said they didn't figure they needed a special pipe to Heaven; anybody ought to be able to turn on the faucet, and no man deserved pay as valve tender. I must say the results were as practical as the operation. There were no Mormons on relief in Paradox or in the hamlets we occasionally visited across the line in Utah. Just the outward look of their well-kept ranches indicated an inner solidity.)

Today Mike's Sunday interest was in his stomach, not his soul. On Sundays Mrs. Williams, who ran the hotel in West Paradox, served a chicken dinner. Price fifty cents. I was just as tired of my own cooking as Mike was. We returned our borrowed horses, got in the truck, and drove back to our quarters to clean up for the Event.

We lived in an outbuilding on one of the farms where we were feeding cattle. It was a long, narrow, plank-walled shack divided into three boxlike rooms. I don't know for what purpose it had been originally intended, but now it served as catchall for broken harness straps, barrels, cracked fruit jars, old machinery parts, tools, cowhides, and other miscellaneous items our landlord thought he might someday get around to using. He considered himself very generous because he allowed us the place rent free. However, we had to pay him an outrageous board bill for our horses, and he openly expected us to show our generosity in turn by branding his calves and hunting his stray milk cows. He was an alfalfa grower. He had a frail-looking wife and thirteen children whom he hustled about their chores by chucking pieces of stovewood at them. Give the devil his due, though: he worked as hard as they did.

We used only two rooms of our mansion. In a cleared space in one was an old brass bedstead on which we slept. From this a hazardous trail led through the junk to an adjoining room where we had a three-legged cookstove that gave off more smoke through its cracked lids than it did up the rusty chimney. The wind charged through the gaps in the plank walls, scattering its load of red sand with fine impartiality. Our clothes, our bedding, our food, our dishes—every single thing in the place was impregnated with it.

We did possess, however, one attraction of which no other establishment in the valley could boast—an absolutely genuine enameled bathtub.

This piece of aesthetic equipment had once belonged to a wildcat oil company that tried to drill a well in Paradox, encountered a bed of salt whose thickness they never did penetrate, and so gave up. When they moved away their belongings were auctioned off. Our landlord, for reasons I can't divine, had purchased this tub and stuck it in our shack.

No pipes led in or out of it. We remedied the latter defect by boring a hole in the floor directly under the drain, so waste water could run out and sink in the sand. We whittled a stopper out of a plug of wood. By simply lugging in several buckets of water from the well, heating them on the stove, and pouring them into the tub, we were fixed. True, the vessel, like everything else, was generally lined with red sand, but so were we, and the results seemed to justify the occasional effort. Indeed, in the expanse of well-being brought on by the possession of this singular object, we now and then let our neighbors come over and use it, provided they would cut their own wood for heating the water.

I feel obliged to admit that there was another enameled bathtub in the valley which likewise had come from the oil well. However, its owner used it as a hog-scalding vat, and we felt it did not rank as an honest competitor.

Our stint of fence building had made Mike's feet sore, and he soaked them so long that he couldn't get his boots back on. So he donned a pair of carpet slippers, and off we went to the hotel, feeling very natty in clean overalls and fresh bandannas.

Mrs. Williams' hotel, a five-room building of pine logs, was located in the town of Paradox, in the west end of the valley. The symmetry of the village had been ruined when Mrs. Williams bought an automobile and built a garage on the south side of the street. Previous to that all the buildings—two residences, the hotel, a combination post office and general store with a gas pump out front, and a chicken coop—had been on the north side. The one-room schoolhouse was beyond the city limits in the farm belt, nearer the center of population.

A strange coupé was parked in front of the hotel. The name of a veterinary-supply company was lettered on the door. "Ah!" said Mike with a gleam in his eye. I understood him perfectly. The poor salesman, though he knew it not, was about to provide us with our favorite form of entertainment.

We went into the lobby, which was also Mrs. Williams' living room. It was a small chamber, painfully neat, with a hooked rug on the floor, lace curtains at the two narrow windows, a spindly geranium in a paper-covered pot, three creaky rocking chairs, a horsehair sofa, and an old-fashioned round tripod table on which burned a kerosene lamp.

The veterinary-products salesman was sitting gingerly in one of the rockers. He was paunchy, pink-faced, thin-haired, and pleasant enough. Before he could pump much information out of us—they all tried, and Mike always gave them garbled directions for finding the farmers about whom they inquired—Mrs. Williams called us in to supper.

We took our places around the square table with its worn, frazzle-edged cloth and vase of artificial flowers. Mrs. Williams ate with us and was considerably fussed when Mike and I, in spite of the citified guest, insisted on carrying the dishes to and from the kitchen for her. She was a fat, jolly woman with shiny cheeks and gray hair cut short in a most unbecoming boyish bob. We liked her enormously, especially the way she got red in the face and said, "Oh, go on with you!" whenever we joshed her. Quick, efficient, and clean as a cat, she had been at one time an Army nurse. She was Paradox' unofficial guardian of the public health and considered far superior to the district doctor who lived forty miles away and was held in some disfavor because of the high mortality rate among his patients.

Mrs. Williams' assistance was wanted mostly for childbirth, the valley's largest natural industry. Her delivery fee was a sack of wheat for a boy and a sack of corn for a girl. Most of her summonses came at night, delivered by hard-knuckled, leather-lunged men arriving either on galloping horses or in rattling cars. This tended to disturb the sleep of her clients, but they had the good sense not to say so.

After dinner we maneuvered the poor salesman into a particular chair in the lobby. Lulled to a false sense of security by our solicitude, he lighted a cigar, crossed his legs, and leaned back to tell us a story. We didn't hear it. We kept listening to Mrs. Williams moving about the kitchen. Pretty soon she began murmuring baby talk to what might have been a cat named Sammy. It wasn't a cat, however. It was her pet deodorized skunk who had just arrived through his private hole in the kitchen floor.

Attracted by our voices, Sammy ambled across the dark dining room and surveyed the lobby from the shadowed doorway. He had a favorite chair, and whoever sat in that chair was obliged to scratch him. His enormous fluffy tail waved gently. He was a handsome animal with garish stripes. Still, a skunk is open to suspicion, especially by those who know not his capacities. Mike and I watched him out of the corners of our eyes, almost breathless with suspense.

Suddenly Sammy sailed out of the shadows and landed on the salesman's lap. The drummer's voice chopped off in midsentence. A wild grimace distorted his face. His hands twitched violently and then were as still as if his blood had turned to stone.

Sammy tramped about on the man's paunch, gave a friendly sniff at his livid mouth, then curled up and settled down. Beads of sweat stood out on the salesman's brow. He was afraid even to breathe lest he bring on an attack.

"Ah!" said Mike with vast satisfaction. "A freezer!"

Novices on whose lap the skunk abruptly dropped were of two types: "freezers" and "bolters." Bolters would let out terrified yelps, knock the indignant Sammy to the floor, and race for safety, falling over the furniture in their panic. Only once had we encountered a "battler," a mild-looking deputy tax assessor who, regardless of consequences, had nearly choked the poor skunk to death before we could rescue it.

Seeing from our faces that he had been victimized, the salesman gradually recovered. He picked Sammy up as delicately as if the skunk were a cracked egg, deposited him alone in the chair, and retreated to a far corner, puffing his cheeks and rumbling under his breath. We tried to mollify him by telling him how others had reacted to similar encounters, but he refused to see anything funny in it, so we left.

At the gate Mike paused, staring thoughtfully across the valley. I knew he was sorting out each detail of the escapade and storing it away in his mind. All at once he gave a snort of delight and slapped his hand on the gatepost. The cataloguing was complete.

He might never mention the matter again, but from now on it was completely his, to be chuckled over months or years later, rich company for some lonely trail.

Mental images such as these are an integral part of most riders' lives. Their days and nights are often monotonous. When a change crops up they look it over from every side, chew on it, squeeze out all its significance, and add its essence to their inarticulate philosophies. For they are philosophers. They can be because they are not hurried, because they take the time to examine such small things as a skunk on a salesman's lap.

When we woke the next morning it was raining, a thin, cold drizzle from a low, gray sky. We saddled up and rode to one of the feed lots where the cows were calving. Our chins were sunk in our slickers; our fingers were blue and wrinkled on the bridle reins. As our horses slopped through the mud we saw two . . . three . . . four newborn calves that had been chilled to death by the rain. Soon we found one whose mother had died. Even if the tiny orphan lived it would be no good. It might learn to steal a swallow or two of milk from another calf's mother before she discovered the intrusion and butted him away, but at best it would turn into a potbellied woolly-haired runt, not worth the grass it ate.

Still, we couldn't bear to leave it there to die. I slung it over my saddle in front of me, took it to the farmer's house, and gave it to the children. I knew they'd dry it off and bed it in straw, as they'd done with two or three other dogies (orphans) we had given them. They made pets out of the little fellows and taught them to drink skim milk from a bucket. I was pretty sure that as soon as the calves were big enough the farmer would appropriate them and kill them for veal. It would cause heartbreak there on the farm, but life was hard and meat was scarce. An outsider, even though he'd presented the calves to the children in the first place, couldn't interfere in such intimate family matters.

We spent a week or so drifting the cattle out of the different feed lots. The strongest ones we kicked into East Paradox; the weaker ones we turned into the river pasture. We had to move ourselves too—our tarpaulin-covered bedrolls and canvas war bags—so as to be near the animals. Our new quarters we took up in the town of Bedrock, at the foot of towering cliffs, where the canyon of the Dolores breaks into the valley.

Unlike Paradox, Bedrock was perfectly symmetrical. On one side of the street was the store and post-office building, its boards weathered by sand and sun to a rusty gray. Balancing it on the other side of the street was a single-room cabin covered with tar paper and supporting at its back a lean-to. Out in the sagebrush was a suburb known as the Boar's Nest, a crazily leaning log shanty occupied now and then by a couple of cowboys who helped us during the heavy work of branding and driving to the mountains. In the distance, safely back from the river, were a couple of hay farms.

The tar-paper house in town was rented from an absentee landlord by a broad-girthed, solidly muscled, red-faced, gray-haired, ornery old tartar whom I will call Bill Jones. He must have been all of sixty-five and he would fight anybody at the drop of a hat. Once the storekeeper sold him some runny, rancid butter. Bill returned it. The storekeeper, who was also a blacksmith and correspondingly stout, got huffy about it. To show him the error of his ways, Bill shoved the butter in his face, made him choke down as much as he could, and shampooed him with the remainder. It was a lovely spectacle, still talked about—especially by Bill, who was no blushing violet when it came to recounting his innumerable and tedious feats of prowess.

We batched with Bill. We bought all the food, cut the wood, packed a barrel of water in our pickup once a week from a well nine miles away (the silt-laden, alkali-charged river wasn't fit for drinking), and did the cooking. In return Bill let us sleep in his lean-to, which was so small a cocked elbow made it dangerous.

The cabin was further crowded by a red-haired, frightened youngster who had run away from home and was hunting his first job. Sheltering the lad, whom he'd never seen before, was typical of Bill. Any broke, hungry cowboy or miner who drifted through could hang his hat in the tar-paper shack. Not that Bill was a soft touch. He could recognize at a glance a professional grub-line rider (as out-and-out moochers were called), and they got short shrift from him. But if you were really down on your luck, if you could stand his interminable bragging and weren't frightened by the way he stamped and swore when you hung the fry pan on the wrong nail, everything he possessed was yours.

We had not been long in Bedrock when the April sun, pale though it seemed, sent melting snow waters booming down out of the high country. When the river reached the lazy channels of the valley it dropped its load of mud. The first green shoots of spring appeared on these bars. The grass-starved cattle waded out for a bite. The quicksand trapped their feet. The stronger ones pulled free, but the weaker ones couldn't. Down they sank, their thrashing driving them deeper. Down until finally their rounded bodies stopped them and they half stood, half lay in the mud, looking helplessly at solid land only a few feet away.

We couldn't fence off these danger spots; the flooded river was apt to change course overnight and build new bars where we least expected them. The only way to protect the cattle was to ride bog twice a day. Believe me, it was work.

The very first morning we went out we saw two dark spots on the mud flats and spurred to a lope. Sure enough, they were cows and not driftwood, as I had hoped.

We dismounted. Both animals were exhausted from their struggles to escape. Soon they would let their noses drop into the water and would drown. Finding a driftwood log, I laid it on the mud beside one of the animals. It kept me from sinking into the quicksand myself as I teetered out and thrust a board under her chin to hold her head above the muck. Mike repeated the performance with the other cow and then galloped to the nearest farm for a shovel, a long chain, and a team, for we knew that our saddle horses could not pull the cattle out.

It was a temptation to hook the chain to the creatures' heads or horns, but we didn't dare try. The two husky draft horses were liable to pull so hard they'd break the cows' necks. So I went to the closest one, carried the shovel out on the log beside her, and dug her legs free. I had to fight for every shovelful. The gummy stuff yielded stubbornly with long, sucking *plo-ops*. All the while the frightened cow was bellowing and swinging her head, trying to get her horns into me.

At last I had her mucked reasonably clear. Mike passed the chain along her side, under her tail, and back on the other side, fastening it in front of her chest and looping her in a kind of sling. Then I hooked on with the team.

E-e-easy now! A sharp pull would break the cow's legs. The two wise old horses leaned slowly against their collars. The chain tautened. The cow bawled hoarsely. But nothing happened. I began to sweat in the raw wind, fearful that I hadn't cleared away enough of the mud. Then all at once she came loose with a pop like a giant cork.

I skidded her up the bank, her wet sides leaving a crushed, gray streak in the weeds. She lay still, panting and drooling. I got the horses out of the way, went to her, and removed the chain. She heaved upright. No gratitude, just frenzy. Head down, she charged. Fortunately her cold, cramped legs were clumsy. I dodged to one side. She tried to swerve after me, couldn't. She stumbled. Down she fell, the last of her will spent in this final, desperate burst. We mounted, picked up the reins of the team, and jogged on to the next one. Maybe she'd get up again. Maybe she wouldn't. Anyhow, we'd done all we could for her. . . . But I didn't like to remember her lying there as I crawled into my warm bed. I hated to ride out the next morning, for fear I would find her dead. Every day we pulled from one to fifteen head out of the mud, and half of them perished anyhow. We couldn't help wondering: if we'd got to them a little sooner; if we'd done something a little differently . . .

We had plenty of other work besides bog riding. During winter the cattle, cows and steers, were allowed to mix more or less indiscriminately. But their summer ranges were distinct. When the snow vanished from the mountains the yearlings and the steers would be trailed out the east end of Paradox Valley and aimed toward Lone Cone Peak and the high, aspen-dotted meadows of Beaver Park. These ranges were too high, however, for breeder cows—at least my stepfather's experience led him to believe that cows flourished better at altitudes of less than nine thousand feet. The cow herd, consequently, was shoved out the north side of Paradox along a breath-taking trail through the Dolores Canyon and its tributary, the San Miguel, reaching eventually their summer homes on the brushy plateaus of the Uncompahgre Forest.

The cow-and-calf winter headquarters were in the bottom of the San Miguel Canyon. Their principal winter range was a weirdly rugged, tortuously eroded stretch of country lying between the Dolores and San Miguel rivers and Paradox. Here the huskiest cows and heifers ran wild, but the poor ones were fed in the valley. Late in the spring the boys from the cow-and-calf ranch came over to round up the Paradox bunch and brand the calves.

We were always tickled to see them. We swapped stories, caught up on gossip, and helped them with their riding and branding. During those busy days we had to have extra help for bog riding, and Bill Jones was the logical choice.

Bill might or might not comply. He was a lazy old devil and he always seemed able to provide for his limited wants from some mysterious source. Money alone would never sway him to work.

There was a way to get him, though. Bill spent most of his time either angling for catfish in the river or reading every wild-West

pulp magazine on which he could lay his hands. In this last he
was not alone. Most cowboys choose the same literature, getting,
I suppose, a nice chesty feeling out of seeing their drab trade glorified to the tune of crashing guns and red death.

We could always tell when Bill was wrought up by his reading.
He stamped around like a prodded boar and swore worse than
ever. We utilized the trait by buying a couple of specially exciting
magazines and leaving them on his bed. The next day Mike went
to work on him with his glib tongue. Bill, very cowboy conscious
now, capitulated and agreed to ride bog for us for a wage of two
dollars a day. We also hired the red-haired boy staying with him
to be his helper.

Bill soon found out that there is a difference between actual
mud and fictional glory, and he didn't like it—despite the fact
that he got caught the same way nearly every year. In an effort
to weasel out he began grumbling about being underpaid. We
didn't listen. He was receiving standard wages and he knew it.
Then he switched to long and bitter plaints about the high rent
of his tar-paper shack. Cash contributions from all the dwellers,
he hinted broadly, would be welcome.

Our consciences, as we prepared for bed in his lean-to, almost
plagued us into complying, but we didn't want to donate more
than our rightful share. After a dexterous skirmish we pinned him
down. His rent was twenty-five cents a week. That ended our con-
science pangs. We were feeding the old reprobate, cutting his
wood, hauling his water, and paying him a month's rent every
day he went out to look at the bog. Very firmly we told him he'd
have to keep his bargain. He was so furious he didn't speak to us
for days. But he was as honest as he was ornery. He never shirked
on his bog riding merely because he'd been sold down the river
on what he figured was a dirty deal.

The boys from the cow-and-calf ranch left with their herd
before we dared start the steers for the high country. After they'd
gone the days dragged longer and longer. We shod up our horses,

ready for the drive to the Lone Cone. We counted the last sacks of cotton cake; we prowled the rocky gulches looking for any stray spear of feed that might ward off starvation yet another day. Finally in May we rode up into the foothills "to see," as if we could make the grass come faster by cursing it. The peaks still loomed white and stark. But maybe—maybe the lower ridges were clear.

Always when it seemed that more delay meant disaster we saw the serviceberry begin to throw out its white blossoms, the tiny green leaves that appeared overnight on the scrub oak, and, best of all, the faint, sweet color of grass that showed first under the protecting brush. Back we went to Paradox at a high lope, hired the extra hands we needed, and feverishly assembled the strongest of the steers for the first drive. It was time to go!

VIII MOVING UP

WE WENT FIRST TO THE BOAR'S NEST
to get Cy Orr. We did it reluctantly, half afraid that the tiny old
man might die on our hands before we reached the Lone Cone.
However, Cy had always gone with the spring drives; leaving him
behind simply because the black shadow was plain upon his days
would have hurt him more than anything that could happen on
the trail. My stepfather would have skinned us alive if we had
even hinted to Cy that he stay home.

We found him sitting in front of the shanty, soaking up sunshine. He had no more meat to him than a yucca blade. A single
line of long iron-gray hairs ran from his underlip to the point of
his chin. This slim beard lent his strong little face an incredibly
evil air, though no gentler man ever lived. How old was he? I
don't know, and Cy claimed he didn't either.

"I had one chance to lea'hn," he often related. "That was on
a trip to South Ameriky." (It was Cy's story—and he told many
an incredible one about himself—that he had been born in England and apprenticed as cabin boy in a sailing schooner.) "When
we were out in the middle of the ocean the captain said to me,
'Boy, you're thi'teen today, an' I'm a-gonna give you the damned-
est thrashin' you eveh had.' He did, too, but I sweah I've fo'gotten the date. It was a long time ago."

By some unrelated stage Cy traveled from South America to Texas, picked up his slow, nasal drawl, and headed north with a trail herd of beef steers. While the crew was passing through Colorado a man was killed, and Cy selected to take the blame. He escaped, fled to Paradox, and lived with the Indians, the first white man to see the valley, according to his tale. It may be so; certainly no one living in Paradox today can remember when Cy Orr was not about.

In Paradox he became a professional horsebreaker. He was a wonder, and outfits all over the country hired him to take the rough off their strings. Even after he retired from active trade he remained light and quick as a sunbeam. I have seen horses rear and fall backward with him. Before the animal crashed to the ground that wizened old man was out of the saddle and standing on his feet, the bridle reins firm in his hand as he clucked at the animal in his soft, reproving way.

I am positive he could commune with stock. In the course of years he gathered together fifty or sixty cows which he ran in the Dolores Canyon. Morning after morning he sat on a rock watching them graze, and when they bedded down he spread his blankets on the ground near by and went to sleep with them. If he grew thirsty he milked any one of them into a pint whisky bottle. They were ordinary range Herefords, the kind that stampede like deer at the sight of a walking man, but somehow he had taught them to tolerate him.

This soft streak wasn't apparent on the surface. His cabin, the Boar's Nest, was crusted with filth. His blankets lay on a springless wooden bunk in an indescribable wad. Bumblebees—so help me—nested in his pillow and set up a thunderous buzzing when he lay down. But they didn't sting him. "They'ah gentled," he said.

Perhaps it was this physical dirtiness which killed him. Cancer infected his left eye. My stepfather, guessing the trouble, took him to a doctor in Montrose. Although Cy had often journeyed to

Denver on stock trains, he had never before been in an automobile. As they whizzed windily along in the open car he grew
terrified. "Lemme out!" he yelled. "Lemme out! I'm spittin' in
my own face!"

He was held captive, however, until the eye was examined.
Could it be cured? Yes, if Cy were hospitalized immediately.

Here Cy, who had been cleaned, polished, and subjected to the
indignities of his first physical examination, interposed. "How
long will I live if it ain't treated?"

"Six months. A year, perhaps."

"I can do all I want in six months," Cy said. Out he walked,
and nothing could lure him back.

He lived five years. Slowly the disease spread, eating away his
eyelids and his whole eyeball. It is grisly to tell, but flies laid their
eggs in the cavity, and I am sure it was the maggots cleaning out
the infected flesh that kept him alive so long. Toward the end
the smell grew so terrible no one could stand to be in the same
room with him. He must have been in the extremes of agony, but
not a complaint passed his lips. He had chosen this way to die,
and he never went back on his bargain.

When Mike and I rode toward him this spring day the disease
was not so far advanced. Though it had destroyed the muscles of
his eyelid, he could still see by hoisting the shutter with his thumb
and forefinger. Not that he needed that left eye. The right remained keen as an eagle's, but when he wanted to emphasize
that he was looking at a thing he pried up his left eyelid and
glared. And so he pinned us now with a stare that demanded
full and instantaneous explanation of our purpose.

We told him we were ready to start moving up.

Cy nodded.

"Where's Donnie?" we asked. Donnie Marsden occasionally
shared the Boar's Nest, and we wanted to hire him too.

"Sylvie's Pocket," said Cy. "I'll get him."

We hesitated. Sylvie's Pocket was a hard day's ride away. We knew that Cy was doomed—though the end was much farther away than we thought—and we wanted to do what we could to lighten the burden. We offered to go after Donnie ourselves.

The little man knew what lay behind our solicitude and resisted fiercely. "I said I'd get him," he growled. "Good-by!" He stamped into the cabin, picked up his bridle, and headed for the horse pasture. Mike and I looked at each other, shrugged, and pretended to ride on.

Screened by a clump of willows, we stopped, ready for trouble. The old man never would ride a thoroughly gentled horse. The five animals in his pasture were wall-eyed spooks; a few days before Mike and I had been able to catch one only by roping it. But Cy would not use a rope on a horse. "Scares 'em," he said. Armed only with his bridle, he walked into the field and shooed the horses into his corral.

Slowly he started toward the one he wanted, looking at its feet and not its head—a nervous horse hates a man to stare at its eyes. The animal jockeyed behind the others, trying to dodge. Cy followed, talking a soft gibberish. By and by the horse stopped and stood trembling, nostrils distended and ears back. Cy put his arms around its neck, petted it, slipped the bridle over its head, and led it out. Moving easy as oil, he saddled it and mounted. The horse made a couple of crow hops. Cy sat it like a feather, and the horse gave up. As Cy reined it toward the Pocket he waved his arm to us; the little devil had known all along that we were watching.

Mike let out a gusty breath. "I reckon he'll get to the Cone—in better shape than we do."

We hired Bill Jones to drive the chuck wagon. It was a wagon only by traditional nomenclature. The mechanical age had intruded even into Paradox, and our vehicle was an ancient Ford truck with high, slatted sides and windshield frame devoid of glass. Roads of a sort paralleled most of our route; where we took short cuts through hills or canyons with our herd the truck could loop around and meet us at the campgrounds. We loaded the Ford with a chuck box (a movable pantry ingeniously equipped with tight compartments for tin dishes and food), with our bed-rolls, oats, and bales of hay for the horses. We were taking only one mount apiece on the trip, and the hard-worked animals would need plenty of good food to stand the gaff. The cattle would have to manage on whatever they picked up along the way.

We also hired Buzz Holden, the redheaded runaway who was staying with Bill. The next day while Bill prepared his chuck wagon Buzz, Mike, and I rounded up eight or nine hundred of the strongest yearlings. Gone are the days of the huge, wide-horned four-, five-, and six-year-old steers that once provided the nation with beefsteak. Now that urban families are neither so large nor hearty of appetite, the demand is for smaller cuts of "baby beef." Also, yearlings handle better on the Midwestern feed lots, where they are corn-fattened for market. They are de-horned, too, so they won't hook each other in the railroad cars or at the close-packed feed racks. It has all been refined to a very neat system—except for the mountain growers.

For us it was very unsystematized indeed. Our little creatures, scarcely more than weaned, were used to following grown cattle. Raised on the cow-and-calf range, they had never learned the long trail to the steer pastures around the Lone Cone and Beaver Park. Confused and bewildered, their tendency was to scatter like quicksilver on any provocation, and until they became trail-broken we had our hands full.

To help preserve order we took along a few cows for the young-sters to follow. Also, we had Brigham, now a grown steer of splendid proportions but in the beginning a calf of very low character.

Brigham was a mongrel child with a dark red, mottled hide. His father had been a Hereford bull, his mother a blackish, half-breed Holstein milk cow. We had kept her and another cow at

the summer camp on the Lone Cone, using half the milk ourselves
and letting the calves have half. Between milkings the calves were
held in a little pen so they could not follow their mothers and
steal more than their fair share.

Brigham spent his first summer thus, and in the second summer, when the cows arrived at the camp, he was again penned,
for his baby brother was not yet born. Normally the appearance
of the new calf would have led the cow forcibly to wean the old
one. But Brigham possessed an overwhelming mother complex.
He had no intention of giving up the milk which had been his
all year.

He must have had an overactive thyroid gland. He was an
enormous yearling, almost as tall as his mother. She could not
handle him. When we turned him out of the pen to make room
for his brother he was delighted and followed the cow like a
shadow, drinking at will. In despair we penned him again. He
bawled all day long with increasing vehemence as evening drew
near and he expected his mother's return.

At last the cow appeared. By now Brigham was so hoarse and
dry he sounded like a squeaky gate. Up to his mother he rushed,
fell on his fat knees so he could reach under her, and drained the
milk in great gulps. His little brother staggered over on wobbly
legs, sad-faced and hungry. Brigham shoved him aside. The
lethargic old cow mooed crossly at her older son, fondly at the
younger. Remonstrance failing, she ran round and round the pen,
wringing her tail, with Brigham in hot pursuit. Winded, she had
to stop. She tried to apologize to the baby by licking him with her
rough tongue while her heels kept up a futile tattoo on Brigham's
corpulent sides.

None of this filled the little one's stomach. He grew dull of eye
and dull of hair. The cow, worried about him, hung around the
corral instead of going off to graze. As a result both of them
grew thin and wan while Brigham waxed mighty. Disgusted, we
drove him to a different field. He broke through two fences and

came back. We took him clear to Beaver Park, eighteen miles away, and again he returned.

Not until fall, when we drove the cow to one winter camp and Brigham to another, were we able to separate them. And even then he did not forget. Each spring he made a beeline for the summer camp. He knew every turn of the way, and nothing could tempt him to stray aside. And so he became a priceless asset as trail blazer for our bewildered yearlings.

We kept him for years, and he grew tremendous in size. His mother died, but now Brigham had found his mission in life. He was a leader of cattle. Generally in a mixed herd a lean, tough cow will forge into the front. But not if Brigham was about. He hooked them all back, saw that the yearlings were strung out behind, and pushed on, his great horned head bobbing in massive rhythm to his stride. How much labor, how much time, indeed how many cattle he saved us during those years is impossible to estimate. We laughed at his proud airs and bursting self-esteem— no mere sterile male has call to consider himself as important to the earth and all that moves therein as Brigham did—but we would not have sold him for any amount of money.

Late in the evening we watered our first gather and with Brigham in the lead shoved the yearlings across the river bridge to a large enclosure known as the Wire Corral. By holding the herd there all night we could get started on the sixteen-mile pull out of the valley before dawn the next morning. If we didn't make it to Dry Creek the first day it meant a foodless, waterless night somewhere on the desert.

Foot by foot we went over the corral fence, bolstering weak spots. In the beginning it had been a sound barrier, but time and breachy cattle had left their ravages. We stapled, spliced broken wires, braced rickety posts. Our eight hundred little steers were nervous at best, and the weather was making them more so. A raw wind came up at sunset, filling the moonlit evening with a nameless hum and swish of mystery. The herd began to stir and bawl. They were ripe for a stampede, and no man could guess what might set them off—the flare of a match, a rider's hat blowing away, the stamp of a horse's hoof. When such a thing happens, away they go without a look right or left, heads down and tails up. Their own running terrifies them still more, and they never stop until exhausted. But perhaps our fence, if we made it solid enough, could halt them before they started.

While we were working Cy Orr appeared through the pale twilight with Donnie Marsden. Somehow the mere sight of Donnie always filled us with an irrepressible desire to chuckle. He had a long, limp face and a long, limp mustache under his huge Mexican hat. He was not tall, but that hat, with its high steeple crown and wide brim sagging dispiritedly about his ears, made him look tall. His voice came out of his thin chest with a lugubrious croak, and his dust-inflamed eyes were continuously watering, so that he spent his life looking as if he were on the point of bursting into tears.

Each fall Cy and Donnie took a trip to Denver under pretext of marketing their steers, though between them they never shipped more than a carload a year. As stockmen they were entitled to ride in the freight train's caboose, and probably neither of them had set foot in a regulation coach, but to hear their talk one would think that business trips via extra-fare Pullmans were everyday occurrences in their lives. They were famous at the hotels frequented by cattlemen. Cy had slept either on the ground or in springless bunks so long that he could not bear a mattress. Coming to his room in the wee, small hours, he pulled the blankets off the bed, wrapped himself fully clothed in them as in a cocoon, and went to sleep on the floor, where the chambermaid invariably discovered him the next morning.

Donnie's idiosyncrasies ran to dress. He stuffed the trouser legs of his striped town suit into shiny high-heeled boots inlaid with gorgeous golden butterflies. He wore a fawn-colored shirt of silk, and in some incredible haberdashery shop he had found a bright green tie on which the silhouette of a naked woman appeared in pink. The sight of his wretched old hat and mournful face appearing above this blazing raiment was utterly incongruous. Of course the chippies immediately got their hooks in him. He would blow an entire year's earnings, often as much as a thousand dollars, in one glorious two- or three-day bust, then come home with a violent headache and no regrets whatsoever.

On reaching the Wire Corral, the pair dismounted but made no offer to help with the fence. Cy would not use such plebeian tools as hammer and nails, and Donnie couldn't. He had only four fingers—a thumb and forefinger on one hand, forefinger and middle on the other. The missing members had been pinched off in various accidents, mostly by being caught in a rope as he lassoed some fractious beast.

Once he had even been scalped by a rope when another rider and he were inspecting a suspicious brand on a bull. They had thrown the beast between them. While Donnie's horse, supposedly rope-wise, settled back to hold the lariat tight on the bull's hind legs (the rope was tied to the saddle horn), Donnie dismounted. The horse let the rope slack. The infuriated bull lunged to its feet. Seeing its error, the horse reared back. The hard twist, snapped by their ton and a half of weight, tightened with a whistle, caught Donnie at the back of his neck and peeled the hide off his skull clear to his forehead. Even then, with his own hair hanging in front of his face, he did not lose consciousness. With those warped claws he had for hands he patted his scalp more or less back into place and rode to a near-by ranch, from which an automobile sped him to a doctor.

Cy followed us disconsolately around the corral, flailing his arms on his chest and complaining of the cold. He was bundled to his ears, but it made no difference. On the hottest days he shivered. He blamed it on "malariar," which perhaps it was, and to combat the ailment he drank quantities of whisky, which he manufactured from potatoes in a still carefully hidden back in the rocks. He was always going to age "the very next batch," but when the liquor began to drip raw and warm from the coils temptation overwhelmed him. Driven by some need which I am sure must have been darker than "malariar," he swilled the stuff straight down and, all alone there in the rocks, lay dead drunk for days at a time.

We warned him regularly that he was going to poison himself on the ill-made brew, but Cy insisted he had an infallible method for detecting bad alcohol. Fill a tumbler three quarters full of whisky, he said, cover the tumbler with a piece of raw beefsteak, and let it stand overnight. If the beefsteak remained fresh in the morning the whisky was good. But if the meat was crusted and green with poisons absorbed from the drink, then beware.

I ventured to doubt if beef had any such properties. Cy gave me an incredulous look. Didn't I know that raw meat placed on a black eye drew out the poisons?

I admitted that beef was a time-honored remedy for black eyes but suggested this was perhaps due to the fact that the meat felt cool to the hot bruise, making it desirable in lands far from refrigerators.

Cy shook his head in real sorrow. "Theah's no fool like an edjicated fool," he said and gave me up as hopeless.

He had no whisky with him tonight, however, for he never drank when on a job. But the cold evening soured him. Across a gully from the corral, making the most of the fading light, killdeers were flitting on pale, erratic wings about the edges of an alkali seep, shrilling their everlasting *kill-dee, kill-dee, kill-dee.*

"Look at 'em!" Cy said. "Little old South American birds!" Of course the killdeers weren't South American, but every spring when their migrations brought them back to Paradox Cy made the same speech. "I sweah the world is upside down. It's comin' to an end. It ain't a-gonna bu'hn, eitheh. It's a-gonna freeze— freeze solid."

As if to wait the dread day in comfort, he built a fire of cedar sticks. Hungry and tired, we were glad to hunker around it with him. Bill Jones was probably holding our supper in Bedrock; the horses we planned to ride tomorrow were there, too, but we were reluctant to leave the cattle. They were not bedding down. The wind kept them milling about the corral, bawling restlessly. Trying to calm them, we took turns riding around the fence, singing to them, talking, blowing on our cold fingers.

Donnie droned monotonously about a black horse he had just traded for. He was always trading horses and always getting skinned. But he expected great things of this newest one, which he planned to ride on the drive. Mike, grinning sardonically, started quoting him verbatim about all the other horses whose praises he had sung—until he rode them. Donnie went into a pout and fell silent.

The cold pressed tighter and tighter. A huge dog I had not noticed when Cy and Donnie arrived crept from beneath a creosote bush, attracted by the fire. It slunk toward us on an apologetic belly, wagging its stump of a tail in hopeful overtures. Donnie, always fearful of offending and knowing that some cowboys have strict notions about dogs keeping their places, started to order it away. Cy stopped him and made a place for the dog by the fire. It lay there with its head on its paws, blinking at the flames and now and then growling deep in its throat as a coyote howled on a distant mesa. It was a wolfish creature, strong-fanged and wearing a shaggy coat of many colors.

"Where did you get it?" I asked Donnie.

"Traded. He's a good un."

"What's his name?"

"Pansy."

We all laughed and Donnie looked bewildered, but there was no use telling him that he was the only person on earth who would name so formidable a he-dog "Pansy."

Along toward ten-thirty or eleven the wind died a little. Some of the cattle lay down and the rest weren't bawling so much.

"I guess we can go," Mike said, and we rode off through the moonlight, the horses' hoofs going *clip-clop-clip-clop* on the flinty stones.

It seemed I had scarcely fallen asleep when Mike's hand on my shoulder aroused me. I sat up. The moon was still high, and I was sure it could not be more than three o'clock.

"What's the matter, Mike?"

"We'd better look at those cattle."

We pulled on our boots and woke Buzz Holden. In the process we also woke Bill Jones, who swore furiously but got up and went out to pack the chuck truck. The rest of us walked stiffly to the barn and caught our horses. The air was dead still and we couldn't hear a sound that wasn't of our own making. Yet from somewhere—the ghostly bulk of the cliffs, the luminous glint of the river, from the very earth itself—a strange uneasiness rose to grip us. Without talk we saddled and galloped toward the Wire Corral.

It was empty. A section of fence lay flat, telling plainly what had happened. Mike rolled out a firecracker string of brilliant oaths, and we started hunting the vanished steers.

In another location it might have been difficult, but here the terrain was in our favor. The rolling, cliff-girt valley floor was almost bald, and in the wan moonlight the trail of the cattle through the sand showed like a wound. We soon began picking up little bunches here and there in draws and gulches, all of them chewing their cuds with an exasperating calmness, as though they'd spent the night in drowsy peace.

A rider loomed out of the shadows. It was Cy. He, too, had been routed from the Boar's Nest by that same mysterious premonition which had stirred Mike. Perhaps a psychologist can explain the awakenings by saying both men had gone to bed with the knowledge of what was apt to happen and that worry would not let them sleep. But this rousing when it is necessary to rouse occurs again and again among dwellers in the open, so eerily you are tempted to believe they have secret communion with the night itself—until unsuspected disaster strikes and everyone snores right through it.

I asked Cy where Donnie was. He snorted with delight. "Ridin' his new horse," he said and galloped on.

By dawn we had gathered all but seventy or so of the animals. The strengthening light showed us that the valley floor between the corral and the river was as clean as a hound's tooth. We looked blankly at each other. Where were the rest of the yearlings?

"That Brigham!" Mike exploded. He and I turned our horses about and loped up the valley. We topped a low hill, and sure enough, a thin stringer of dust trailed along the road ahead of us. Brigham was on his way to the Lone Cone, our missing steers trooping behind. He would have taken each one that would follow him to the mountains as surely as we could. But not all of them would follow, and it was to deal with the others that we drew our wages. We stopped Brigham's vanguard, much to Brigham's disgust, and waited for the rest of the herd. Bill Jones appeared with the truck, halted, opened the fragrant maw of the chuck box, set up his Dutch ovens, and wrestled breakfast together. The herd drifted in and we let them scatter out to browse while we ate.

Donnie appeared last. He would not leave his fine-looking black horse but ate his breakfast sitting in the saddle. This was not due to affection. The horse had bucked him off when he first mounted that morning. Throughout the trip it continued to buck him off each time he voluntarily left the saddle and tried to return. Then, having thoroughly humiliated him, the treacherous creature would stand still and let him clamber painfully aboard.

We strung the herd out in a dusty line half a mile long. Poke, poke, poke. Fiction writers to the contrary, there is nothing more monotonous than trailing cattle. The herd moves no faster than the slowest members, and the slow ones—the sick, the weak, the lazy—collect at the rear, where they are known by the descriptive term, "the drags." Leadenly they plod, one foot, another foot, one foot, another foot. Now and then, driven by some vague impulse, an impotent steer rears up on another. The resentful recipient runs petulantly ahead, while the stubborn rider hops ludicrously along on two hind legs, clinging tight with its front ones. There is a brief stir, then the aggressive one gives up, and the herd is again a red level of swaying backs.

One foot, another foot. A steer wanders to the side. The dog trotting at your stirrup lifts yellow eyes to you for permission. You nod. Ears eager, he slips up behind the laggard and sinks teeth into its hock. The steer gives a snort that sounds as if it were jerked loose with a string, leaps into the bunch, and stays there for a time. The dog trots proudly back to your stirrup.

The horses, especially old ones who have trailed many cows, lose patience too. A drag lags. The pony opens his mouth and with his strong, square teeth seizes the creature by the ridge where tail emerges from backbone. Again there is a snort and a jump, a little ripple in the endless sea of boredom.

Your knees grow stiff; you stretch your legs and squirm in the saddle. Dust fogs and fogs in your face. Unable to stand it any longer, you lope toward the front of the herd and trade places with one of the "point" riders. Now you are beside the cattle instead of behind them, keeping the leaders pointed in the right direction and watching for any unwanted strays that might attempt to mingle with the bunch, but the pace is the same plod, plod, plod, and the day stretches into eternity.

We ran into a swarm of gnats. Donnie tilted his head to one side and beat it with the heel of his palm. Then he straightened, shook his head violently, swore, and beat some more. Finally, driven to distraction, he reined over beside me.

"I got a bug in my ear," he said, and his eyes, fiery red from the

dust, sent tears trickling down his cheeks. "It's buzzin' an' buzzin'.
I can't get shed of it."

"I wouldn't know what to do."

"Maybe we could drown it."

"What!"

"Now, look. I'll lie on the ground here. You pour water in my
ear. He's just a little bitty bug. It ought not take long."

I laughed until I cried too. Donnie joined with a pale smile,
but his face was doleful as a bloodhound's. And all that time that
gnat was buzzing and buzzing inside his head. "All right," I said
when I could talk, "I guess it won't hurt to try."

We dismounted. Donnie had a canvas water sack looped to his
saddle horn. He handed it to me and stretched out on the ground.
Mystified, the others grouped around, making remarks which
Donnie, long since inured to remarks, mournfully ignored. I
dribbled water into his hairy ear, perhaps a cupful. It spilled over
the edges and ran into his mustache. His face had a tense, ex-
pectant look. He smiled. "It's drowned!" he said triumphantly.

We went on. Pretty soon I noticed Donnie probing his ear with
a matchstick. "What's the matter now?" I asked.

"He must have dried out. He's buzzin' again."

"Do you want me to sprinkle him some more?"

Donnie shook his head. "It don't seem no use. I reckon I'll have
to wait till he dies." He hesitated. Then: "Haven't you got a bug
in your ear?"

"Not this trip."

"Nobody else has either." Donnie thought about it. "Why am
I always the one?"

The afternoon dragged out. Mike began singing:

> *"The sun went down o'er the mossy hill's crest,*
> *Ta da di-di da, ta da.*
> *The sun went daow-wn o-o'er the mossy hill's cre-e-est,*
> *Ta da di-di da-aa, ta-a da-a-a-ah!"*

He knew only that one line of the song, but he managed to get variety from volume and ta-das. To the tune of his orchestrations we crossed the divide between the head of the valley and the adobe slopes which drop toward Dry Creek. The thirsty cattle, without a drink for twenty-four hours, smelled the creek's yellow-green trickle and broke into a shuffling run.

While they tanked up we made camp in an abandoned rock house that stood near the yawning, debris-filled cement foundations which once had supported the Standard Chemical Company's radium mills. Spiderwebs festooned the beams of the house and the glassless windows; lizards and rats scuttled into the shadows. An ineffable restlessness gripped me, for when we were five or six years old and my father was connected with the mill my brother and I had lived in this house, creating mud towns in the arroyo out front and watching, wide-eyed, the long mule trains as they wound down from the mesas with their loads of carnotite ore for the thundering, odorous reduction plant. We had watched the mountain-bound cattle go by, too, and I had never dreamed that one day I would go with similar herds and camp in the ruins of our old home. Now the mill was gone and my brother and father were gone, but ghosts walked the flat that night while cattle bawled and sheet lightning flickered in the mountains, sending down hoarse warning of an approaching storm.

A pasture near the creek let us hold the cattle without night herding, and we were on the trail by dawn the next morning. But even with that good start we made less mileage than we had the day before. We climbed onto broad mesas spiny with hog-backs and dark with those stunted, grotesquely twisted, shaggy-barked evergreens known locally as cedars but which are really a form of juniper—and in all this telling I use both words with careless impartiality. Wet squalls blew into our faces, and the mountains ahead were blotted out by long gray curtains of rain. The hungry yearlings scattered far and wide through the dwarf

trees, and we rode untold miles holding them together and shoving them forward. Strays—even if it is on its home range a critter
which doesn't belong to your herd is known as a stray—joined our
bunch with galling persistence. We had to cut them out and
whip them away with doubled ropes before we could convince
them they were not welcome.

Night caught us in a broad, shallow, rock-rimmed canyon
known as Long Draw. We pushed the cattle into its open bottom,
found a grove of piñon pine dense enough to turn most of the
rain, and made camp. After downing Bill's supper of Dutch-oven
bread, beans, bacon, canned tomatoes, canned apricots, and a
hair-raising coal-tar product masquerading as coffee, we drew
lots to determine our various shifts at the empty weariness of
night herding. We went out in pairs, one man blocking the canyon in front of the cattle, the other blocking it behind them. The
rock rims prevented their climbing out the sides. Spatters of rain
fell intermittently; lightning cracked. But it wasn't one of those
hot, tight storms so full of electricity that ghostly balls of Saint
Elmo's fire glimmer on the animals' horns and ears, and our tired
yearlings did not take fright. We built little fires to sit by and
listened to the *chomp-chomp* of the steers as they pulled at the
thin feed. Out in the pitch-blackness the click of a hoof on stone
would warn that some were edging by. We would mount, shoo
them back, stretch, shiver, and wonder how on earth an hour
could be so long.

By morning it was raining in earnest. The adobe ground turned
to grease, and a horse could go no faster than a trot without
danger of falling flat. Everywhere gray puddles lay like thin sheets
of lead. The chuck truck mired in one mudhole after another, and
two of us spent most of our time pulling it free with our lariats.

Toward noon we gave up. We had come out of Long Draw
onto the spreading flats of sagebrush which mark the head of
Dry Creek Basin. Seeing a farm, we rode to it and asked the
owner if we could put our cattle in the unplowed field east of his

house. We could, for a price. He also told us we could camp in a
one-room shack he was building in the field for his father-in-law
to live in. It was a miserable place, constructed of raw pine
lumber exuding nodules of congealed pitch. Unfinished, it was
dank and chilly, containing no stove and not a stick of furniture.
But at least it had a roof. We accepted eagerly.

We soon got over the eagerness. To cook we had to go outside
and nurse a fire from soggy wood under a canvas tarpaulin
stretched from the side of the truck. We did manage to turn our
food lukewarm, but nothing could help our beds. Dampness had
seeped into them, and crawling between the blankets in that
dreary cabin was like lying down in an icebox. The cattle were
no better off. There was no grass in the field. Led by the im-
patient Brigham, they tramped back and forth along the fence,
filling the already noisy darkness with their disconsolate plaints.

The next day was the same story. Rain fell in solid sheets from
a windless sky, every arroyo thundered bankfull of chocolate
water. We could not go on. Cy shivered and shook and mourned
the end of the world. Mike, wise from past experience, produced
a greasy deck of cards. We sat cross-legged on the muddy floor
and played pitch, blackjack, and poker until we were so bored
we could have thrown back our heads and howled like coyotes.

Toward evening the rain stopped. Sometime after midnight
the moon broke through the clouds. It woke Cy, or perhaps he
hadn't been asleep. He roused the rest of us. "Let's get the hell
outa heah!"

We were ready enough. We saddled and started the eager
cattle along the trail, shiny wet in the moonlight. It was too
muddy for the truck, but we figured that with our early start we
could reach the summer camp by dark. There was food there, and
we could sleep in the hay in the barn until the road dried out
enough for Bill to follow. Then, leaving our horses in the summer-
camp pasture, we would toss our saddles in the truck and return
to Paradox for another drive.

Except for a few patches of runty cedars and piñon, the way was open and we made eight or nine miles by dawn. A red sun rose with all its promise of a fresh day. Directly ahead, blocking out sight of the mountains, was a high ridge dewy green with the budding leaves of scrub oaks. Those oaks and that sun meant trouble. The day dried the mud to a clayey gum that balled on the animals' feet in heavy, unshakable wads. We dismounted continually to scrape it from the horses' hoofs with our pocketknives, but we could not do the same for the cattle. The drag of it drained their strength. As we crept onward through the morning one after another of the yearlings played out and dropped, exhausted, in the middle of the trail. There was nothing to do but leave them and ride on. If they lived they would hang up in near-by swales and draws until we could pick them up again.

When we hit the oak brush in the hills the whole herd stopped. Those new leaves were manna to their empty bellies. Each animal grabbed a branch in its mouth and stayed there, chewing greedily. We had to beat them loose one at a time. We whipped them with ropes, jabbed them with spurs. The dogs barked and ran and nipped. In brush too thick for the horses to get through we dismounted and plunged on foot into the midst of the cattle, screeching profanity and laying about with clubs whittled from oak branches.

Then, late in the afternoon, the gap through which we were pushing widened abruptly. The Lone Cone stood dead ahead. Although nearly thirteen thousand feet high, it is not a craggy mountain; it is not spectacular. From its broad base lines slope gently upward to a sharp point. By midsummer its cap of sparkling snow would melt away into a soft gray bonnet of rock, ever changing with each dimpled shadow that floated across it. Standing apart from all other high peaks, it is exactly what its name says—the Lone Cone, the loveliest mountain, to my prejudiced mind, in all the world.

On a pine-dotted bench at its feet sat the summer camp.

Winter let us stay there no more than half of every year, but each fall when we left it was like going into exile. The desert was a hiatus. Here was fulfillment: grass and flowers and indolent days with the fattening cattle.

We sat silent on our weary horses, looking and looking. Then a great grin curved Mike's lips and he said all there was to say:

"We're home!"

IX GREASY SACK

SPRING CAME WITH A RUSH OF color. Blue iris—"flags," we called them—lay on the damp flats like acres of spilled sky. Wild roses massed on the ditchbanks; mallow, honeysuckle, and Indian paintbrush—the last termed "bloody nose" by the unromantic Mike—made spots of red in hollows and swales. Hidden by the sage, low clumps of Oregon grape shone with brilliant yellow flowers which in turn would produce tiny purple fruit, delicious foundation for a deep-hued jelly. There were other jelly crops too: chokecherry and service- (pronounced sarvis) berry and wild plum mingling white blossoms with the stiff, useless buckbrush and thorny haw apples in the draws. They were harbingers of fun, these berry shrubs, for in the fall the entire ranch force would move out on picking bees, equipped with shiny lard pails and baskets of sandwiches. Even Cy admired the chokecherry bloom. "Wine!" he said and smacked his lips.

But now we had to enjoy all this color and fragrance on the fly, so to speak. As the snow faded from the north slopes and grass spread its thin green sheen across the hills there were more yearlings and my stepfather's pet herd of registered cows to bring up from Paradox. Between trips we plowed the moist earth by the cabin for a vegetable garden, mopped the worst of the muck from the floors, hurriedly made away with the heaps of tin cans which had accumulated during the fall roundup, and in general prepared for the feminine invasion by my wife and mother and the cook.

Not all the cattle had been wintered in Paradox. The strongest, it will be remembered, had been left on the desert mesas to rustle for themselves. While some of the crew handled the successive trail herds, others of us hunted and probed and slowly gathered together these scattered strays.

We joined riders from other ranches and went out in groups of six or seven, driving fifteen or twenty extra horses, some of them packed with our food and bedrolls. In the course of our wanderings we covered a territory perhaps a thousand square miles in size, and since most of our supplies were carried in small cotton bags—dried fruit in one, coffee in another, beans, sugar, sowbelly, dishes, and canned goods each to its own container— the trips were properly known as "greasy-sack rides."

My partner on most of these journeys was John Scott, self-appointed straw boss of our summer range. Some of my best and some of my worst hours were spent with him. He could track wild animals like an Indian and could tell more lore in a more fascinating way than any man I ever knew. But he was always looking out for John Scott. When I was a youngster he lazily used to take but one bed along on the rides, saying we could sleep together and save the bother of extra packing. Many a night I did not sleep, however. He snored like a lumber mill. He shoved me with his knees and rammed me with his elbows until he rolled me out on the cold, stony ground. In desperation I would steal a blanket, wrap up in it, and crouch by the fire, hating him until my arms trembled and my mouth turned dry and hot. In the morning he was enormously surprised and blamed his antics on nightmares. I never believed him. I think he wanted the bed to himself and manufactured his dreams to get it.

He was grotesquely homely. His thin black hair lay plastered tight to his bony skull. He had a red, bulbous, pock-marked nose and green eyes set so close together it was said you could not put a cigarette paper edgewise between them. He was all things to all men. He buttered your back when you were with him and berated you when you were away. He camped at sheep outfits and cursed his fellow cattlemen to the Mexican herders; he joined the Mormon Church when riding in Utah, and on coming to Colorado could not think of enough evil to say of his religion; he spread vile rumors merely to cause trouble. For all this he had been whipped unconscious more than once, but he never learned his lesson.

I do not believe John could learn. His violent moods were completely beyond his control. A slow sullenness would come over him, and he would spend four or five days without speaking a word. Then, like a blast of lightning, he would explode into insane rage, screaming and hurling rocks, beating his horse and whipping the stock he was driving. Oddly, though he carried a gun in a specially constructed holster in his chaps pocket, he never used it during an outburst. He was berserk and wanted to wreak his hurt with bare hands alone. Too, he was essentially a coward, and a man had no trouble keeping out of his way, but his animals suffered cruelly.

And then black remorse would seize John. He bought presents —a hat, a bridle, spurs—for the men who had been with him when he cracked and surreptitiously hid the gifts in their war bags. He would slip out at night and shoe their horses; he could not ride far enough to do them a favor. He babied the mounts he had abused, fed them sugar, and tenderly doctored the hurts he himself had inflicted. He would work with febrile energy from before dawn until after dark, accomplishing more than all the rest of the hands put together.

Then, burned out, he would sink back to his ordinary indolent level. We wanted him with us then. He knew the country and the cattle as no other man, and when he turned loose the full soul-warming flush of his affability, his most bitter enemies would joke and laugh with him until tears ran from their eyes.

Our greasy-sack rides took us into what we called the "rimrock country," the plateau region of the geology books, where the granite Rockies tumble wildly down to the red sandstone deserts of Utah. It is a land of black forests, cracked by rough canyons. The flat-topped mesas and the tortuous gulches are rimmed by low collars of dun-colored cliffs. Until your eyes grow used to picking out every fleeting movement you see scant sign of life. But it is there, cunning, abundant, strong. No matter where you go, the dainty tracks of deer are ahead of you; every night from every side you hear the laughing yap of coyotes. Sometimes as you drop gingerly down a twisting trail that leads from the dry benches to water you surprise a tufted-ear packet of ferocity, a bobcat, crouched in a tree. There will be a yellow gleam of hate in his slanted eyes, a twitch of his stumpy tail and he is gone, a tawny streak melting into the tawny boulders. The mountain lion, scourge of the desert, is there too. You seldom see him, but you may be sure he is watching you from some high rim.

Man also has found a precarious living here. On some flat where the gnarled trees break away to form a park, or in some canyon where a seep of water oozes from the sand, you come on a scraggly alfalfa field surrounding a weathered shack and a sway-backed barn. This is the abode of a homesteader—"the squatter," as he is disaffectionately known by stockmen.

The Federal government, through various homesteading acts, has given citizens, principally war veterans, permission to move onto the public domain and file claim to a piece of land. By farming and "improving" this claim for three years the squatter acquires title to it. Naturally the best sections were taken first. Late-comers fell back on what was left, and their first desperate attempts were devoted to getting water for irrigation. Why not, they reasoned, dig ditches from the mountains to the open mesas, rather than let all those life-giving streams flow uselessly through the untillable gorges of the desert? It sounded fine. Ditch companies sprang up everywhere, some of them co-operative affairs, some of them pure swindles.

The mere promise was enough to send homesteaders rushing to file claims. And then after years of waiting the water often failed to come or came in such small quantities as to be a mockery. From organizations of angels the ditch companies grew to be execrated. I remember well one sign nailed before an abandoned farm in a highly advertised tract:

HOMESEEKERS, BEWARE!

IT'S WATER YOU WANT—

NOT HOT AIR!

Even the blistered wastes at the upper end of East Paradox were once filed solidly by squatters. A ditch was created on paper but never materialized. The whole story is told in one deep arroyo known as Dutchman's Well. Here a stubborn Dutchman, wearied of waiting, determined to dig his own water from the soil. He figured that by starting in the bottom of the arroyo he would not have so far to shovel. Under the hot summer sun he toiled, lifting the dirt from his hole with a little bucket tied to a frayed rope. Twelve feet he dug in the flinty earth, and then the inevitable happened. A cloudburst struck the hills; a flash flood roared down the wash, and his well was instantly piled chock-full of mud and boulders. It was a great joke to the countryside, and the Dutchman's folly gave an everlasting name to a once-nameless barranca. But it was no joke to the Dutchman. He disappeared, no one knows where. Perhaps he killed himself. It was not unknown for a man to knock at his neighbor's door, receive no answer, push inside, and find there on the floor a grimacing corpse with a bullet hole in its head.

In most cases, however, the people simply walked away. You do not often see the cabins they built—those poor shacks have been hauled off by vandals for their wood—but as you ride along you pass a piece of rotted fence or a pile of rocks taken one by one from the land to make way for the plows. There are dry hollows scooped out of the sage and earthen dams thrown across shallow draws to catch the rain water that never falls often enough to fill them. Most pathetic of all are the dead ghosts of the shade trees. Trees planted with the hope that someday children would play under them, trees watered from barrels hauled miles in wagons.

We have camped under those skeletons, using the dry branches for firewood. But no fire can drive away the sorrow they tell. It tears you apart at night when the full moon rises in an immensity of space and the silence is so thick you hold your breath, straining for some sound that will shatter the loneliness. Under the moonlight the abandoned wagon tracks wind off through the flat rocks. What did that road say to the women who saw it on other nights? "Follow me; I am escape." It must have, for it still says so. Looking at it, you know what is lacking in the worn, tired faces of the few wives whose husbands still hang on. The light of hope—it is gone and their eyes are dead.

And yet, though nine out of ten of these homesteaders failed, they changed our entire scheme of stock raising. The bulk of them came into our part of Colorado after World War I. All at once the ranchers woke up to find that the springs they had used without charge were being taken under their noses. Lush flats where their cows had grazed were torn up and planted to crops. That hateful invention, "bob" (barb) wire, blocked their trails, and if the hungry cattle pushed through it, the owners were dumfounded by lawsuits for damages.

When this had happened years before in the plains east of the Rockies, violence flared. Men were killed and the plot germ born for countless wild-West stories. But in western Colorado courts and law-enforcement officers had already been operating for a generation under forms laid down by miners and by the cattlemen themselves. It did not take the county officials long to realize that voting power lay with the newcomers; besides, the homesteaders had the authority of Congress behind them. Realizing that a fight would result simply in their being hanged, the stockmen confined violence to hard breathing through their noses and set about meeting the squatters with the squatters' own weapons.

They, the cattlemen, also filed homesteads under their own names and the names of their men. When they had to they bought out a settler and grouped the tracts into large pastures. Soon the best of the countryside was streaked with fence lines, and the added expense enforced rigid economies of operation. The owners had to learn how to get the most meat off an acre; they had to keep death losses to a minimum. And so they developed better grades of stock and undertook a close supervision of their animals unknown in the careless days of the old-timers.

Other factors hastened the breakup. The sins of the stockman plumped heavily into his lap. All the West knows what it was —overgrazing. I remember my stepfather telling me that when he and other ranchers came into the section they looked at the endless sea of grass and told each other it could never be eaten out. But it nearly was. They escaped only by the skin of their teeth— and by fencing what was left. As they pulled in their horns a new visitor appeared, a despised visitor who could succeed where even the homesteaders could not. He was the sheepherder with his stinking, woolly flocks, and now indeed the old days were gone.

It has been a vast change. Not long ago all the cattle between the Cone and the Utah line were handled by great roundups occurring two or three times a year. The ranchers sent out several chuck wagons and eighty or ninety men to work the herds from the desert to the mountains. I can still see the scene knife-sharp, for I was just getting into my teens when the roundups ended, and every detail remains with the indelibility of boyhood. The cattle a tight knot on the bunch ground, dust spewing as the riders raced back and forth. The canvas-covered chuck wagons, the restless horse herd in a corral made of lariat ropes. The spiraling smoke from the cook fires, the hot coals heaped on the lids of the Dutch ovens, so the "doughgods" inside would bake as evenly on top as on the bottom.

The riders arrived in relays to eat, dismounted, unsaddled and rubbed down their foam-flecked horses. Then they stumbled stiff-legged to the fires, spurs rasping and their dirty old chaps sagging around their hips. They sat cross-legged on the ground, wolfing the soggy food as though life itself depended on speed. Finished, they stretched out on their backs for a ten-minutes snooze, with one knee drawn up, their heads stuck under a shade bush, and their hats pulled down over their faces. Pretty soon it was time to go. They walked to the corral for fresh mounts. The animals milled and plunged. A yellow rope flicked in the sunlight; a loop dropped over a horse's head. It reared, pawing and squealing. The cowboy braced the rope against his hip, heels dragging as he choked the horse to a stop. It stood trembling, ears pricked and the air whistling through its nostrils.

A lot of the men were as scared as the horses. It was customary for at least half of a cowboy's roundup string to be "rough"— broncos raw from the range. The riders swallowed, hitched at their belts. Finally, nerve screwed up, they mounted. The horses, sometimes five or six at once, sunfished and went to bucking in all directions. It seemed that one always managed to go through the cook fires, scattering embers, spectators, pots and pans in a welter of profanity. The cook leaped out with a dish towel in one hand and a skillet in the other, dancing his wrath and yelling the uncomplimentary remarks that only a cook can master.

The last day of the roundup was generally a wild one. The bulk of the riders were gone with the gathered herds, and only fifteen or so men remained to clean up the edges. They had spent a month or six weeks with little sleep, poor food, and hard work, and many of them were ready to come uncorked. Some obliging bootlegger—this was during Prohibition—always found the camp under various guises. One operated as a washing-machine salesman, loading the maws of his demonstration models with pint bottles of "corn."

It was an explosive sort of rotgut, and under its influence enmities sparked hot. There were often fist fights and occasionally worse. Two brothers carved each other up a bit with knives before they were separated and the instigator run out of camp. Another time we lay rigid under a wagon while the disgruntled loser of a bare-knuckle battle unlimbered a Winchester .30-.30 and shot five times at an unarmed opponent, wounding him in the elbow. It might have been a little ridiculous, except that the hurt developed blood poisoning and the man died just as dead as if he had been shot through the heart.

A bitter rainstorm dampened one "last night." Fifteen or more of us piled for shelter into a tiny single-room shack. There wasn't enough space for all to lie in one layer on the floor, so John Scott and I bedded on the table. Three or four drunks became obstreperous and interfered with those who wanted to sleep. They were ejected and the door locked against them. In revenge they climbed on the roof and pushed the loose stone chimney down into the glowing fireplace. The avalanche hurled hot coals throughout the room. Burned sleepers leaped to their feet howling bloody murder, and in an instant the cramped space resounded with an indescribable melee. We surged outside, hunting the perpetrators. The affair ended in a monstrous uproar, during which the cabin burned to the ground. Shelterless, half frozen and disgusted, we saddled up and rode home. I was fourteen or fifteen years old; ever since then the word roundup has conjured a lively picture in my mind.

Yes, the great roundups are dead, and the "greasy sack" is their emaciated heir. Considerable riding remains to be done, however.

Much of the homestead land has reverted to the public domain, unfenced, unwanted, unfit for anything except grazing. And the squatter did not cover all the ground. Millions of arid acres remain almost as they were when the first cattle reached them.

Not long ago the Taylor Grazing Act placed this "open" land under supervision of the Federal government. The step, although it has caused grumbling, was necessary and should have come sooner than it did, for Western grasslands will need half a century or more to recover from the brutal raping of the past decades. The cattle, also, have changed. Blocky, white-faced Herefords have replaced those original gaunt, untractable longhorns which seemed to produce only horns, tails, and appetites.

Old-time cowboys sneer at Herefords as namby-pamby creatures to be herded by flat-heeled farmer boys on draft horses. But even a Hereford will develop a wild streak if given plenty of room and little handling. The hind end of a runaway steer looks the same as it always did, and the process of overhauling it is not very different from what it used to be. In the main it is a matter of a good horse and a long rope, plus lots of patience and that particular kind of "savvy" which is gained only through experience. Young riders with all their dash and zip are not apt to be so efficient as older, quieter hands.

Our greasy-sack rides conformed more or less to a pattern. Cattle have a strong home instinct and hang close to a chosen spot. If this were not so, if they roamed as far as their legs could carry them, ranching except in pastures would be impossible.

We knew where to look and also when. A cow normally grazes like a deer at night, goes to water in the morning, and holes up in thick brush or timber during the heat of the day. We would separate into pairs and go out at the first crack of dawn. Slipping quietly along a fresh trail, we would grab the bunch—the animals ran in groups of six to a dozen—before they could break for the brush. We would drift them to an appointed meeting place, throw them in with our partners' gather, cut out the strays, and

put the ones we wanted in a holding pasture until we had cleaned
the district and were ready to move on.

Sometimes we were able to rent a homesteader's field, such as
Rial Winton's north quarter near Mud Springs Draw. Although
a squatter, Rial had prospered. His homestead was neat as a pin;
he had a few cattle of his own and "sense enough to nail his fence
wires to the inside of his posts." (Many an inexperienced homesteader carelessly stapled his barbwire to the outside of his posts.
Then if an animal in the pasture pushed against the fence—and
sooner or later one did—the staples popped out, the wires sagged,
and the critter went through. Wires fastened to the inside of the
posts did not give so easily. Accordingly, we made our first judgment of a new settler by the method in which he hung his wires.)

One spring Rial greeted us with a bare-mouthed grin and
sunken cheeks. He hadn't a tooth left in his head, though he was
no more than forty years old.

"Well!" said John. "The jaw cracker is in town!"

"Yay, boy!" lisped Rial. "No more rheumatithm fo' me. Kinda
tirethome livin' on thoup, though."

The jaw cracker was the traveling dentist. He went from town
to town, dragging his shop in a trailer behind his automobile.
Whenever he appeared, all the possessors of toothaches, recurrent
headaches, neuralgia, rheumatism, lumbago, or morning stiffness
flocked to see him. He jerked out their teeth—in fairness it must
be admitted that the patients asked for the treatment, though
perhaps the dentist would have recommended it anyhow—and
sent them home to let their wounded gums shrink into shape.
On his return trip he measured his now-hungry clients for plates,
made the dentures in his home office, and shipped them out
C.O.D.

It is amazing how many people were helped by this rigorous
procedure. Few dry farmers or cowboys ever touched a tooth-
brush or had a cavity treated until it pained so badly they could
not stand it, in which case a little fruitless home dentistry with a

pair of pliers was not unknown. Inevitably their teeth decayed. Often the removal of the diseased members toned up a person's entire system. News of the cures spread far and wide; anyone suffering from a mysterious ache listened and acted on the dentist's next trip. Moreover, store teeth lent prestige. They were handsome—far more handsome than the owner's former yellowed fangs—and their sudden appearance in a smile created the effect of a new Schiaparelli gown on Fifth Avenue. This desire for beauty and social acclaim, both by male and female, led to many an otherwise unnecessary extraction.

The teeth also led to odd complications. John Scott told again and again with boundless delight about the time Rial put his teeth on a chair, forgot them, sat down in the presence of company, and soundly bit himself. And I shall never forget the pair of cowboys who carefully laid their plates side by side on a log at bedtime and the next morning were unable to tell whose were whose. They quarreled bitterly until the smell of breakfast overpowered them. Agonized by hunger pangs, they popped the dentures into their mouths and determined ownership by fit.

Although we liked Rial Winton, he had six or seven miles back in the piñons a homesteading neighbor named McIsaac of whom we did not approve. McIsaac was a tall, stooped bachelor with a sharp face and a tiny rosebud mouth so tightly pursed, John said, that you couldn't drive a needle into it with a sledge hammer. Riding the dry, ragged breaks around his place took a full day, and one noon John and I decided to fortify ourselves by lunching with him. It was known that McIsaac treated himself handsomely. He had fresh eggs and butter, bacon and store cheeses stored in a cool bucket hung in his well.

Mouths watering, we rode to his door. He looked at us without words, though it was the custom to ask any mealtime passer-by to "step down." Today's host is likely to be tomorrow's visitor, and the exchanged meals balance out in the long run. But McIsaac let us sit on our horses until we were forced to the acute embarrassment of asking for nourishment.

"It'll cost you fifty cents each," he grumbled.

We dismounted and went inside. Suddenly we froze. Coiled in the middle of the floor, black tongue darting, was a thick tan-and-gold bull snake. John seized a broom.

"Nix!" said McIsaac. "That's Roger."

Reluctantly John put away the broom. Bull snakes are not poisonous and are even welcome around fields and barns where they do yeoman service in keeping down rodents. But having Roger underfoot while we lunched was something else. John's shaggy brows bunched over his green eyes.

Broad hints about the well availed us nothing. We ate crusted beans, sour stewed apricots, stale baking-powder biscuits, and warmed-over coffee. While we were choking it down McIsaac produced a can of condensed milk, poured some in a saucer, and set it on the floor. Over slithered Roger and began to drink. McIsaac replaced the can on the shelf without asking if we wanted any for our coffee.

That was the last straw. John stood up abruptly, kicked aside his chair, flung a silver dollar on the table, and stalked outside. All afternoon he fumed like spilled water on a hot stove.

"Chargin' us for his garbage an' then feedin' milk to a snake!"

When we reached Winton's we found Rial in the clutches of an itinerant hide buyer. The fellow, hook-nosed and dark of visage, had arrived in a sorry pickup truck and was dickering for the steer hides Rial had hung over his corral fence. An inordinately persistent man, he bargained with his entire body, waving his arms, thumping Rial's chest with a scrawny forefinger, washing his hands together, thrusting his pendulous lips almost into his prospect's face, and whining loud enough to be heard a quarter of a mile. Rial was trembling with disgust.

John's ugly face creased in thought. "Mister," he interrupted, "there's a feller up the road has lots of hides."

"So?" The black eyes glinted.

"His name is McIsaac, an' he keeps those hides hidden in his strawstack."

The buyer smirked. "Some of the brands maybe ain't his."

"Maybe. Anyhow, when you ask him about hides he'll deny havin' 'em. You know how careful a man's got to be these days."

The buyer nodded. Apparently he had been in this boat before, and it is a human failing to believe the worst about another person.

"Just go to that strawstack," John continued, "an' start diggin'. When you prove the hides are there he'll do business."

"Business is what we want!" The buyer hurriedly completed his deal with Rial, climbed in his pickup, and wheeled off.

"John," Rial said, "you ought to be skinned yourself. Mac never in his life butchered a stolen cow. He hasn't a hide on his place, and you know it!"

John shrugged. Then, having formed a mental picture of the scene and found it good, he gave a vindictive snort of pleasure. "Favor a snake, will he?"

We can only imagine what happened. Toward dusk the hide buyer returned. He leaned out of the cab, sputtered an unintelligible something, and drove furiously on. Rial, who was near the gate hoeing his potato patch, insisted the man's eye was bruised and swollen. And when we rode by McIsaac's place the next morning we saw straw scattered far and wide over the stackyard. I have often wished it had been possible to see and hear that meeting.

Another camp we liked was deep in the piñon forests where the ragged breaks of Bull Canyon pitch and plunge toward the sullen red gorge of the Dolores River. The rough wagon road twists

through the trees, dips toward a seep of water. A hand-lettered
sign appears:

WILD HORSE, COLO.
Population . . . 2

This was the abode not of a homesteader but of a tough, seam-
faced, loud-laughing Irish cowman, Len Farrell, and his meek,
silent, twenty-year-old helper. They wintered two or three hundred cows here and in summer drifted the animals onto North
Mountain, a timbered spur running out from the Cone. Until
spring, when we stopped by on our greasy-sack ride, they saw no
one for weeks at a time. Their home was a tent. A most unusual
tent too. Farrell had purchased it from the side show of a traveling circus. Khaki-colored and spotted with patches, it had a
huge round base, high side walls, and a roof that sloped to a tall,
conical point. The circular earthen floor was packed hard. There
was ample room for a cookstove, a large table, and half-a-dozen
bedrolls. Saddles, pack panniers, and grain boxes lined the walls.
Ropes draped overhead served as hanging places for clothes,
bridles, quirts, and so on. Bales of hay made sweet-smelling seats;
the stove chuckled with the rustling wind, and a coal-oil lantern
hung to the center mast pole sent shadows dancing across the
high, peaked canvas. A delicious intimacy lay on the place, invit-
ing late talk and bubbling good humor. Inevitably it was here
that John Scott spun his best yarns.

There he sat on a bale of hay, his palms resting on its edges,
his hard, knobby body leaning forward. His green eyes snapped,
and his crabbed red face grew full of magic. The ugliness disappeared, and he swept us irresistibly into a fairyland of word
and sonorous tone, of soft gesture and biting allusion.

"We were settin' in the pool hall at Norwood one afternoon
playin' draw poker. You know how it is." (Yes, we knew: the
cone of white light spilling on the stained baize-covered table, the
drifting smoke, the dirty chips, the smell of stale beer and sweat.)

"Bugger Red was dealin'." (John squinted one eye shut, licked his thumb, and passed out the imaginary cards. It wasn't John doing it; it was Bugger Red. And then he put us in each player's chair, showed us the cards, muttered under his breath, looked avaricious, flung down a hand, scratched, and rolled a smoke. His ear for dialect, his mimicry of mannerisms was so shrewd, so mercilessly exact that we howled with laughter.)

"Pretty soon the door opened and a city feller come in. He was wearin' choke-bore breeches (jodhpurs), an' he was beef plumb to the hock—three ax handles an' a piece of rope across the beam, I swear. He kinda rolled along on the balls of his feet, like he was tryin' to carry an aigg in his crotch without bustin' it." (John walked. He leaned his hands on the back of an imaginary chair, peered at the imaginary table, and invited himself into the game.)

"We told him to set. He giggled high in his nose like a lost filly colt. But he wasn't lost. No! He picked us bare as a dry farmer's feed lot. Bugger Red got up mad an' went out. Pretty soon he come back, grinnin' behind his teeth. 'Boys,' he said, 'they's a badger fight on.' Then he pretended to remember the stranger an' let on like he'd said more'n he meant.

"The stranger's ears flew up. 'Badger fight? What's that?'

"Bugger wouldn't tell him. The feller begged." (Now John was the stranger; now he was Bugger. He wore himself down and admitted that a badger was going to be matched against a bulldog under the grandstand at the fairgrounds. What a battle it was going to be! Only . . . it was against the law. If the town marshal got wind——)

" 'I won't breathe a word!' says the stranger, 'and I'd certainly like to see that fight.'

" 'Well, come on,' says Bugger, and away we went." (Away went John, a whole troop of people now, whispering, laughing, and nudging.)

"We got under the grandstand, an' there was Pete Larkin's big white bulldog, growlin' like a wasps' nest. Up above him, on a plank scaffold about head high to a man, was a barrel lyin' on its side. The mouth was covered with burlap, an' a chain ran out of it. Everybody was nervous, lookin' an' listenin' for the law." (John threw up his head and peered over his shoulder. Entranced, breathless, we peered over ours.)

"Bugger says to the stranger, 'The badger is in that barrel with the chain around his neck. But nobody's got the nerve to pull him out. The marshal would fine the feller for startin' the fight. It's too bad. Them badgers is somethin' to see, comin' out of a barrel with their fur up an' their lips back.'

" 'I'll pull it out!' says the stranger, lickin' his chops an' sweatin' with eagerness.

" 'I knowed you was a sport!' says Bugger, clappin' him on the back. He handed over the chain. 'You got to yank hard an' quick, so the badger will sail plumb out an' land free!'

"The stranger gets a strangle hold on the chain an' braces his feet. 'Ready?' whispers Bugger like a hen-house thief." (We all nodded. We were ready too.)

" 'GO!'

"The stranger rares back like a bogged mule. Out sails a little old thunder mug, plumb full. 'Aow-w-w-w!' yowls the stranger an' falls flat on his back."

John falls too, sputtering and choking. . . . The story, incidentally, is a true recital of a favorite cow-town practical joke, but it was never as funny in actuality as it was in John's telling. Certainly the episode is crude, and so, too, on the surface, is a good deal of a cowboy's talk. But these men, living close to nature, with natural bodily functions an integral part of their jobs, unavoidably draw the rough, rich imagery of their conversation—their incomparable similes and metaphors—from the things they see. Using such native materials, John Scott, uneducated, unlettered, and scarcely able to write his name, made of his coarse yarn spinning a brilliant art. He may not have been the greatest dramatic raconteur of all time, but I have yet to see anyone who can match him.

Not all our camps were so pleasant. As we worked toward the fringes of the range we left the homesteaders far behind, stopping wherever we could find a drink and build a holding pasture by dragging logs across the narrow mouth of a rocky pocket. Sometimes the water we found was so muddy and bitter we could drink it only by turning it into coffee and ladling in sugar. As the season advanced and the days grew hotter we often had to hunt the cattle by moonlight.

Bleakest place of all was Wild Steer Mesa, a slabbed tableland rising like a cocked hat in the triangle between Paradox and the Rio Dolores—River of Sorrows, so named by the Spaniard, Escalante, in 1776, when a Negro favorite of his exploring expedition fell into the stream from a bluff near the present town of Dolores and was drowned. We camped high on the mesa's shoulder, for there was no way of reaching the river a thousand feet below. A uranium prospector had built a tiny cabin here, and on its walls some disgusted visitor had written, "Fly blown in Wild Steer, June 2, 1924."

What those flies and mosquitoes lived on between our annual visits I cannot imagine, but they certainly made up for lost time when we appeared, driving horses and men alike into a helpless frenzy. During the day we lay under the trees, listless in the heat, smoking, slapping, and squirming. And each year John told the story which I suppose has been told all over the West:

"Why, these mosquitoes ain't nothin'. You ought to see 'em in Greasewood. They put scouts along the trails, an' when a man shows up you can hear 'em holler, 'Here comes meat!' They fly over in droves that shade the sun. They sound like a millrace. Oncet I thought to fool 'em by takin' along a copper wash boiler. When I saw 'em headin' my way I crawled underneath it. But do you think that stopped 'em? No sir! They lit on it an' began to

bore like woodpeckers. *Rat-a-tat-tat*—it near broke my eardrums.
I picked up a rock an' when they drilled through I clinched their
beaks over like you would a nail. It weren't no use. They reared
back, picked up the boiler with their beaks, an' flew off with it.
The rest really did go for me then. If a forest fire hadn't come up
an' smudged 'em off, I never would of got away."

Finally the cold evening brought relief. We dozed a few hours,
then jogged off to "moonlight 'em," as this night riding for cattle was called. A full moon turned the sage flats to platinum;
trees and cliffs were ink streaks under the pale sky. Our ears
strained for every pop of a twig, our eyes for every moving
shadow. But mostly our horses did the finding. They knew the
game. Suddenly one would throw up its head, its body taut and
eager.

We spread out and slipped down-wind. Out on the flat a
cluster of dark spots stirred like wind-rippled leaves. Cattle! They
had seen us! They broke for the rough hillsides and dense timber,
where in the darkness we could not overtake them. We raced to
cut them off. A gully yawned ahead. We let our muscles sag
limply, ready for a fall. But the ponies got over, hurtled on.

Sometimes we headed the cattle; sometimes we didn't. If we
failed we let them go until another night, swearing at the sound
of them crashing through the rocks. If we succeeded we surrounded them, holding them motionless. Their flanks rose and
fell with their nervous breathing; their heads turned and twisted,
hunting escape. Gradually they grew used to us. Because most
cattle by nature prefer to follow rather than lead, one man rode
in front of them toward the pasture we had made in a near-by
canyon. Another got behind and drove, being very careful to
make no sudden noise or gesture that would startle them into
flight. The rest of the crew vanished over the lip of the hill, bound
for another likely flat.

And so the drives went on, a sweep here and a sweep there,
long hours of monotony and swift minutes of bright excitement.

Dust and jostling red backs, the night wind sharp in our faces or the sun like a pile driver on our backs. Day after similar day, but always with this contentment running through them like a golden thread: soon we would turn again into the mountains, into summer.

X SANDROCK

HUNGRY AS THEY WERE, THE little steers we belabored each spring into the mountains were unable to eat all the grass that sprouted under their noses during the quick, lush months of summer. We had to buy more cattle or else waste range. Over to Utah we went, to a wild, weird land of sandrock, where each year the sprawling Scorup-Somerville Cattle Company produces more yearlings than it can fatten for market.

We traveled luxuriously by car. We would soon have to hit the trail on horseback, and during these preliminary trips of "look-see" it was a great relief to cover the choking, sun-baked country in one day instead of ten. Radiator boiling and chassis groaning, we staggered up the dirt road that coils out of southwestern Paradox. Over the hump and into tawny La Sal Canyon, its steep sides such a rubble of dun boulders, dark junipers, and thick scrub brush that in places a dog can't wriggle through. We rode sour-faced, thinking of the unadulterated hell we always had when our tired herd hit this miserable stretch.

The road twists across the state line high on the southern shoulder of the La Sal Mountains. The land comes down from the peak in a smooth roll that gradually slides off into an endless plain of sagebrush. It looks level, that plain: a sea of gray monotony broken by black islands of piñon pine. But mean little canyons and dry washes slink through it everywhere, making horse travel a complex problem of navigation. Melting snow or rain turns the gummy earth into a morass of mud that at one time or another hopelessly mires every car and wagon in the section, turning their drivers into profane, purple-faced fatalists. It is a richly productive land, however, in such favored spots as can be watered. Over near Dove Creek, on the Colorado part of the plain, drought-routed farmers from the Dust Bowl have found a haven where they grow beans, beans, and still more beans. With armies to feed, business is good.

These arable spots are pinpricks. Most of the plain is given to the wintering of cattle and sheep. Colossus of the latter outfits is the La Sal Land & Livestock Company, whose headquarters camp straddles the road on the shoulder of the mountain. The map shows a town: La Sal. It is not a town. It is a sheep company: store, garage, warehouses, boardinghouses, barns, networks of corrals, and mile after mile of fodder-producing fields set like bright emeralds in the gray sage. It is a good Mormon concern run in a good Mormon way by its horse-trading boss, Charlie Redd. Big-boned, pink-cheeked, and affable, Charlie Redd can call more men of assorted types by their first names than an electioneering congressman. But this hasn't kept his herds—they number far into the tens of thousands—from being stampeded on dark nights, or strychnine from being put in his sheep salt. His barns, warehouses, and haystacks are periodic prey for arsonists. This country used to be cattle land, and the old enmities die hard.

We rattled on west through low, drab hills to the north-south highway which taps Mesa Verde National Park. South we swung for several miles, coming at last into Dry Valley, which looks exactly as it sounds. Here the CCC, by drilling deep water wells, has added thousands of acres of grazing land to the usable total. And still the CCC is locally despised for its pampering paternalism. This entire corner of Utah is a stronghold of rugged

Mormon individualism—than which there is nothing ruggeder—
and all that its stubborn inhabitants ask is to be let alone so they
can take care of themselves.

We were hunting the most stubborn one of all in his little rock
house on Indian Creek. Dim wheel tracks strike west from Dry
Valley. We reached the turnoff and halted, openmouthed with
astonishment. Once there had been nothing here. Now there was
a rough plank structure resembling a privy. It had "Post Office"
daubed on its unpainted front, and next to it was a white sign
lettered:

Entrance To

HOME OF TRUTH
Marie M. Ogden
DIRECTOR

All else was blankness. A few fat lumps of sandstone sat glumly
under the brassy sky. The distant forest of piñon was like a black
skullcap pulled tight on a wrinkled forehead.

Jack Lamb, blocky little livestock marvel who was traveling
with us, shook his head. "Maybe the Truth does live here," he
said. "Nothing else could."

We drove on. After a couple of miles we ran onto a group of
wooden shacks so mean and raw they seemed to melt right into
the landscape. In the midst of them rose the skeleton of what was
going to be for that country (if it was ever finished) a most
ambitious building. We decided it must be a temple.

Not a builder was in sight. "I guess the Truth's got no body
to it," Jack said. "What the devil do you suppose this is all
about?"

We could find no one to tell us, so we went another mile and
stumbled onto another group of shacks. Thoroughly baffled now,
we peeked through the windows. We saw handmade tables and
chairs and candles but no person. There were promising signs,

however. A short distance away a long-handled pump suggested a well, and on the crest of a low hill a few gray, ragged tents flapped in the hot wind.

Out of one of these tents popped a thin little man. He wore a short-sleeved, open-collared white shirt, low oxfords, and duck trousers, garments utterly unsuited to southeastern Utah. The temperature stood well over a hundred degrees, but the tent dweller had no hat. His face was the color of boiled lobster. Down the hill toward the pump he came, swinging his arms in long arcs. In one hand he carried a white enameled pitcher.

I walked toward him. He was staring straight at me, but it became evident he didn't see me at all. I stepped cautiously aside.

"Hello!"

He jumped a foot into the air and threw back his arm. I thought he was going to chuck the pitcher at my head. Then slowly his eyes focused.

"Good day," he said.

We both drew a long breath and looked each other over. "What is this place?" I asked.

"The Home of Truth. Do you wish something?"

"Well, no. We were headed for Al Scorup's ranch on Indian Creek and——"

His face congealed, and he drew himself up stiff as a board. "Mr. Scorup is one of the Damned."

"Oh," I said, thinking of Al's massive frame and bulldog jaw. "Who damned him?"

"You'll have to talk to Mrs. Ogden."

And so our interview ended. Only bit by bit during ensuing years did we pick up the story of this colony—at least the story as local residents tell it; I do not pretend to understand the colonists' viewpoint. I know this, however: Mrs. Ogden is a charming woman to talk to. At one time she was a prominent welfare worker in New Jersey. There the ancient cry of the prophets came to her: the world was doomed to destruction by war and strife and madness. But over in Utah, her revelation said, was a spot where Truth would prevail and its devotees prosper in the eternal sunshine.

She selected Indian Creek for a site. Unfortunately Al Scorup was already there, but he did agree to sell his ranch if she happened to have half a million dollars lying around. This set her back a bit. The colony was a communal affair; when a member joined he turned over all his property to the leader and was thereafter provided with shelter, food, and clothing. A hundred or so Truth Seekers had fallen in line, but they couldn't ante half a million dollars.

Mrs. Ogden made a counterproposal. She would establish her colony on Indian Creek as planned and Al would be allowed to join. His ranch would escape destruction, and what did he think of that?

Well, Al said, it seemed to him that maybe the colonists would booger his cows, and he reckoned that for their sakes he'd better not do it. So the pilgrims moved into Dry Valley, and Al's outfit was earmarked for Armageddon.

Right away the colony ran into a tiff with local authorities. Dark rumors spread that one of the leaders had died and the followers were worshiping his corpse. Of course the believers didn't consider the departed member dead; he had merely gone beyond to scout out the deal for the future. When he returned he would step once more into his mortal clay. Naturally it wouldn't do to destroy said clay, so it was stored in a locked building to which, so the claims ran, only Mrs. Ogden had ingress.

This was too much for the countryside. Out bustled the county coroner. Word of his coming preceded him, and the pilgrims spirited the corpse—if it was a corpse—away into the rocks. The coroner's posse beat the brush to no avail and went home. The departed brother was restored to his shrine; the coroner charged in again, was similarly foiled, etc., etc. Finally a working compromise was evolved. The coroner examined the controversial article. Whatever it had been, he announced, it was now nothing but a mummy of undetermined ancestry, well embalmed by the dry desert air. As everyone knew, there were hundreds of other mummies lying around in the ancient cliff dwellings that dot the land. If the colonists wanted one of their own the coroner didn't see why they shouldn't have it. So matters rested.

Meanwhile, many a canard was broadcast about the Home. To answer them Mrs. Ogden purchased the weekly paper at Monticello and entered journalism. In between times the dwindling membership (of the original hundred only ten or so are left) go on pilgrimages to Shay Mountain, a soaring hump fifteen miles away. While the followers pray about its base, the leader ascends to the top for the revelations by which she guides her flock.

From the Home of Truth we proceeded uncertainly west toward Indian Creek. During the last four or five years the road has been improved—that is, made discernible—but before then it was a case of hunt and peck. Wherever you could force an automobile, that was the highway. We hopped ledges, racked in and out of dry washes, threaded trees, skirted sinkholes, and at last came to a bewildered stop on a wrinkled tableland of "slick rock." Slick rock is a Utah staple. The eternal wind whisks the dirt off whole hills and vales, leaving nothing but the framework, like a coyote with its hide peeled off. This bared rock holds no trails. Before we could progress we had to get out of the car and walk ahead with our noses to the ground, hunting scratches left by previous travel.

The maze unraveled, we nose-dived into a subsidiary gulch, wallowed through sand, and reached the main canyon. Here the desert's most dulcet sound reached our ears—running water. This was Indian Creek, draining northwest from the Blue Mountains

to the titanic gorge of the Colorado River.[1] The creek has hewn
an exquisite canyon, flat-bottomed and full of greenery. Smooth,
dusky red walls soar on either hand; ridge spurs shoot up into lacy
obelisks and Gothic spires.

Nine miles of hayfields, their soil deep and rich and red as
blood, line the chocolate-colored stream. As we passed the fields
mowing machines were clanking busily. Slings attached to those
crane-necked masts known as Mormon derricks lifted feathery
loads of hay from wagons to stacks. How those tall spruce poles
had been brought from the mountains over that frightful road I
cannot imagine. Nor did I stop to wonder. After the thin, baked
smells of the desert, this perfume of water and flowers, moist
underbrush and new-cut alfalfa was a lotus drug, and all we had
mind for was to breathe.

The road crosses Indian Creek, or rather Indian Creek crosses
the road, and we promptly bogged down. We left the car, waded
ashore, and walked on, the pink sand sifting into our wet boots.
To our left Cottonwood Canyon broke through Indian Creek's
red walls, and the combined gorges widened into a broad, cliff-
girt valley. Here stood the ranch: a few whispering cottonwood
trees for shade, a sway-backed corral, and a flimsy, open-sided
shed for the farm machinery. There was a little steel bin to keep
rats out of the horses' oats and a pair of mud-daubed bunkhouses
built of crooked piñon logs. A cookshack and dining room, with a
black iron kettle out back for making lumps of yellow soap. An
orchard of apple and peach trees, trellises of grapevines and roses,
and a tiny sandstone house where Mr. and Mrs. Scorup live.

No, it does not look like much. But consider this: for more than
a hundred and fifty miles, clear down to the junction of the
San Juan and Colorado rivers, across them to the Arizona line
and beyond, there is no other house. There is no road, no tele-

[1]On maps the Blue Mountains are called Abajo. Such discrepancies are
frequent in southern Utah. For some reason the surveyors failed to get together with the settlers; as a result the charts bear names local residents
never heard of.

phone, no electric light. This is all. This and the measureless, unmapped miles of sandrock.

Al Scorup came stumping out to meet us. He had been on horseback since dawn, and fatigue sent twinges through old fractures in his knee and foot, making him limp a little. His veined, slabby cheeks were smeared with dust, but his pale blue eyes were as hard and bright as glass.

We told him what we had learned in Dry Valley: that he was due for destruction. His mouth formed as nearly perfectly a V as a mouth can form, and his thick shoulders trembled with his soundless chuckle.

"I'll risk it," he said.

The thing we had come for was happening. A cloud of golden dust hovered in Cottonwood Canyon. Another cloud stirred sluggishly along Indian Creek below the ranch. Underneath each cloud was a herd of two thousand head of cattle. Their drivers had left the ranch seven or eight weeks before. They had split into pairs, some of them going a hundred miles or more to the junction of the San Juan and Colorado. They had found a few cows on a rocky bench, a few more in a box canyon. They had thrown the animals together, drifted them on, joined other riders, swelled their herds from dozens to thousands. Some of the animals they shoved toward summer range in the Elk Mountains, others toward the Blue Mountains; still others came on toward Indian Creek.

No Chinese puzzle was ever more intricate: two ponderous herds moved ten or twelve miles a day over uncharted trails, formed and reformed at scheduled spots on a scheduled time by men who had no contact with each other for weeks at a time. Now those two herds were meeting right on the dot. A machine is a precise thing; cows and horses are not. Yet this precision was comparable to trains in a switchyard.

I ventured to remark it.

Al looked at me in mild surprise. "Of course they're here," he said. "I told the boys when they left in April that I wanted them back today with four thousand head." And that was that.

There wasn't sufficient graze for the herds around the ranch itself, so they were held a short distance back in the forking canyons. A commissary crew came on ahead: several mules loaded with water cans, bedrolls, and grub panniers. The packer was a redheaded boy with a silky red beard and one sleeve torn off his dust-powdered shirt. He unloaded his stock and dumped the bedrolls in a pile by the saddle shed. Similar outfits kept arriving, half a dozen of them, each bossed by a tattered, unshaven youngster. They had supplied the riders during the roundup; their mules were called "long-eared chuck wagons." No wheeled vehicle can manage that country.

Toward sunset the cowboys themselves started drifting in, thirty villainous-looking creatures, gaunt and sun-blackened. Each found his bedroll in the pile by the saddle shed, lugged it into the orchard, and spread it under the trees, for the twenty-odd hay hands had long since filled the bunkhouses to overflowing.

Most of the riders were scarcely old enough to vote, and now they were in a wonderful humor at being "home." They raced to the creek, stripped, and plunged into a knee-deep pool that had been dammed up behind a low bluff. It was startling to see the color of their bodies. A cowboy doesn't bare himself to the sun, even by rolling up his sleeves. His face, throat, and hands are like mahogany. The rest of him is milky white.

They lathered themselves still whiter, snapped each other raw with their towels, yelled, sang, put on clean clothes, and came trooping back. The log dining room could not accommodate all of them at once, and supper was served in relays. How they loved that meal! For nearly two months they had eaten nothing but beans, beef, and Dutch-oven bread. They had not stepped inside a building or put their feet under a table. Now they had steak, potatoes and gravy, fresh garden vegetables, milk, pie, and cake (but, in accordance with Mormon custom, neither tea nor coffee) heaped on plates they didn't have to balance on their laps. They could live in such luxury for another day or two, then back to the desert they'd go, to room and board in whatever cave was handiest.

Dinner finished, each man carried his utensils outdoors to a table set beside a fire pit, where a huge kettle of water boiled. Some of the younger blades wiped dishes for the three sturdy black-haired girls who did the cooking. The hay hands sharpened the sickles for tomorrow's mowing. Sparks flew from the whirring grindstones; turkeys gobbled on the fence rails, and up on the mesa a pair of coyotes made enough racket for an entire pack. Utterly contented, the cowboys lounged in the violet dusk, swapping yarns about their various drives or repairing their roundup-tortured gear.

One or two of those saddles deserved a second look. The leather on cantles, skirts, and fenders had been carved into pictures of the great buttes of Monument Valley, of the natural stone bridges in White Canyon, of steers and horses. This was the work of Buck Lee, part owner of a ranch down toward Mexican Hat in a fantastic land of eroded sandstone known as the Garden of the Gods. Buck is almost a legend in southeastern Utah. His oil paintings and leatherwork have been exhibited in the state capitol at Salt Lake City. It is not esoteric art; cowboys will save money for years to buy one of his hand-tooled saddles.

The tales Buck spins are equally good. He is forever baffling credulous visitors with something like this:

Buck once had a pet grizzly bear, almost as tall as a horse and better to ride because it could cover country a horse couldn't touch. This bear had only one ear and a bad temper. Once as Buck was riding his grizzly through the rimrock he met another bear, even larger. The two lit into each other with bloodcurdling roars. Buck was under them, over them, on both sides. Finally they stopped to rest for another round, but Buck decided enough was plenty. He leaped aboard, dug his spurs straight in, and away he went with the other grizzly in hot pursuit. Scared stiff, Buck grabbed his mount's ears and hung on for dear life. It wasn't until he had gone eight or ten miles that he realized he had an ear in *each* hand. . . . There the story ends, and the infuriated listener—Buck's dry, infinitely detailed manner of telling makes the adventure sound real as rain—is left to divine the end for himself.

One of the Indian Creek cowboys took no part in the evening gossip. He lay under a bush too sick to eat. For three days he had been able to stomach only canned milk; now he couldn't hold down even that. But he wasn't too sick to work. When his turn at night herding came he saddled up and rode off without the least notion of asking for someone else to relieve him.

It was an ordinary thing. Physical distress is part of the job. For instance, there is Johnny Plummer, one of the old-timers. His horse fell with him one blistering summer and broke his leg in two places. Somehow Johnny caught the animal again, dragged himself into the saddle, and rode sixty miles to the ranch. He arrived out of his head, parched as a crackling. The trip had taken him two days, and he was without water the entire distance. His only comment: "There were times along the way when living didn't seem worth the trouble." A dumb-animal instinct for self-preservation, maybe. But without it there would never have been a state of Utah.

And then there is Harve Williams, a keg-chested, powerful man with a boulder-round face perpetually covered by a stubble of black beard. Harve owns a small interest in the company and is foreman of the Bar X Bar part of the range. (The company runs three brands: the Flying V bar ($\underline{\vee}$), the Bar X Bar (—X—) and the Lazy TY ($\vdash$). Once or twice each winter and again during the summer Harve strikes into the desert with several loose horses and a pack train laden with oats and non-perishable food. He finds a box canyon with a seep of green water in it, fences off its mouth, and leaves a couple of horses there. Near by

he locates a cave. In the loose sand of the cave's floor he digs a hole and buries part of his grain and grub. In that dry climate supplies keep indefinitely; rats and prairie dogs cannot raid the cupboard because the fine sand slides back under their paws faster than they can dig it out.

On Harve goes, repeating the performance until he has caches scattered throughout the desert. Now he is fixed for several months of riding. When he gets hungry or wants a fresh horse he heads for one of his storehouses. The half-broken cayuses he left in the fenced canyons, seeing no one for months on end, have gone wild again. Small matter. Harve fights the brutes into submission, gnaws on some of his dried food, and, tending to the cattle as he rides, moves on.

On those nights when the herd was held at Indian Creek there was a great coming and going. About the time the full moon topped the monster butte across the canyon someone stumbled over my feet, muttered " 'Scuse!" and disappeared through the mottled shadows. I sat up. Canvas-covered beds glimmered like patches of snow in the orchard. Here and there a bed would stir, a tousled head rear up, a pair of arms stretch sleepily. That mysterious sixth sense which wakens a cowboy with the surety of an alarm clock was rousing the night herders. They pulled on boots and jumpers, the only articles of clothing they had removed on going to bed, and tiptoed toward the corrals. A cigarette glowed; spurs jingled; a horse snorted. There was a lazy roll of hoofs, and the new watch rode off to relieve the boys who were holding the cattle. Soon the spelled crew jogged home and the performance was repeated in reverse.

Before dawn we were all out. We sliced a workable-sized bunch of cattle off one of the main herds and brought them to the cut grounds near the creek. As soon as it was light enough to see we began to segregate the animals we were going to take to the Lone Cone. We selected one, and then Scorup selected one for us. Of course we took the best we could find, and he threw us the worst. In the end the animals probably averaged the same as if we'd drawn an arbitrary line through the middle of the herd and said everything north of the line was ours. But this I-pick-you-pick method is customary; it prevents shenanigans by an unscrupulous buyer or seller, and it gives each party a chance to go home secretly feeling he's got the best of the bargain.

We brought up another bunch of cattle and another. Dust fogged; the sun climbed; sweat-streaked horses were changed for fresh ones. Four or five men cut at a time, their wise ponies slipping back and forth through the close-packed animals. A flick of the reins, a touch with the spurs, and the horse knows which steer is to go. Slowly, so as not to excite the rest of the bunch, he crowds the yearling to the edge of the herd. Suddenly the steer senses all is not well. It tries to dodge, but with a swift leap the horse blocks it off. The steer whirls. Spinning on a dime, the horse heads it again. The rider jerks off his hat, slaps it in the brute's face. Back and forth they lunge. Men working between the main bunch and the "cut" (the segregated animals) dash up and take over.

A pirouetting horse bumps a toe and tumbles head over heels. There is a sharp stir as everyone turns toward the fallen rider. But almost instantly he is on his feet again. For a moment he stands doubled over, hands pressed against his breastbone as he gasps back the wind that has been knocked out of him. Someone hands him his hat; someone else leads back his trembling horse. On he goes.

Riders who have been holding the restless bunch trade off and take their turn at cutting. Dust grits between your teeth; the heat is a tight band across your head; your throat grows so parched you can't even spit. Anger flames into explosive oaths as a renegade steer, lean as a snake and just as quick, outdodges you again and again. The whole bunch breaks away, rolls down into the creek, and has to be driven back.

In the midst of this confusion Al Scorup sits like a rock on an old white horse. The waves surging about him seem scarcely to touch him. More than half a century in the desert has given him an iron grip on his temper. But now and then when a man muffs what seems to Al an obvious maneuver his big frame swells with impatience. His outbursts have their storm signals. Although he normally adheres more closely to the Mormon bans on strong drink and tobacco than do his young riders, he carries a plug of "chewing" in his jeans. When his control grows thin he cuts off a sliver. The cowboys, seeing his hand start toward his hip pocket, know it is time, as they say, to "git motorin'."

Wild though the cutting seemed, it nonetheless went on more smoothly than our similar operations in Colorado. Al Scorup will not stand for unnecessary zest. Beef is gold, and every pound counts. Over in Colorado the younger riders, full of the slam-bang impetuosity of their age, were apt to forget this and go after a fractious steer with a delighted whoop. But not on Al's range. His spoken wrath, like everything he says, sounds soft, but that doesn't mislead his men. They know he has been through the mill and that it has given him an uncanny way of sensing how the stock is handled even in his absence. As a result there are few of those wonderful rollicking races that sweat dollars right off a cow.

Take the matter of dogs. A smart hound slipping up behind a contrary critter and sinking teeth into its hock brings the animal to life right now. With steers this is fine. But a nipped cow with a calf, instead of running, will turn and fight the dog to a fare-ye-well. A dozen other hoarse-bawling mothers join her, and they chase the poor pooch all over the flat. Then you have to chase them to get them back again. It is fun; it wakes up the herd, but the confusion costs its pound of flesh. Al, whose cattle are mostly cows, will not allow a dog on the place. Still, there are times when some sort of boo is necessary. The Utah cowboys put pebbles into gasoline tins and shake them. The clatter spooks the cows without rousing them to fight. "Mormon dogs," we called the contrivances.

The Mormons have their own way of branding calves too. In Colorado we would jam all the mothers and children we could find into a corral or hold them on some handy flat. Then, lariats whistling, captives bawling, and cows milling, we'd rope the calves and drag them to the fire. Al's cowboys went at it more quietly. They have small corrals spotted all over the range, set with one or more sides against a cliff to save logs. Only a few calves, gathered while still little, are put into this at a time, with just enough cows added to keep them calm. The riders dismount. Working afoot, they slip up behind a youngster and seize it by the hind leg. Before it has time to blat more than once or choke itself dizzy fighting a lariat, it is thrown and burned. This is not a very dramatic execution of what can be a hurly-burly business indeed, but it does save wear and tear. Nor, incidentally, does it mean that the Utah cowmen are inept with their ropes. The way they tie into a renegade steer is enough to stand an ordinary calf catcher's hair right on end. But more of that in another chapter.

And so the cutting at Indian Creek went on, as calmly as any conflict with half-wild creatures can go. At last the herds were worked. The segregated bunches were headed toward their proper destinations. The camp in the orchard melted away, and only a raw brown circle trampled out of the sagebrush was left to show what had happened. Our part of the yearlings crept out into Dry Valley. Al's cowboys would drive them as far as Looking Glass Rock. There we would take over. It would be nearly July before we reached the mountains, which was timing it about right, because until then the Forest Service kept us off the high bunch-grass pastures we wanted to use.

Pair by pair the Scorup riders disappeared into the desert. It was impossible not to want to go with them and see the things they had told us about: the shadowed gorges into which no man has ever set foot, the flat-topped mesas rimmed by such over-whelming precipices that only birds and aviators have looked on their summits.

Most intriguing place of all is Dark Canyon, a cool fairyland in a blistered waste. Here stockraising is carried on absolutely backward to anything we had heard of before. Generally you take cattle up into the high country during summer. But at Dark Canyon they are driven down. The lower you descend, the more alpine the scenery becomes. A crystal stream threads the gorge; grassy meadows dotted with fir trees appear in concavities formed by the massive walls. Little black-and-white woodpeckers, gray flycatchers, doves, and bluebirds call between the cliffs. Flowers grow in profusion: asters, candytuft, and ox-eye daisies; gaudy red paintbrush, blue lupine, and tall pentstemon such as we knew high on the shoulders of the Lone Cone. There are musk roses, too, primroses and sego lily, the delicate three-petaled state flower of Utah. Besides beauty, the sego lily has honor: its edible root kept many an early Mormon from starvation. Also part and parcel of Utah's history is Brigham tea, a scrubby, wirelike green bush from which Brigham Young learned to brew a "healthful" substitute for real tea. Sheer above this garden wilderness tower walls of tan, pink, and white sandstone. But even in Dark Canyon it is not summer forever. Winters are cold and snow lies deep. In the fall the cattle have to be driven *up* to the mountains, to winter range on the heat-seared, piñon-shrouded mesas surround-ing the gorge.

The day came when Al Scorup put my wife and me in charge of a lean, sun-charred young rider named Cy Thornell. Cy loaded us on a couple of tough, unhandsome ponies, packed bedrolls,

food, and water on two mules, and undertook to show us his
particular scenic pet, a Godforsaken region called the Needles
and known only to a handful of cowboys. We climbed out of
Indian Creek on a dismal trail, winding between two fingerlike
buttes named the Six-Shooter Peaks. The color red permeates
everything: cliffs, plains, hills, and canyons. Even the cedar trees
are powdered with red dust, kicked up by tireless whirlwinds.
We had to hang onto our hats. The breezes here blow hard
enough to carve rock, and they do your skin no good at all.

As we neared the eastern brink of the Colorado River Canyon
the land grew rougher, wilder. Here is the beginning of that
incredible epic of erosion which reaches its climax in Grand
Canyon, Arizona. Yawning gorges split the earth. Water draining through these tortuous cracks often hews itself a brand-new
channel. This leaves the old canyon isolated, a looping, senseless
gouge in the landscape. Other canyons, junction-bound, swing
close together with only a thin ridge a thousand feet high between
them. We had to screw our nerve an extra notch, we found, to
ride along one of these narrow necks. An eighty-degree slope beneath one stirrup we were used to, but having it beneath both
stirrups was something else again. Our confidence in our horses of
necessity grew to blind faith. Then the canyons, not ready to join
for another mile or two, swing apart, and the dividing ridge
broadens pearlike into a mesa thousands of acres in size, an island
hung in a gulf.

It is an unforgettable experience to watch dawn from one of
these canyon rims. The eastern mountains stand in hard, sharp
lines against the sunrise. A golden glow models buttes and trees
in high light and shadow. The world is awake—except the
canyon, its bottom still lost in fathomless black. Slowly the sun
climbs higher. Deep down the purple shadows stir and swirl.
Light breaks through the blackness, tinting the walls. As if your
very eyes were sculpturing them, the great ribs and pinnacles and
buttresses take their form.

On our way through Salt Canyon we passed ruined cliff dwellings set high on dizzy ledges. Southeastern Utah is full of these ancient communities, many of them unexplored, some undoubtedly yet to be discovered. "Moqui houses," the cowboys call them.

They reminded Cy of a story—true this time. Not long ago, he said, a rider jogging along here came across two men "staggering around like blind dogs in a meat house." The cowboy called to them. They threw up their heads like wild animals and charged him. Instantly he realized they were out of their minds with thirst and might even kill him for the water he carried in a canvas sack slung to his saddle horn. He drew his revolver and by firing over their heads made them halt. Handing them the water sack, he forced them at gun's point to drink in slow sips. When their madness was somewhat wet down he tried questioning them, but they seemed suffering both from amnesia and delusions. They even refused to accompany him to his camp. The best he could do was point out a trail which would lead them to safety.

A month or so passed. The cowboy chanced on a Salt Lake paper which carried a story by two eminent archaeologists who had been exploring pueblo ruins in Salt Canyon. They told in detail about an armed maniac who had opened fire on them. But by persuasive argument, their account said, they kept this strange desert madman from murdering them. Crooning soft words, they even persuaded him to give them water. Then they escaped from him and made their way to civilization!

I began to think we were as lost as the archaeologists had been. We pushed through maze after maze of bristling rock which the wind had carved into whorls, turrets, windows, and arches of complex design. Wide, flat-bottomed valleys bordered by abrupt walls ran every which way. They crossed each other, paralleled each other, started and stopped with no apparent excuse. You enter the head of one—or the foot; the distinction is meaningless, for they are apt to slope either way at any given point—you

follow it several miles, and suddenly it ends in a blank cliff. They
have no external outlet. What little storm water collects in them
disappears through gaping sinkholes in the ground.

One of them was named Cyclone and lived up to its designa-
tion. A howling gale roared into our teeth. Finally Martha asked
Cy if it would ever stop.

He shook his head. "The wind gets in here," he said, "and then
rushes round and round trying to find a way out. It never does."

Martha sighed, took a cold-cream tube from her pocket, and
smeared her face with grease. The blowing red sand collected in
it until she looked like a Greek tragedienne frozen in a mask of
brick.

"You might as well give up," I told her. "Utah has you
branded forever."

Cy was more chivalrous. "Anyhow," he comforted, "you're in
country no other white woman has ever seen."

We climbed out of Cyclone Canyon over a trail that was little
more than an eyebrow on the face of the cliff. Now, indeed, we
were in a bewildering maze of rock, named like so many Western
locales for the devil—the Devil's Lane, the Devil's Kitchen, the
Devil's Horse Pasture, and so on. But in this case the term has
justification. The first man who penetrated the region stayed
there alone one winter with a tiny bunch of cattle. When he came
out he was desert-drunk, mumbling and grumbling to himself,
swearing up and down that he had seen and conversed with
Old Nick in person.

You can see most anything there in the heart of the Needles.
Sharp monoliths leap hundreds of feet into the hard blue sky.
Serrated ridges of flaming rock twist in all directions. We picked
out figures resembling elephants, sphinxes, battleships, men, shoes,
organs and choirs, gargoyles, and what not, all on so gigantic a
scale that size lost significance. Against the towering cliffs the
piñon trees looked like dwarfed shrubs.

We camped that night under an overhanging slab of rock in

Lost Canyon, at one of the only two water holes we had seen in forty miles of riding. The spot is a favorite cowboy hostelry, equipped with the familiar cache of grain and grub. Decorated, too. Using charcoal as a medium, many a lonely guest has expressed himself by writing or drawing on the smooth stone. Most of the art was of either an equine or amorous nature, some of which, when he caught my wife looking at it, embarrassed Cy horribly. The writings were mainly names and dates, followed by succinct remarks on the weather, pinto beans, gnats, and life in general.

The wind died, but the air stayed full of sand. Into this golden mist the sun sank, a blood-red ball. Out of the creeping purple shadows the buttes soared like jets of flame. Until dark hid the scene and coyotes began mourning at the stars we were content simply to look. Then, as we sat around a fire of cedar sticks, questions began to rise.

How could this desolate land be profitable for ranching? At least 75 per cent of it is solid rock. Vast reaches can be utilized only in winter, when enough snow falls to provide water. It takes a hundred acres to feed one cow, and she has to be tough. A man needs to be tough to follow her too. Those superb cattlemen, the Texas trail drivers, weren't able to do it. A co-operative livestock venture by Mormons from Bluff City was wrecked in those red sands. Yet John Albert Scorup hadn't been. He had come here alone when he was a nineteen-year-old boy, lost and starving and scared. Now he and his riders follow his cows over a million and a quarter acres of staggering desolation between the San Juan and Colorado rivers, a vast triangle of land that even today is not completely mapped.

How in God's name had he managed?

I asked Cy. He shrugged, saying, "He decided he wanted a ranch here. And you know how he is—never sense enough to know when he's licked."

That remark has, of course, been worn threadbare on persever-

ing people. But it fits Al Scorup like a shoe. Some of his stubborn-
ness seems plain silly. Yet he has won through when other
bullheaded folk—indeed a whole bullheaded colony—sank down
into failure. It is a grim, relentless sort of story about a man who
is essentially as gentle as a baby, and it deserves a chapter of its
own.

XI MORMON COWBOY

TO KNOW AL SCORUP YOU MUST
first know the sort of thing the early Mormons did, particularly
that group which in 1879 undertook the most amazing and most
fruitless effort in pioneering history.

In 1879 Brigham Young, Lion of the Lord, was two years dead.
Singlehanded, he had carried out one of the greatest colonizing
exploits of all time. His settlers had strung sturdy hamlets
throughout the valleys of Utah, had spilled over into Arizona,
Idaho, Nevada, California, even into Mexico. Fresh recruits were
coming from across the seven seas. But with all their zeal they had
left untouched one blank spot larger than Massachusetts. This
was southeastern Utah, cut off from the rest of the state by the
deep diagonal of the Colorado River Canyon.

This isolation could not last. The Denver & Rio Grande Railway was pushing into southwestern Colorado. The fabulous
fiddle-footed trail drivers of Texas were crowding their bonanza
herds of beef into every open section of the West. Already two
"Gentile" (non-Mormon) families had moved as far as the
Colorado-Utah border, and more would inevitably follow. Better
that the followers be Mormons.

Accordingly, John Taylor, Brigham.'s successor, sent a scouting
party to see what the new land was like. They swung far south

through Navajo country and came to the east-west San Juan River from underneath. The muddy, sullen stream, when they finally reached it after weeks of danger, looked so good to them that they returned overoptimistic and reported that the valley was feasible for settlement. But, they warned, the circuitous route through the Navajo Nation was too long, too difficult, and too subject to Indian attacks for an emigrant train. If possible the settlers should go straight across country from "Dixie," as the populous regions of southwestern Utah were known.

No man had ever traveled those deserts or had the foggiest notion of what might be encountered. Nonetheless, a "call" for colonists was issued, and, like all Mormon calls, it amounted to a compulsory draft. No matter how fine a farm or successful a business the selectee had created at home, when the finger was put upon him he went. He sold his possessions for what he could get, bundled his family and a few bare essentials into a wagon, and moved on to what he knew not. Incomprehensible? Perhaps. But the followers of the Church of Jesus Christ of Latter-day Saints had—and have—faith. The kind of faith that cannot be laughed off or reasoned aside. Strip it of the unfriendly epithets that have been given it—bigotry, bullheadedness, intolerance, and harshness—and you still have an essence as hard and sure as the rocks they turned into gardens. It defies explanation, but certainly it commands respect.

And so in the fall of 1879 eighty-odd families were called to settle the San Juan. Several thousand dollars were appropriated by the Territorial Legislature and by the Church to buy materials wherewith the colonists could build a road as they went, thus paving the way for future emigrants. The train was ordered to assemble on the desert at the tiny hamlet of Escalante and a man named Charles Hall sent out to locate a route.

He was a strange surveyor. He simply journeyed east to the Colorado Gorge, looked down two thousand feet to the river, noticed that the walls weren't quite perpendicular, and returned to report that the road was a cinch.

His astonished companions disagreed violently. More parties were sent out. One group, tying blankets together into ropes, descended the cliffs, forded the river, and ascended the opposite wall. There they found themselves in a maze of canyons, cliffs, and tortured slick rock. It took them ten days to go six miles. They came back pessimistic.

By this time, December, more than two hundred persons with their wagons, horses, and cattle had assembled at Escalante. Now remember that this wasn't a trip of their own choosing. Not a one of them but had left a comfortable home, friends, relatives, dreams, and ambitions behind. All our other storied pioneers have gone forth of free will, with high and selfish hopes. The Astorians meant to capture a fur empire; the Oregon trailers had the promise of rich and fertile fields; the forty-niners roaring into California and the fifty-niners into Colorado thought each to himself of his golden nuggets. But these Mormons could look forward only to toil and hardship.

There they sat. A heavy fall of snow in the mountains behind made retreat difficult but not impossible. Although they had been given blasting powder, picks, and crowbars to build a road, their scouts said the road could not be built. What to do?

Messengers were sent for advice to Church headquarters. The order was flat and final. "Go ahead at all costs!"

Faith. Believe what you must believe. A scout named George Hobbes presented a minority report that a way could be made. That was enough. The Saints pushed ahead to the brink of the growling canyon.

They could see water, but they could not reach it. There was no grass, no wood. The party had to split into two groups and herd their starving livestock far and wide across the desert, hunting out potholes of brackish liquid. Children and women were set to grubbing sagebrush and shad scale for the cook fires, lashing it into rope-tied bundles and staggering to camp with it on their backs. On December 17 forty-seven men started hewing a path down the naked stone.

They found a cleft a hundred feet deep in the ragged cliff top. It led them out on the face of the rock through a tiny notch between the sheer walls and a pinnacle left standing by erosion. Maybe the notch would serve as a gateway. Anyhow, they had to try. They blasted the opening wide enough for wagons and from it took the name of their crossing—Hole-in-the-Rock.

Below the Hole the workers had to descend on ropes. The ropes wore out and they built a narrow trail down which they could crawl on hands and knees. By using all their powder they were able to blast a long diagonal across the upper cliffs.

Their powder gone, the men resorted to "dugways." In the Southwest today a dugway means any road scraped in a hillside, but when the early Mormons first hit on the expedient it was considerably less—a mere rut dug deeply in the slope. The inside wheels of the wagons fitted into this slot so snugly that the vehicle could not fall out—maybe.

Patiently working twelve hours a day the Saints chipped a zigzag of ruts into the solid rock. But there was one stretch too steep even for dugways. The workers could stand on it only with the aid of ropes held by their comrades. They drilled a line of perpendicular holes and set oak stakes into them. Driftwood logs were lugged up from the river and laid in a wall along the stakes; the space between the wall and the slope was filled with rocks. Now they had a road not blasted into the cliff but built *out* from it.

A drop of two thousand feet—less than half a mile. It took them six weeks of superhuman toil to negotiate it. And all the while, unknown to them, was another route to the north where scarcely any blasting would have been necessary, a route so fine that when it was discovered a few years later it was promptly called Dandy Crossing.

Did the Saints think their lot was hard? One wonders. They had a fiddler with them, and how those early Mormons loved a fiddle! It could accompany anything, their stately hymns, their rollicking dances. Yes, they danced at Hole-in-the-Rock. Every night. Their roof was the sky and their ballroom floor the smooth, slick rock polished by an eternity of blowing sand. When the moon shone it was their light; when it didn't they built great fires of grubbed sagebrush. They were zealots, indeed, but not so sour as zealots are generally pictured. Romances bloomed. Babies were born there in the desert—three of them before the San Juan was reached. One, a girl, was named Desert.

At last the road was completed. The loose horses were driven down it first. Nine of them slipped and plunged to death on the boulders below. But every one of the eighty-odd wagons, wheels locked and stern checked by long ropes, was lowered in safety. Cottonwood logs were lashed to the vehicles, and they were floated across the stream. The cliffs on the opposite side did not prove so difficult. Only two grueling weeks were needed to work a way up them.

And now the Saints were within seventy-five miles air-line of the San Juan. But they could not go air-line through the torn and twisted country. Their windings took them twice that far, laborious creeps averaging less than three miles a day. And each day there was a causeway to build, a shoot-the-chutes to negotiate, a dugway to chip, a tight-laced forest to hack through with axes. We have heard much about the difficulties of the overland trail from the Missouri to the Pacific, but countless caravans traveled half the continent in less time than it took these Saints to cross the corner of one state. On all the overland trail there was not one obstacle comparable to what they conquered at Grand Gulch, the Slick Rocks, Clay Hills, or Comb Wash, to say nothing of Hole-in-the-Rock.

In the spring of 1880 two hundred and twenty-five exhausted persons—one of them the little girl who was destined to be Al

Scorup's wife—reached the San Juan. First they built a little fort, and then their homes: one-room cabins of crooked cottonwood logs. There were no doors in the doorways, no glass in the windows. The sun seared the flats, lanced off the cliffs. Sandstorms whipped the town, named Bluff City after the banded cliffs of red-and-white sandstone which towered above it.

Each year the colonists built dams and ditches for irrigation, and each year the San Juan swept them out. Finally artesian wells were developed, but by then it was almost too late. Time has made cruel mockery of the town's heroic founding. Of the original farm land so hopefully plowed, the river has left less than a tenth. The population has diminished almost as steadily. Today a hundred-odd people call Bluff home—the "City" has long since been dropped from the name. An occasional automobile kicks up a plume of red dust on the narrow road which leads to the railway a hundred miles north. There are a few bright patches of alfalfa, a few milk cows, a few saddle horses standing droop-headed in the shade. That is all. That is the metropolis of southeastern Utah.

Starting from this place, working with these people, John Albert Scorup carved out his ranch.

He did not come with the original settlers. In 1880 he was eight years old, living near the town of Salina in the Sevier Valley of central Utah. His parents were Danish converts to Mormonism who had come across the plains on foot with a handcart company, wheeling their belongings with them in a little wagon. The elder Scorup landed a job as herdsman for Salina's communally owned band of sheep and set up housekeeping in a dugout with a few wooden dishes and a hand-woven linen bed sheet, wedding gift from a friend. His name wasn't Scorup then; it was Christensen. But Scandinavia had proved fertile ground for Mormon missionaries, and the Sevier Valley was full of Christensens, resulting in all kinds of confusion. Hunting a more distinctive name, Al's father selected Skaerup, after his native village in

Denmark. Later the name was altered to Scorup; how or why, no one recalls today.

It is possible that young Al, third of eight children, knew something about the new colony of Bluff City. The Salt Lake *Deseret News* carried occasional advertisements for farmers to settle there, though the pulling power was practically nil. Al could read and even cipher a little—in spite of his education and not because of it. The schools were poor, and he managed to attend only a month or so at a time. Father Scorup had moved from the dugout into a house and had scraped together a little herd of sheep of his own. It was sink or swim now. The mother helped by marketing butter and cheese and hand-woven rugs; the older boys were frequently called from the classroom to work with the flock.

Al didn't like those sheep. He preferred cattle. When he was seven he invented a game about them, using willow sticks for animals and branding irons made of wire. His partner in this, as in all else, was his older brother Jim. The two of them hung around cowboys from the time they could ride and were doing men's work at local roundups before they were well in their teens.

In 1891, on a horse hunt, Al attracted the attention of Claude Sanford. This fellow Sanford was typical of the small-time livestock speculators floating around the country in those days. They would buy a bunch of cows, stick the herd somewhere, and then try to resell it on a rising market. Now in the eleven years since Bluff City's founding the Texas trail drivers had discovered that great, gray plain of sage along the southern part of the Colorado-Utah boundary and had clogged it with tens of thousands of snaky longhorn cattle. Inevitably some of the animals slopped over into the canyons around Bluff.

Sanford bought 150 of these cows, put them in the piñon breaks south of White Canyon, which drained west from the Elk Ridge of the Blue Mountains. Then he drifted over into central Utah. The cows were without attention for quite a while, and he wanted someone to take care of them. This young Al Scorup looked like a good hand, and Sanford propositioned him: one third of the calves in return for his work.

It was a poor deal. In that rough country cows scattered far and wide for forage, and the bulls didn't get at all of them. The calf crop was bound to be small; one third of it, the way the live-stock market had sagged, wasn't much pay. But Al, only nineteen years old, had a single-track mind and plenty of confidence in himself. He wanted cattle, and this looked like a chance to get some. He agreed.

The decision created a furor at home. The Scorups were a close-knit family, and none of them had ever been a day's ride from the others. Besides, they had the Mormons' good love for the land, the love which Brigham Young so well understood when he urged his followers to reverence the soil not merely as a means of sustenance but as a way of life sufficient unto itself. When you planted a farm you rooted yourself with the crops. The cattle business was nomadic; cowboys roamed foot-loose and fancy-free. And those Texas "Gentiles" were an irreligious, quarrelsome lot. Al's mother cried all night, trying to dissuade him. But when she saw his mind was set she made him a couple of patchwork quilts for a bed. He strapped them on an extra horse, put a five-dollar bill in his pocket, and struck southwest. Nearly three hundred miles he rode along twisting, circuitous trails and at last came to Dandy Crossing over the Colorado River.

The Dandy merits a digression. Although still remote from any automobile road, it is the only practicable ford in the hundreds of canyoned miles between Greenriver, Utah, and Lees Ferry, Arizona. The Indians knew about it, of course. On a high ledge, where White Canyon breaks into the Colorado, there is a spectacular prehistoric cliff dwelling. Paiutes and Navajos used the ancient trail. A few early white explorers, following the river in boats, floated by the crossing but attached no significance to it. The first outsider actually to settle there was a murderer named

Cass Hite, and he was shown the way by that villainous Navajo chief, Hoskannini.

The story starts, in a way, with Kit Carson during the days when that old scout rounded up almost the entire Navajo tribe and kicked them into a "bull pen" in eastern New Mexico—a sort of Western version of a concentration camp. But there was one subtribe which never submitted. Its members lived on what is now the Utah-Arizona border, in a valley they called Tse-bi-gay, or "inside the rocks." It is a land of titanic sculptures. Sheer, smooth buttes of red sandstone rear more than a thousand feet above the pink sand of the desert floor. Today it is known as Monument Valley.

Legends began to trickle out of Tse-bi-gay of a fabulous silver mine, Pish-la-ki, reputed source of the soft white metal from which the Navajos fashioned their jewelry. Did the mine ever exist? Probably not, at least not as the vein of pure silver described in whispered tales. Certainly the Navajos have not used its output for scores of years. Their exquisite silverwork is hammered from Mexican dollars, which lack the alloy that makes our own coins so hard. But where did the metal come from in antiquity? Did the Indians get it by trade from Mexico? Was there a Pish-la-ki, rich as fables? Or did they refine silver on a small scale from surface workings such as the Spaniards developed in New Mexico and Colorado before there was a United States? These questions cannot be answered with certainty, and that grain of uncertainty, however small, was enough to send many a prospector to his death.

Partly it was the land which killed them. Monument Valley is surrounded by hundreds of miles of desert. Parching winds blow endlessly; the sun is a molten ball in a copper sky. Water holes were far apart and jealously guarded by sullen savages. The Navajos of Tse-bi-gay—the "Irreconcilables," some poetic officer at Fort Defiance called them—had not forgotten what Kit Carson had done to the rest of the tribe. Furthermore, if they had a silver mine they emphatically did not want these intruders to find it. Few prospectors ever came back from their search.

If the miners did not profit, some of the Navajos did. A small party of prospectors headed for an unknown destination can easily suffer "accidents" and their equipment be appropriated by the "finders." This gave the chief of the tribe, Hoskannini (or Osh-ka-ni-nie—the phonetic spelling of his name varies), an idea. He obtained from somewhere, perhaps Pish-la-ki, several pieces of high-grade silver ore—"money rock," he called it. He or his bucks showed the samples where they would do the most good. For a price paid in advance the Indians agreed to show the excited listeners to the mine. A meeting place on the desert was arranged and the unsuspecting victims instructed to come fully equipped for a long journey—for of course horses and pack outfits were worth more to Navajos than coin.

The men never returned from the trips.

All told, twenty or more persons vanished thus into the desert. The authorities at Fort Defiance were frantic. Hoskannini's wily hand was suspected, but no proof could be established. Then along came a couple of men named Mitchell and Merritt. This was about the time Bluff was being settled. Indeed, the pair tried to get some of the colonists to join them in the search for Pish-la-ki, painting rosy pictures of wealth which failed to sway the steadfast Mormons.

Some accounts say the men actually found the mine; others say no. Anyhow, they seem to have made two trips, a high average, but on the second both were killed. One of the pinnacles in Monument Valley is known as Mitchell Butte in commemoration of the event. And this time there was no doubt as to who was responsible. The authorities came rushing in to arrest Mr. Hoskannini, but the consummate old villain outguessed them again. He escaped over the San Juan River, and somewhere around Dandy Crossing his trail was lost for all time.

Meanwhile (chronology here is vague), one Cass Hite drifted

into Tse-bi-gay. He was a miner from Telluride, Colorado, where he'd got into some sort of trouble that recommended speedy departure. Monument Valley seemed a good place to lie low, and he might even utilize his time trying to find Pish-la-ki. He had a way with Indians. He even lived in Hoskannini's hogan for more than a year, but he failed to locate the mine. However, Hoskannini did one thing for him. He took Cass Hite down White Canyon and showed him Dandy Crossing. Whether this occurred during the chief's flight or on an earlier occasion is not certain.

Cass liked the lonely place. He panned the gravel bars along the river and found a dab of flour-fine gold which, during the ages, had washed down from the Colorado Mountains. He decided to settle. When the Bluff City Mormons discovered the ford and began using it on their travels between old homes and new he built a rock store to catch their trade. Placer miners who were prospecting the river made the spot their headquarters. Cass established a post office named after himself; mail and supplies were hauled in from the west once a week. Two of the miners undertook to operate a rowboat on call from one shore to the other.

During the course of the years Cass collected quite a poke of dust, both by trade and by mining of his own. He showed it around now and then, and suddenly the rumor spread that he had a secret mine. He was followed, threatened, bribed, and cajoled to reveal its location. Of course the mine didn't exist, but when he said so it was believed that he was being sly. To keep from being pestered to death, he finally touched off one of the weirdest gold rushes in American history.

He said that the gold came from riffles farther down the canyon. The tale spread like wildfire. Hundreds of miners rushed into the grim gorge, tore its gravel bars to pieces. Eventually even staid Eastern capital fell prey to the excitement and organized the Hoskannini Mining Company. Sixty bright-painted wagons drove back and forth with its mountains of freight. The group spent $100,000 getting ready to operate and another $100,000 building

a huge dredge. After endless difficulties the monster was transported to the river and set to scooping up gravel. It soon failed.
The gold was there, but it was too fine and too scattered to be
recovered in commercial quantities, as Cass Hite well knew. You
can still see sodden bits of that old dredge and others in the
muddy river, mute monuments to a man who started a stampede
simply because he wanted a little peace.

He got his peace, but in a different way. In 1891, the year
Al Scorup reached the crossing, Hite went up to the town of
Greenriver on a spree. He spreed too hard, killed a man, and was
jailed for life. A couple of years later he was paroled because of
bad health. He returned to Tickaboo, twelve miles below Dandy
Crossing, built a cabin, and embarked upon a hermit's career.
One day in 1912 a pair of cowboys passed by and found him dead
in bed.

Al Scorup was interested in neither gold nor murders. He swam
his two horses across the roaring chocolate-colored river, climbed
out the south side of White Canyon, and began rounding up the
Sanford cattle, now almost as wild as deer. He soon ran through
his supply of pinto beans and salt pork. He owned no gun with
which to kill game, and his five dollars didn't go far at Hite's
store. In desperation he sold a big three-year-old steer to some
placer miners for twenty dollars. It took eleven dollars of the pro-
ceeds to buy a forty-eight-pound sack of flour.

Scared, homesick, and on the verge of starvation, the nineteen
year-old boy saw he'd have to hunt an out. He shoved the cattle
into a canyon and rode to Bluff, where he landed a job with the
Texans. "The Mormon cowboy," they called him—none of his
coreligionists in southeastern Utah had yet embraced the profession—and tales of his uncanny prowess spread from camp to
camp. He helped trail beef into Colorado and earned seventy-five
dollars, enough to supply his White Canyon camp.

On the Fourth of July he returned to Bluff. Holiday festivities beckoned; while he was in Fletch Hammond's store the town's thirteen unmarried women formed a giggling committee of the whole to look him over. There was no glamour about his trade to account for the interest. The Bluff girls were used to cowboys —Texas cowboys. But this rider was a Mormon, tall and big-boned and handsome. He had been well brought up too. He would not spit tobacco juice on the whitewashed walls of the combination dancehall and church as the Texans were wont to do. The ladies begged him to stay for their party.

Al refused. "I've got to see to my cows," he told Emma Bayles, daughter of the hotelkeeper. "But," he added, looking at her again, "I'll be back."

A long time passed before he kept that promise. He jogged off for White Canyon, feeling pretty good. He had a few dollars in his pocket, grub on his pack horse. Water and grass were unusually plentiful that summer, and the calf crop ought to be sizable. Lost in his rosy thoughts, he was wholly unprepared for the half-dozen armed Texans who surrounded him when he rode into his camp.

"We've scattered your cattle, bub," they told him over a gun sight, "an' we're takin' the graze. You'd better drift."

The boy didn't say a word. Even had he been armed, he could not oppose all those men by force alone. But there were other possibilities. He turned his horse northwest toward his home at Salina and by crowding himself hard made the three-hundred-mile ride in five days. There he asked his twenty-one-year-old brother Jim to come back and help him.

Jim was a hard-twisted youngster with a more volatile nature than Al's—freer to fight, freer to laugh, and lacking Al's pighead-edness when it came to butting his skull against a stone wall. Jim was willing to go to White Canyon, but not just for the hell of it.

"One man'll live thin enough on a third of that herd's increase," he demurred. "Two men won't get anywhere at all."

He was right, of course. Al scratched his head. There was only one answer—get more cattle. But how? Neither brother had a spare dime.

Finally Al hit on an idea. He shopped around among local ranchers, telling of the range which spread out from White Canyon, of lush summer pasture on the Elk Ridge of the Blue Mountains, of protecting breaks in the winter country where sun-cured grama, buffalo grass, and shad scale would preserve marketable weight gained in the uplands. He did not mention Texans. He had developed his notions about what was waiting for them. They tried to run their poor-quality longhorns as cattle were run on the flat plains of Texas—kicking the animals onto the range and letting them rustle for themselves. Al didn't think the system would work in the rock jungles of Utah. Pretty soon, he figured, the Texans would fail and the range be free again. So he kept mum; there was no use alarming Salina ranchers with tales of competitors.

His salesmanship is almost incredible. He proposed to take local animals across hundreds of miles of desert to unexplored land. Yet in the end he persuaded the ranchers to give him three hundred cows, to be run on a one-third percentage basis.

The animals obtained, Jim agreed to go. The boys were in the saddle nineteen hours a day and considered themselves lucky if they moved the motley herd twelve miles a crack. It took them most of a rainy December to reach Dandy Crossing, and there they found the sleet-chilled Colorado in flood.

They couldn't hold the hungry cattle on the barren hillsides until the water receded. And they wouldn't turn around. Straight into the chocolate-colored torrent they forced the herd. Now, cattle can switch directions in deep, running water more easily than a horse can. A swimming pony, lacking the big, round body which lends a cow buoyancy, is apt to tip over if turned too quickly. When the Scorups' cattle got out into the river they grew terrified and broke back. The boys—neither of them could swim a stroke—weren't able to stop them. All they could do was splash their horses out of the freezing river and try once more.

Again the herd broke back. It looked hopeless until Al thought of the Hite rowboat. He hired it and three or four leather-lunged miners. For the third time the cattle were whipped into the flood, but now the boat floated along on the downstream side of the leaders. When the animals tried to turn around the miners beat them with oars and hats, waved Mackinaws, and screeched themselves hoarse. The cattle straightened out. But the icy current was numbing the calves; some of them quit struggling and drifted downstream. The men in the boat rescued several; Jim and Al went after others. They spurred tired ponies again and again into the river, lassoed a calf as it bobbed by, hauled it ashore. Down the bank they'd race to get ahead of another, plunge in, and snag it too. Even then a lot of the little creatures were so chilled that unless they were warmed in a hurry they would die. The boys again put ropes on them and at a gallop dragged them flat on their sides along the sand bars. The friction restored circulation; every calf, except a few missed in the river, was saved.

Al had no desire to run head-on into the Texans south of White Canyon, so the brothers turned north. It was unknown land, so rough the Texans had not bothered to look at it. Nor had the placer miners ventured into it, for the convulsed sandstone formations bore no gold. No man could say what lay ahead, but the Scorups pushed on regardless, their landmark a mountain which resembled the wooden shoes their parents had worn in Salina. They called the mountain the Wooden Shoe and stopped their tired herd in its shadow, the first white men to penetrate that jumbled wilderness.

By night they slipped south across White Canyon and stole the Sanford cattle back from the Texans. They made their home in a sandstone cave and filled out a slim larder of sourdough, beans, and dried fruit with venison. By riding as long as daylight would let them see and often longer, they kept their trail-gaunt cattle alive, drifting them from one grassy pocket to the next.

For five years they lived that way. When they needed money for supplies they went to Bluff and got temporary jobs with the Texans, but most of the time it was just sand and wind, and wind and loneliness. Instead of increasing, the herd grew smaller. The owners, when the boys reported once a year, raised the devil, but somehow Al held them in line. Jim, who loved company and laughter and good times, grew despondent and wanted to quit. Al, heavy-handed and implacable, would not let him. Once when Jim sneaked off and went home anyhow, Al rode after him and forced him back.

But Al was right about one thing. The Texans couldn't cut the mustard. They gave up and moved out of the country with what part of their herds they could gather. Bluff City businessmen, thinking to prosper where the Texans had failed, formed a pool to buy the remnants of the Southern cattle. They meant to rule the roost too. They crossed White Canyon with sixteen hundred head of stock, knowing perfectly well there wasn't feed enough to go around. The Scorup kids were competitors and would have to leave.

Their cattle outnumbered more than three to one, the brothers, in all logic, should have hunted a hole. But they didn't. They slipped their animals by twos and threes into hidden pockets. By riding twice as long and twice as hard as the Bluff cowboys they always managed to reach grass first and turn the Pool stock off into the rocks. When spring came more than half the invading cattle had starved to death; from then on the ranchers stayed on their own side of White Canyon.

Not long afterward the Bluff Pool acknowledged Al's superiority to their own crew by hiring him as their foreman! His pay was $37.50 a month, and on the strength of it Emma Bayles and he were married. Their first home was a single-room, dirt-roofed rock house in Bluff City, rented for thirty cents a week. But even thirty cents loomed large. The brothers had turned the leased cattle back to the Salina ranchers and were trying to start out on their own. While Al worked for a grubstake Jim stayed with the little herd on the Wooden Shoe.

When he could get time off Al came over to help brand calves and gather strays. It was on one of these forays that the brothers discovered the three huge stone bridges near the upper end of White Canyon. Jim led in the first outsider to see them, a mining engineer named Long. He refused Long's offer of a fee for the trip, asking only that the western bridge be called Caroline, the English form of his mother's Danish name, Karen. Long named the largest bridge after his wife, Augusta. The third they called simply Little Bridge, an error in judgment, since its 194-foot span is wider than Caroline's. Rainbow Bridge had not yet been discovered, and these soaring arches were the wonders of the day. In 1906 Al guided in the expedition whose survey led to the section's being set aside as Natural Bridges National Monument. Later the government manufactured Indian titles for those given by the discoverers. Al has never gotten over his peeve about this; after all, one of the original names had been his mother's.

Finally a break came. West of Bluff is a sixty-mile maze of dry cedar forest. In places the gnarled boughs of these trees are interlocked so tightly that a rider cannot penetrate them. But here and there the jungle is laced by deep canyons containing water and by little parks where sparse grass and a weed called "cow alfalfa" grows. Cattle belonging to the old Texas outfits escaped into this wilderness, went wild, and multiplied. So, too, did Bluff stock. These huge longhorns, as large as elk and twice as mean, belonged technically to the Pool—if they could be caught.

Al thought he could do it. The Bluff ranchers didn't, but he talked them into paying him five dollars for each one he brought out. Into the cedars he went with three reckless young punchers. All winter long they roped and dragged out at rope's end every fighting, blood-crazy longhorn they could reach. The take was two thousand head—ten thousand dollars, less the wages paid Al's riders!

The brothers could expand now. They shopped around for bargains. The Bluff Pool collapsed, and they bought it out. By 1910 their cattle, numbering thousands now, ranged from Elk Ridge to the junction of the San Juan and Colorado rivers. Every spring mountain ranchers from Colorado rode down to dicker. Buyers and sellers would squat on their boot heels in front of the livery stable, yarning and pitching silver dollars at cracks in the board sidewalk. When they got tired of that they would go to the edge of town and race horses. After a while, with a nod of a head, they would complete a deal involving thousands of cattle and tens of thousands of dollars. It never occurred to any of them to put the terms on paper.

Still the Scorups lived with their cattle, sleeping in caves and subsisting on wild game and food cached in the sand. It was the only way they could keep summer drought and winter blizzards from beating them, just as those bugaboos of the desert had beaten the Texans and the Bluff Pool. They brought the first Hereford bulls into southeastern Utah. To get what they wanted they had to ride each year to the Sevier Valley and spend a month trailing the ponderous brutes to Dandy Crossing. The bulls didn't like swimming any better than had that first herd of cows, so the boys developed a "persuader." A bull was tied to the stern of a rowboat; one Scorup at the oars pulled its neck out like an accordion; the other got behind the reluctant animal on horseback and laid on with a willow switch. Now and then a bull, aggravated beyond endurance, would take to fighting in the middle of the river. They were grand melees—horse, bull, and boat going around and around—but by some miracle the men weren't drowned, and they never lost an animal.

It was on one of these bull-buying trips to the Sevier Valley that Jim met Elmina Humphreys, a Salina schoolteacher. With true Scorup tenacity he set about winning her. It was no whirlwind courtship. Calling on Elmina involved a horseback ride of six hundred miles. They were engaged seven years before they were married. Al wanted them to establish their home in Bluff, but Jim refused.

"Life is too hard for a woman over there," he said. "Elmina is going to stay in Salina with her folks."

Life was indeed hard in Bluff City. Since the men were generally away on the range, the women had to do all the chores—raise garden, milk cows, chop wood, and trade with the Indians. Each spring floods sent the townspeople scurrying to the hills and then left them mud-fouled houses, buried fields, and wrecked ditches to return to. By 1913 automobiles were common sights everywhere else in the country, but when the first Ford steamed into Bluff in 1913 it scared the Indians around the trading post so badly that they dived headfirst into the San Juan and swam in a panic for the opposite shore.

Al knew all this and did his best to soften things for his family —it had grown now until it included six children, all girls. He was ruthless with himself and with Jim, but the enormous sentimentality corked under his crusty exterior made him putty in the hands of his womenfolk. He bought them that first Ford, though there wasn't a road they could drive it on. He built them the finest house that could be built in a place like Bluff, and because local drinking water was bad he drilled a fourteen-hundred-foot artesian well in the back yard.

He didn't see his family very often. Occasionally he would ride clear in from the Wooden Shoe for a single evening at home. He'd have to be back at work when dawn broke. At midnight, with tears streaming down his weather-hardened cheeks, he'd tiptoe into the girls' rooms, kiss each one, then saddle up and lope away into the darkness. When he would be back he never knew. Perhaps he would be packed back, tied across his saddle. Dead men were brought into Bluff that way with grim frequency. It had almost happened to Al the winter a wild steer, near the junction of the rivers, tore off his kneecap and shattered his leg. He roped himself to the saddle horn to keep from falling off his horse when he fainted with pain, as he did every hour or so, and rode three days to reach town.

But the worst of living in Bluff were the Indians. The San Juan was the boundary line between Utes and Navajos, and members of both tribes swarmed through the settlement wearing nothing but a breechclout and a stare. The Mormons kept on fair terms with them, but nearly half a hundred " 'Mericats" (non-Mormons, in Indian dialect) were killed in the early days, including seventeen cowboys at one swoop in an ambush in the mountains to the north. In time the Navajos grew more tractable, and the Utes were sent to a reservation. But one subtribe of Paiutes refused to go.

Among these Paiutes was a small group of incorrigibles led by a young hellion named So-wa-gerie but called Posey by the whites. Posey's main occupation was horse stealing. Now and then he also had to steal his wife back from his brothers-in-law, for they didn't approve of their sister being married to such a scoundrel and regularly spirited her away. For diversion Posey would go into town at night and make faces through the lamplit windows, just to see the women and children jump. No reprisals were ever made. He brazenly told the Mormons that if he was bothered his followers would massacre the settlement. It was no idle boast. Help was sixty miles away over almost impassable roads, and a handful of Indians, picking a time when the men were absent, could wreak havoc. Bluff City lived on tenterhooks from one alarm to the next.

Things finally came to a head. One of Posey's friends, a buck named Tse-ne-gat, killed and robbed a Mexican sheepherder. A United States marshal rode into Bluff with a posse, and the battle was on, right at the gates of the town. Five or six Indians were shot up and two cowboys badly wounded. Posey cut the telegraph line, blocking any message for help, and settled down to a siege. For several days skirmishes raged, but both sides had a high respect for their individual skins, and a lot more ammunition than blood was spilled. It was a typical frontier uproar—except that it took place in 1915, when the frontier was theoretically dead as a dodo.

The settlers at last managed to repair the telegraph. Following pioneer tradition to the last inch, in came General H. L. Scott and a piece of the Army, bugles blowing. The leaders of the Paiutes were captured, and there the frontier aspects of the situation end. Al Scorup, who had been in the thick of things from the start, wanted to hang the Indians to the highest tree in town, but this was too abrupt for modern law. Posey, Tse-ne-gat, and a few other ringleaders were sent to Denver for trial.

By 1915 enlightened civilization, its scalp intact, had come to the conclusion that the red man had gotten a dirty deal from his conquerors—which is certainly true. But it is also true that there are bad Indians just as there are bad white men. Forgetting this, missionaries, newspaper editors, and civic-betterment clubs throughout the West took up cudgels for the captives. Their journey to Denver was a triumphal tour. They were wined, dined, and made honorary policemen. In a burst of sentimentality all of them were freed and sent back to Bluff, where one immediately perished as a result of overindulgence during the trial. Posey, more contemptuous than ever of white man's laws, returned to his old ways. In 1923 he got into another gun fracas with a posse and this time he was pumped full of lead. He crawled into a cave, stuffed his wounds with weeds, and died there, still facing his attackers. Not until then were the Paiutes persuaded to settle on a special reservation of their own. They were given nine thousand acres in Allen's Canyon, of which today they farm about eighty.

Before this, in 1917, Jim and Al Scorup had a chance to buy for ninety thousand dollars a ranch near Salina where Loss Creek breaks into the Sevier Valley—land on which they had once

herded sheep for their father. With it were extensive grazing
rights in the Fish Lake Mountains. Here they could indulge their
passion for purebred Hereford cattle and raise their own bulls
for use in southeastern Utah.

Jim plumped for the deal. Twenty-six years had passed since
Al had persuaded him they could make a stake in the empty bar-
rens. Twenty-six years of pounding back and forth across those
endless miles of rock until he knew and hated every dip in them.
Well, they had a stake now, and if they bought the Loss Creek
property he could go to Salina, live in a house instead of a cave,
and see his wife and four children more often than a week or so
at Christmas time. "Al, Al, let's do it!" And Al did. Tickled as a
kid with a new toy, Jim went home.

He had scarcely arrived when Elmina, his wife, died of pneu-
monia.

Meanwhile, Al heard that a ranch on Indian Creek capable
of running seventy-five hundred head of cattle was for sale. He
looked it over and liked it—and maybe buying it would give Jim
something to fasten his mind to. They talked it over, but Jim was
listless. "If you say so, Al, it's all right. Only—well, I don't want
to live over there any more." As a matter of fact, he didn't want
to live anywhere any more.

Heavyhearted and baffled, Al went back to Indian Creek. He
signed Jim's and his name to notes covering the bulk of the half-
million-dollar purchase price. The balance was taken up by their
fast friends, Andrew and Will Somerville, the latter a gangling,
redheaded man with a booming laugh and a peculiar habit of
wrinkling his nose which earned him, to his disgust, the nickname
Snuffy. For another fat sum they acquired Dark Canyon to the
south. Eventually the Elk Ridge and White Canyon outfits were
included to form the Scorup-Somerville Cattle Company, a
sprawling outfit stretching for more than a hundred and fifty miles
along the fierce east breaks of the Colorado River, an empire half
again as large as the state of Rhode Island.

On November 1, 1919, the ranches were turned over to the new owners. On November 9 three feet of snow fell on the winter range, burying every spear of feed. And all winter it kept snowing. Back in Salina, Jim quit fighting and went to bed. Al dropped everything when a messenger reached him at Indian Creek, and on horseback bucked the clinging drifts for forty-eight hours, trying to reach Moab and an automobile which would carry him to the brother whom always before he had been able to buck up when things were black. But this time he was too late. When he arrived at Salina Jim was dead. The doctor didn't know why. But Al knew. It was heartbreak, though the certificate read "influenza and complications."

There was no time for grief. Back to Indian Creek he went. By April the corpses of fifteen hundred starved, frozen cattle dotted the range. The rest were skin and bones, and the postwar slump was shattering the livestock market. Cattle the Scorup-Somerville Company had bought at sixty-five dollars a head plummeted in value to twenty dollars. In Salina and Bluff, in the distant stockyards at Los Angeles and Kansas City, cattlemen laid bets that the outfit could not pull through, that the Mormon cowboy was licked at last.

Well, he wasn't licked. He sharpened an old pencil stub, sat down under a kerosene lamp at Indian Creek, and in his cramped handwriting figured out a drastic financial reorganization. Every worker on the place, from foremen to hay hands, backed him to the limit. During one entire year Harve Williams drew only ninety cents of the wages due him. Eighty cents he used to buy cigarette papers to stick on his lips as a shield against the chapping winds. He doesn't remember now how he squandered that other dime.

Al didn't buy himself so much as a new pair of pants those years, but he did send his six daughters through Brigham Young University, and he did bring up Jim's four orphaned children. His closest friend, Snuffy Somerville, died; Emma, his wife, was stricken with paralysis and lay helpless for three years until death released her too. Al grew a little grimmer, a little more silent. Though over fifty years old, he spent sixteen hours a day in the saddle. It is monotonous in the telling—more rocks, more caves, more wild cattle, more broken bones. Maybe it was monotonous in the doing too—though things have a sharp edge when they mean survival.

And survive he did. The ranch—the largest in Utah—stands solid today, perhaps the only old-time cow outfit in America still ruled by its original founder. It has changed very little from the day Al Scorup first came there with his two quilts and his five-dollar bill. There are more cattle now, but no more houses. The land is even lonelier than it was. The placer miners along the river are all but gone; Cass Hite's store is a pile of rubble. The Texans are gone; the Bluff City ranchers are gone. But Al is there.

He could rest now, if he would. Rarely will he leave Indian Creek, however, except to visit his daughters, all with families of their own. He has remarried, and his wife tries to take the care of him that he will not take of himself. After all, he is over seventy and could stand a little pampering. But the old life is strong in him. He still gets up at four o'clock in the morning, as he did when his only home was a cave, splashes his yet unwrinkled face with cold water, and goes down to the creek to watch the dawn. This is the hour he likes best. While the great buttes take shape out of the darkness his plans for the day take shape with them. I can see him standing there now, bare-headed, his pale blue eyes looking far across the desert.

"It has been my worst enemy," he said of that beautiful, merciless land. Then his deep voice softened and he added slowly, "And my best friend too."

And yet sometimes I wonder who really won. The desert? Or Al Scorup?

XII SUMMER AGAIN

BETWEEN UTAH AND THE CONE, either at La Sal or in Paradox, we rebranded the footsore Scorup yearlings. It was a noisome, dirty chore, its harsh rigors meagerly softened by a device known as a branding chute.

Early in the morning we started bringing small bunches of the cattle to a corral. A gate opened from the pen into a corridor whose wooden fences funneled together until the chute between them was scarcely wide enough for an animal to wriggle through. At the end of the chute was a V-shaped squeeze with a movable panel of fence. This cunning artifice was activated by a long wooden lever thrusting out from the fence like a jib boom. When a steer entered the squeeze a dismounted cowboy—the fattest of the crew—reached over his head, grasped the lever, and pulled it down with all his strength. The movable panel clamped on the astonished steer, who at once began to bawl and thrash. Its struggles jiggled the fence; this in turn agitated the lever. A strong steer could really give the man at the end of the pole a shaking.

A yearling was helpless, however. While it was pinned tight a man wearing one glove and gripping another like a pot holder thrust a hot branding iron between the fence bars and did his painful work. He "vented" or "fired out" the old brand by burning a diagonal line through it and then stamped two parallel lines like an equal sign on the shoulder. These bars were our trail brand and much quicker to apply than the pitchfork design we used on cattle we raised ourselves. Although simple in the extreme, the bars could not be altered safely by a rustler, because the vented brand served as part of the pattern.

The remonstrances of the burned steer alarm the animals behind it. They try frantically to escape by backing up through the narrow chute. Workers prevent this by thrusting wooden poles behind their legs. Other workers, perched on the top rail of the fence, kick them forward into the squeeze with spurred boots. The chute lever swings down; the branding iron dips; there is a frying sound. The smell of burned hair mingles with the sweetish odor of heated, close-packed cattle. The fence creaks; yearlings bellow; men call back and forth. The dust—always the dust—swirls in endless clouds. You wipe streaks of it onto your face with your dirty hands; you hack it out of your parched throat. Shirts stick to sweaty backs; your skin grows puffed and red from the heat of the fires and the blaze of the sun. A rider jogs up on a bowed-neck horse, dragging wood for fuel with his lariat. The chute gate opens; a fresh-branded steer comes bucking out into the receiving corral. "Bring on another!" And another. One a minute, all day long from sunup to dark. You sleep that night, so dead-beat you fall into your bedroll without even taking off your filthy clothing.

For a day or two we let the hurt cattle rest—we could use the pause too—and feed. Then on to the trail again: the long red ribbon of road through East Paradox, the adobe slopes and cedar forests of the foothills. And at last the Cone, spreading its graceful serenity over the weathered old buildings of the summer camp. Tall yellow pines shaded the ranch; a scattering of brush lay on the flat out front. The draws dipped lazily away, and a small lake sparkled behind the earthen dam we had years ago piled across a brooklet. The womenfolk were by the gate, watching us come.

We rode up, grinning from ear to ear. It was summer. There is no other word for it.

On the surface the camp presented little to account for our enthusiasm. The main house was built of upright pine planking, stained by the years until it was as brown as a tree trunk. It supported a lean-to, where the cook slept, and contained three large, airy rooms: the warm kitchen, with its wood box and fat black range whose fancy scrollwork winked back at the pots and pans hanging from nails driven into the walls; the dining room, with its long table and an oil painting of a dead magpie lying on its back —very still life by the wife of one of my stepfather's cronies—and the master bedroom, its closets consisting of projecting cubicles fenced off by faded draperies. Here all the dogs and cats assembled of an evening with my stepfather and mother around the smoke-blackened fireplace. Rifles and shotguns stood in the chimney corner; a gasoline lantern dangled from a wire overhead, hissing softly as it threw its harsh white light over a small table piled with books and ledgers. Flamboyant Navajo rugs colored the rough pine floor. The bathrooms were out yonder.

A porch shaded by pungent hopvines ran the length of the building, and each of the three rooms opened onto it. Bumblebees droned sleepily, and now and then the occupants of the porch's two creaky rocking chairs caught a whiff of bacon or ham or, during cool fall weather, of raw beef from the screened meat box by the kitchen door.

The house teemed with life. Bitches and cats produced their young under the porch. Hummingbirds and swallows built homes beneath the eaves. Flickers, bluebirds, wrens, gaudy little sparrow hawks, chipmunks, mice, and wasps nested in hollows around the stone chimney and in the long plank walls. From dawn to dark the old building was murmurous with their thumps, squeaks, chirps, and buzzings. Fortunately the various domiciles were blocked off from each other by rocks and boards, by altitude and suspension, and by flattened pieces of tin which we nailed up here and there against climbing marauders. Even so, the hordes of mortal enemies that reached maturity under that one roof were astonishing—and a matter of great pride to my stepfather, who kept a year-by-year tally on the inexhaustible tablet of his memory.

By dint of many underhanded attacks on male chivalry Mother had finally succeeded in surrounding the house with a lawn. She would hide a wheelbarrow, shovel, ax, and scythe near whatever piece of native jungle she wanted cleared next. Then she lay in wait. When prey appeared she seized a shovel and flew to work. Just when the alarmed victim was trying his hardest to look the other way she would call, "Oh, John"—or Mike, or Ed, or David, or whoever it happened to be—"would you help me *just* a minute?" And there we were, caught.

She had one willing accomplice in my brother Dwight. With infinite labor he constructed a rock garden against the rail fence surrounding the yard, and into it Mother and he transplanted innumerable ferns and wild flowers. Domestic varieties were dotted about the lawn; hedges of painfully trimmed wild roses grew up, and in time even the cowboys admitted that the place was quite handsome—though they never developed the least inclination toward keeping it so.

Scattered about the boundaries of the lawn were the rest of the ranch buildings, including a pair of plank-floored, plank-walled tents for overflow. There was a commissary for food supplies, a cool milkhouse with a floor of stone flagging, and an icehouse full of sawdust, where ice cut from the lake during winter by a neighboring homesteader was stored. Beyond the vegetable garden stood the cowboys' compact log bunkhouse, with its stone fireplace and four iron bedsteads. Still farther away were the open-front barn, built of huge unchinked pine logs slowly rotting away, a chicken shed, and corrals with high pole fences and swinging gates.

I suppose the spot was lonesome, though this never occurred to us. The closest town, Norwood, lay twenty-one miles to the

north, a sad little hamlet sixteen miles removed from the unrelia-
ble narrow-gauge railroad over which we shipped our cattle. Norwood's sole excuse for existence was as supply center for the handful of prosperous farms surrounding it, prosperous because they
were served by the country's one successful ditch line. Their well-
being was not reflected in Norwood's rutted street or in the drab,
sun-curled paint on the false fronts of the stores. We went there
when we needed supplies or to pick up the mail. In wet weather
the clay road regularly tipped us into some ditch, and many times
each summer we had to abandon the car and hoof it up the last
rain-drenched hill into camp.

Within a long morning's ride of us were the summer camps of
two or three other cow outfits and the limp fields of perhaps twice
that many homesteaders. From the numerous progeny of the latter Mother each summer hired a girl who was, in local idiom, "to
come and help." There was considerable competition for the position. Not because of the wages. The girls had only the briefest
glimpse of their monthly pay check before Pa rode over and appropriated it. Not because they learned cooking, sewing, and the
undreamed-of fields of books and magazines. No, they wanted to
come because the floor mopping, vegetable cleaning, laundry, and
dishwashing were easy. They did not have to milk cows, pitch hay,
butcher hogs, plow, or chop wood. For a whole summer they
could loaf.

Our homesteading neighbors were not intentionally brutal.
But, except for a few families who had arrived early enough to
obtain a favorable piece of land, they were helpless in the iron
grip of poverty. Ill-educated and overworked, some of them were
perilously close to mental deficiency. If the parents cuffed and
swore at the children, if toward each other they used vile talk and
fought fist and nail, it was because their raw nerves demanded
these sharp releases; because, remembering their own childhood,
they were quite without realization that there might be other
methods of exacting obedience.

Yet they were not deficient in affection or pride. One of our neighbors struggled to keep his homestead solvent with a series of labors no mere animal would ever have endured. Lacking fodder one winter, he tore up his mattress and fed the straw filling to the milk cow. Lacking shoes, he wrapped his feet in gunny sacks when he went into the snow to work. Starving, he secretly killed and butchered his burro, bringing the meat home with glad tidings that he had shot a deer. The children never guessed the truth; the knowledge that they were eating their pet donkey would have caused sorrow and humiliation, and they still believe that old Jack wandered off during a storm and died.

One summer when his wife desperately wanted money for a trip to visit her ailing father the squatter walked to town where a fair was on. Handbills had advertised a boxing match—anyone lasting three rounds with Slugger So-and-So to get twenty-five dollars. The husband entered the ring. He was knocked down seven times, lost three teeth and part of the hearing of one ear. But when he walked home he had twenty-five dollars to give his wife.

On another summer there came to them in the annual course of events still another baby. Mother went over with a few presents and found the child in its crib—a wooden, blanket-lined canned-goods box. She picked it up. Its dress was made from a flour sack. Around throat and sleeves was lace crocheted from cotton store string. "I didn't want my baby to come into the world without one pretty thing," the woman explained. Perhaps these items are in the archangel's book along with the kicks and curses.

Nonetheless, the mental vacuum in which the children grew up is incredible. To be sure, there was a one-room schoolhouse near by (whose short sessions were held in summer, since winter snow made travel to it impossible), but few of the scholars finished its six grades, for their services were needed at home. And right at home they stayed, their little bodies bent and hardened under adult labor—and occasionally adult abuse—of the cruelest sort.

They reached maturity without entering a church or sitting down before a white tablecloth. They never flushed a toilet or saw a railroad or stepped on a cement sidewalk. Their only contact with the simplest "necessities" of modern living came through the pages of the "Wish Book"—the mail-order catalogue—and they rarely bought what they saw; they only dreamed.

One summer my wife and I had to go to Denver. We felt it was an opportunity to show the town to Rose, an eighteen-year-old girl who was then working at the ranch. Now Rose had a lot of pride in her shapely body. She wasn't going to let anyone know she was fresh from the sticks. She went about the city with her head up and her eyes open, governing herself by imitating every move Martha made. But once her aplomb was shattered. The two of them entered an apartment building on some errand, crossed the lobby, and went into a small room. Carefully observant, Rose halted when Martha did. Suddenly the door shut and the room shot upward. Rose let out a shriek and seized Martha's arm in a drowning man's clutch. It had never occurred to my wife to warn her in advance that there were such things as elevators.

The marvels we supposed would impress her—tall buildings, clanging streetcars, the illumination of the downtown section at night—apparently failed to do so. Meanwhile, tiny details that we dismissed with the thoughtlessness of familiarity absorbed her—the neat curbstones marking off the streets, the regulated greenness of lawns in the residential section, alleys and ashpits ("Ain't that handy?"), the color of a Negro's skin. And, above all, the wonders of Mother's city house—toaster, vacuum cleaner, sink, the miraculous jets of fire from the gas stove. I thought she would wear out the light switches, snapping them on and off to see the bulbs leap to life at her touch. We could scarcely get her out of the bathroom; imagine lying full length in a tub while it filled with warm water all by itself!

The ultimate overwhelmed Rose the morning she stepped into

her first department store. Though knowing she would be beaten for it by Pa, she had kept her monthly pay check, intending to buy a few of the things she had seen pictured in the "Wish Book." And now here was the place.

Just inside the door she gasped and stopped dead. Her eyes flashed from this counter to that, to the next and the next. And suddenly all the pride, all the pretense were gone. She stood there trembling violently, tears pouring down her cheeks. She did not buy. She could not. There was too much, too much. Every afternoon and every morning she went back to that store. Back and back, looking and looking. Not until the day of our departure for the ranch, with the doors of paradise closing in her face, did she make her first hesitant purchases. Sometimes, thinking of her now, I wish in black remorse that we had not taken her. Or are souvenirs—an empty lipstick container, a dry perfume bottle, sand-wrecked high-heeled pumps with saucy bows, silk underwear carefully folded out of sight in a battered straw suitcase—are these things enough to help when the freezing night creeps down from the mountains and snow spreads its ghostly phosphorescence to the horizon that will never be crossed again?

The ranch at the Cone occupied a rather anomalous position. Although we called it the summer camp, it was not the place where the bulk of the cattle was summered. This seeming contradiction can perhaps be made clear if one pictures the entire year's operations as taking place on a range shaped like a lopsided hourglass. The larger bulge held the sparse rimrock of the winter country; in the smaller bulge was the tall bunch grass of Beaver Park, eighteen miles beyond the Cone. Sitting in the neck between them, controlling the trickle of cattle, was the summer camp. And so, since we could reach either way from it, it had become our summer headquarters, and we blithely called it a cow outfit, though there were times late in the season when a baffled visitor might not see an animal anywhere about.

As the cattle came up from the low country they were put in the Cone pastures to rest and fatten up while we waited for the forest rangers to open Beaver Park for grazing—the park was in Montezuma National Forest and hence under government supervision. The herds stayed under fence, and a few hours' riding each day sufficed to care for them. Wonderful, indolent rides which Martha could at last share, as I had been promising her for so long. Hard gallops through the gentle draws, slow climbs up the winding trails to the ridge tops. "Jingling" (rounding up) the horse herd in the cold morning when dew sparkled on the grass and the rising sun washed the hills with a clear yellow light. Picnic lunches on some sun-struck slope—it was never hot, for the camp's elevation was over eight thousand feet. And then coming home through the long shadows to the crackling fireplaces and the fat boy baby who had put in his appearance a few months before and spent most of his time rolling naked on the warm grass of the lawn. This wasn't cowboying; this was paradise.

Often during the rides a guttural thunderhead reared over the hilltops with a lash of rain. Drenched, our coatless shirts plastered to our skins, we might take shelter under a dwarfed piñon or in an abandoned cabin. But we stayed away from those massive, scattered yellow pines dotting the flats like welcoming umbrellas. Rising above all other things, they acted as lightning rods. For miles about the summer camp there was not a single pine whose trunk did not show the fierce zigzags of the sky's electrical claws.

Even a squat, twisted juniper, if it stood alone, was dangerous. Once during a storm a pair of us stopped under one for a smoke, then rode on. We had scarcely left when a shattering crash almost knocked our horses from their feet. Looking back, we saw our tree burst into a flame that slowly sputtered out under the rain to a sluggish column of smoke. Fence lines, too, could be a threat. If lightning struck one before the posts were wet enough to act as grounds the current might race for miles along the wires. Now and then a cow or two, huddled in a corner, was electrocuted this way.

Still, we liked those sharp mountain storms. There is a wild exhilaration in racing through the rain while white lightning fries the heavens and your horse shies at the cannonading thunder. And then, about the time we thought we were going to freeze solid, the sun came out. The birds emerged, too, singing their heads off; puddles winked merrily; leaves sparkled, and the smell of freshness was almost unbearably sweet.

Little chores kept the cowboys from growing insufferably lazy. We had small stands of timothy, alfalfa, and barley to care for, pitch-laden pine wood to gather for the fireplaces, and smokeless aspen to saw and split for the cookstove. And although we didn't have many calves at the summer camp, there were some. We should have branded a few head each day while they were still little, as the boys at the cow-and-calf range on the Uncompahgre Plateau did by necessity, but since our dab was small we put it off with the excuse that there was always tomorrow.

We paid for the procrastination. Tomorrow eventually came, and we were faced with doing the whole job in one day. We routed ourselves out at sunup—we had fallen into the evil way of sleeping until six-thirty or seven every morning—gathered the desired cattle, packed them into a corral, dragged up a lot of wood, got the fires blazing, thrust in the irons, and in general did our best not to notice how husky some of those early spring calves had grown. Very politely, pretending we really didn't care, we started arguing about who was going to rope and who was going to flank.

Somehow John Scott always managed to connive his way into grace. Grinning, he tightened his saddle cinches, mounted, and rode into the herd. His lariat flicked; the loop settled about a calf's neck. With a lightning twist John wrapped the rope around his saddle horn—a dally. The plunging calf made a bolt, but

John had used as little rope as possible, and the animal had not much room in which to maneuver. It hit the end of the slack, snapped around. The smart horse turned without guidance toward the fire, dragging the calf behind.

A flanker runs out. He reaches over the calf's body, grasps the inside front leg with one hand, the loose skin of its flank with the other. He heaves up, at the same time boosting from underneath with his knee. This throws the calf off its feet and it falls flat on its side to the ground. The flanker drops on its neck with one knee, seizes its front ankle in a hammer lock. At the same instant a helper catches one of the thrashing hind hoofs. He pulls back on the leg, sits down without being able to choose his landing place, which is generally a pile of cow manure, and thrusts the calf's other hind leg forward with one foot. The scissored animal is helpless. A man runs up with a branding iron. Another castrates and earmarks it—in a close-packed herd, ownership of a particular steer is more easily determined by the pattern into which the ears are cut than by the hard-to-see brands on their sides. In our case we cropped both ears off square. Meanwhile the rope has been freed and John goes off after another victim.

This one is big and strong. Just as the flanker heaves on it the calf gives a mighty spring. The flanker falls, and the calf comes down on top of him, tramping him soundly. Meanwhile the reaching helper is blasted in the belly with both hind hoofs. Swearing furiously, the men crawl to their feet and catch the calf again. One hauls on its tail; the other bulldogs it—twists its head around —and at last, minus considerable wind, clothes, and bits of skin, they wrestle it down.

"Damn you, John, get the next one by the feet!"

"Oh, you want 'em delivered already wrapped!" John mocks, but for a time he catches the calves by both hind legs, upsets them, and drags them in on their sides, so that the flankers can pounce on them without difficulty. But it is easier to rope animals around the neck, and soon John slips back into his old ways.

A lone man with plenty of time can go through the entire process unaided. While his trained horse holds the roped animal he dismounts, throws the calf, and lashes its feet together with a "piggin string." After he has four or five securely tied down he brands them, frees them, and captures a new batch. He can do this out on an isolated flat with improvised materials, but he should never become too skillful at it. The beholder of his aptitude is likely to wonder on whose calves he received his practice. A man with much branding to do is well advised to seek company.

Since growing calves change quickly in appearance—cowboys soon learn to recognize an enormous number of individual animals, though to the untrained eye they all look "as much alike as Chinamen"—and since the youngsters are comparatively easy to manage, they are more often preyed upon by rustlers than are adult cattle. There is a deterrent, however. The discovery of a calf wearing one brand and following a cow that bears another calls for prompt explanation. Accordingly, the thief operates on animals that are old enough to wean from their mothers. By this time the prey is generally branded, and the rustler must rework the design into one of his own. But he can't just think up a handy pattern, appropriate it, and burn it on helter-skelter. A brand, like a commercial trade-mark, is private property and jealously guarded under a form of copyright registered with the state government. The Colorado brand book contains something like thirty-five hundred entries, and no one in your part of the state is allowed to use a brand similar to yours.

A lot of those thirty-five hundred entries are hopelessly complex, having been created by men with great imagination and few cattle. To be practical, a brand must be simple enough to allow quick application. At the same time it should be distinctive and hard to alter. The ideal has never been found. In the first place, the mark is often poorly administered, blotched, or misshapen as the calf struggles under the iron. These indistinct patterns give the rustler his chance. He reblotches them into something resembling his own registered brand, and who is to say with certainty, months later, that the illegible scrawl isn't his?

Furthermore, a good brand artist has considerable ingenuity. For example, we once used a pitchfork with a square bottom (Ψ) and thought it adequate. But an affable neighbor of ours named Dan H. Pickens registered his initials as his trade-mark, a *D* and an *HP* connected. He then proceeded to operate on our pitchfork. Soon many animals wandered about bearing a D⊦P. "Damn Hard Pickin's," Dan jocosely called the fruits of his toil.

He was caught at last and granted leisure time in jail to think up new devices. To foil similar attempts we rounded the bottom of the pitchfork and added a two-bar to the hip, like this Ψ≈. Afterward we enjoyed comparative security—with emphasis on the word comparative. The completely tamperproof design cannot be developed.

And so the branding went on in the ankle-deep dust of the corral. Throw, burn, cut, and drag up another. A tallyman—a wide-eyed boy or some old-timer too feeble for calf wrestling—shaved a patch off one of the weathered poles of the corral with his pocketknife. On the whitened surface thus created he kept count with a pencil stub as the flankers called out the tally— "One Pitchfork steer!" "One Bar C heifer!" "One Circle Cross steer!" "Pitchfork—steer again!" Smoke and stink and heat. Released, the hurt calf bounds to its mother, who is standing as near the dread fire as she dares, mooing her apprehension and anger. She smells the little one, licks its bloody ears, leads it away.

John drags up another. "This is the one we've been looking for!"

"What one?"

"The last one!"

We stretch stiffly, scatter the embers of the fire, and turn the glad cattle out to the freedom of the pasture. We push the irons back and forth through the dust to clean and cool them. Our mouths are so full of dirt that even our teeth are like little knobs of mud. From head to foot we are caked with grime and blood. Well, there is plenty of clean water in the lake. We roll smokes, stumble to the sleepy horses tied outside the corral, and ride home. The days sink back into long hours of golden indolence.

Indolence, yes, but not complacence. The swift hand of trouble lurked too near. Some of the accidents were hilarious—except to the victim. One evening when the family was away Jim Danks, professional roundup cook, decided to stew a chicken in the old-fashioned pressure cooker on the range. Jim could master even cakes and pies over an open fire, but elaborate culinary appliances were beyond him. However, he had the confidence of ignorance. He loaded a fat hen in the cooker and fired up. Instead of slowly bleeding off the steam when the chicken was done, he threw the lid clamps wide open. The cooker erupted like a trench mortar. Jim was painfully scalded, but we could not be sympathetic. Whenever we tried, the vision of that hen cannon-balling against the ceiling, where it left a perpetual grease spot as token of Jim's travail, rose to destroy our solemnity.

Nor could we cluck with proper melancholy when Bud Wilmot tangled with the wasps. Bud was a tall, lanky, ugly man whose reddened eyes welled more moisture than even Donnie Marsden's. For some reason he wore two pairs of trousers. One, thin and tight-fitting, he buckled about his waist. The others he called his "brush-bustin' breeches." Baggy corduroys many sizes too large for him, they were held in place by frayed suspenders. Between the two sets of trousers was a gap of several inches.

Bud was a contentious sort of person, always landing on a remark and shoving it around like an angry bull. One day he led us down a brushy ridge. Instead of watching where he was going, he was looking back over his shoulder, arguing. He ran into a branch. On the branch was a yellow jacket's gray paper nest. It shook loose and dropped into the gap between his trousers. I am sure he suffered quite as much as he afterward said, but the memory of his gymnastics, the howls and leaps as he rolled in the brush, divesting himself of his painful pants and then running wild with shirttails flying and the wasps in furious pursuit, prevented any sober harkening to his tale of woe.

We were sobered often enough, however. All about the Cone were myriad prairie-dog towns; a running horse putting a foot in one of those burrows fell "tail over teacup." Not one of us but bore scars of such a tumble, and sometimes the scars went deep. An ill-broken horse fell with Charlie Terrill. His foot caught in the stirrup. The frightened animal lunged upright and dragged him at full speed through the rocks, kicking him at every jump. He twisted loose finally and lived, but he never rode again. And Charlie was lucky. Down in Dry Creek Basin a horse fell with a homesteader, rolled across him, and broke his back. He wasn't far from home, only a mile. He tried to crawl there on his belly, dragging himself by his elbows. He must have lived many hours, for when searchers, alarmed by the eventual return of his empty-saddled horse, found his shattered body it was only a few yards from the gate.

A runaway bronco smashed into a wire fence with Sam Gordon, veered sharply, and raced along it. Sam's saddle turned, pinning him between the horse and the fence. His head hit every post like a drum; between the posts were the reaching claws of the barbs. . . . Bald-headed, pigeon-toed Harry Craver, the handy man at the summer camp, mounted a horse that was too frisky for his stiff joints. It whirled and cracked him against the gate. When we reached him he was dead. . . . Lightning struck a party of picnickers on the Cone, killing two. . . . A flash flood trapped a cowboy between the unclimbable banks of an arroyo. . . .

There is no point going on. It is only listing names for a reader.

But the dead men were more than names to us, and their ghosts rode in the back of our minds, whispering, "There, but for the grace of God——" Perhaps this explains in part why the soft, lazy, uneventful hours at the summer camp seemed so fine, why we clung hard to them, grinning in delight at all the ordinary little happenings that each day reminded us life is good.

XIII ROPES, GUNS, AND PRACTICAL JOKES

ONE DAY AFTER MIKE HAD COME TO my wife's rescue and showed her how to put the cream separator together he said, "I suppose you know what to do when a cow loses its cud?"

"They don't," said Martha suspiciously.

"Oh yes. You never saw a cow lyin' in the shade that she wasn't chawin' her cud."

"No, but——"

"They're born with that cud, an' it's the only one they got. It grows as they grow. They carry it in their stomach like a man carries tobacco in his jeans. When they want a chaw they cough it up. Only sometimes they cough too hard an' it gets away."

"I don't believe you."

Mike wagged his head. "You will, sometime when the menfolk are out ridin' an' you're alone to take care o' the farm stock. A cow'll lose her cud an' stand around the gate bellerin' like she was gonna die. She will, too, if she don't get a new one. Ain't that husband o' yourn told you how to make cuds?"

"He——"

"You better learn. Here, I'll show you. You take a pebble fer a base. Wrap it up good in a tough coverin', like a piece o' cloth off the mop. You got to flavor it so they'll take it. Turnip water, that's best. Soak the mop in a bucket o' turnip water. Cover it good with alfalfa an' lace 'er into a tight little ball with lots o' rubber bands."

Shaken, Martha took refuge in scoffing. "And then they gobble it right up?"

"Some do; some don't. If they balk you've got to shove it down their throats. It's quite a fight with a wild ol' range cow. But, shucks, you won't have much trouble with these gentle milk penners around the house. Just squeeze the cow's underjaw with one hand. That makes her open her mouth, and real quick you ram in the cud, elbow deep. I reckon it does seem kind o' slimy at first, but you're a ranch wife now, an' you wouldn't want to lose a cow by bein' finicky, would you?"

Martha appealed to me. "By golly, that's right," I said. "I'm glad Mike told you."

She appealed to John. He stared at her. "Of course!" he snapped. "We all carry a couple of extry cuds in our saddle pockets. You best have some too."

Finally she appealed to my stepfather. He overwhelmed her with scientific terminology, including a penciled diagram of a cow's multiple stomachs and arrows to trace the digestive processes. Battered by this mass of evidence, she could be seen now and then in nose-wrinkled contemplation of some ruminating cow. The shadow of a cud haunted her days, and a long time passed after truth dawned before she forgave us this assault on her credulity.

Many a ranch visitor can agree with Mark Twain, who complained in his *Autobiography,* "When grown-up persons indulge in practical jokes the facts gauge them. They have led narrow, obscure, and ignorant lives, and at full manhood they still retain and cherish a job lot of leftover standards and ideals that would have been discarded with their boyhood, if they had moved out into the world and a broader life. . . . If I could say they were burglars, or hatrack thieves, or something like that, that wouldn't be utterly uncomplimentary."

The great humorist was calling the kettle black. As reporter on a pioneer newspaper in Virginia City, Nevada, Twain fully shared, both on giving and receiving ends, this most typical form of frontier fun making. He outgrew it after several sad experiences, but the Western communities he castigates never did. Whatever its psychological wellsprings—and Twain was partly right in his estimate—practical joking, or "jobbing," as it is known locally, remains a favorite diversion in the isolated towns and ranches of the cow country.

One sleepy afternoon we were driving a bunch of cattle from here to there. Riding with us was Herb Blake, a blond, husky, handsome young man fresh from New York City. Although he had never before stayed overnight on a farm, he possessed a consuming ambition to be a rancher. Through various connections he at last landed at the summer camp and undertook to learn the trade.

He learned.

Alert to every move and gesture, he watched John and Mike, unaware that they were baiting a trap. In apparent effort to amuse themselves, they were idly lassoing various cows by the hind feet or by one horn. Then they would shake the rope loose and repeat. Herb was fascinated. Just that morning John had given him a rope to carry, tying one end of it with an iron knot to the saddle horn. It was not long before he grew eager to share the simple-seeming sport. He essayed several throws at the horns of a ponderous bull and missed, for he was using a small loop, scarcely two feet in diameter, such as he had seen the cowboys employ, and his control was not up to its precise manipulation.

At last John said, "Do you really want to ketch that bull?"

"You bet!" (Herb had noticed that cowboys seldom say "Yes" in agreement, but rather "You bet.")

"Build a bigger loop."

Herb expanded his noose until it was huge enough to catch a house. He heaved. The loop—it could scarcely have missed now —settled squarely about the bull's neck. Triumphant, Herb gathered in the slack. "I've got him!" he cried.

John grinned a satanic grin. "You sure have!"

The majestic brute continued its way, and Herb's outweighed pony perforce went with it. To his horrible chagrin the boy realized he could not shake his rope free. He began to sweat. Shadows were lengthening; we were ready to turn the cattle loose in their new pasture and go home. With a convulsive gulp Herb fumbled at the knot holding the rope to the saddle horn, but it had been tied to stay.

"Lend me a knife!" he begged.

"You can't cut loose an' let that bull go off draggin' a rope," John said. "He might tangle in the brush an' choke."

"I'll ride up close and cut it where it goes around his neck. Please!"

John reached in his pocket. His shaggy eyebrows lifted. "By gosh, I come off without my knife!"

Now a cowboy uses a knife many times each day, to make shavings for starting a fire, to cut strings of rawhide for mending his pack panniers or stirrups, to splice rope, open cans, castrate calves, slice bacon, or merely to whittle as an aid to thinking. He would rather leave home without his hat, but today we all denied having knives along, and Herb was innocent enough to believe us.

"I tell you what," said John. "We'll ride to camp an' come back with somethin'. Of course we'll have the chores to do an' supper to eat, but you hang on. We'll be along."

Away we went. Screened by the trees, we halted and looked back. The cows had scattered out, grazing, and the bull was following. Herb tried to spur his horse up close, reach out with his hand, and pull the slipknot free. The bull twisted and ran. At last it grew wroth, pawed the ground, bellowed, and prepared to fight. Alarmed, Herb kept his distance. Every thirty seconds he looked over his shoulder to see if help was on the way. I expected him to step out of the saddle—as many another man would have done—and let the bull take the horse where it willed. But he stayed on, resolved to protect his mount and gear as best he could.

At last John said, "He's a sticker. Reckon he's learned by now about carryin' knives an' ropin' stock?"

"I reckon," said Mike, and we rode out to rescue a thoroughly subdued young cowpuncher.

Not long afterward we went on a greasy-sack ride into Dry Creek Basin. As we were drifting our gather toward the Cone we passed a homestead. One of the youngsters came pumping his new bicycle valiantly through the dust of the trail to watch us go by. Of a sudden he let out a screech, leaped from the seat, and began pitching rocks at the vehicle's rear wheel.

Mystified, we rode over to see what was wrong. By some weird chance the boy had picked up a rattlesnake. It lay tangled in the spokes, its tail buzzing like a shaken can full of dried peas. John dismounted and drew his revolver. He held the gun at full length in both hands, sank down into an ungainly crouch, squinted one eye over the sight, and after an agony of concentration that had us all holding our breaths, he blew off the snake's head.

Herb was enraptured. This was the first rattler he had ever seen. He drew it out of the wheel spokes, examined it minutely, dismembered its rattles, and buttoned them in his shirt pocket for a souvenir. That night as we squatted around the campfire the talk turned to snakes. Each of us produced his direst yarns about their bites. We told how they don't always give a warning rattle before striking; we overemphasized the need of shaking one's boots before donning them in the morning; we related with full melodrama the old folk stories about reptiles crawling into a man's bed for warmth on cold nights. Herb's eyes all but bugged out of his head.

We started to bed. Herb lovingly placed in his boot the long-barreled six-shooter he had felt compelled to buy on coming to the wild West and slid with a yawn between his blankets. All at once he went rigid, toe extended. Then suddenly he came unwound, leaped upright, shrieked "Snake!" seized his revolver—and shot his bed full of holes! Gingerly, then, he took the blankets by the corner and threw them back. There lay the end of a rope where Mike had concealed it under cover of our stories. He had even twitched it at the proper moment, but the results surpassed our fondest expectations. We never forgot them—and I daresay Herb never has either.

Herb's original attitude toward six-shooters rouses the glamorous legend of the cowboy and his gun. The cowboys themselves are quite aware of it, and not altogether displeased by the fictions it has caused. Moreover, their mode of life gives them justification for continuing, on the surface, the romantic fact of gun toting. The weapons can be used for providing food and taking pot shots at predatory animals. A bullet is sometimes needed to put an injured horse or cow out of its misery. Or even an injured man. It is a common remark among cowboys that, if hopelessly crippled by an accident far from home, they would rather kill themselves than live a few hours longer in agony. Only in very rare instances have such suicides occurred, however.

Perhaps half the cowboys on the Cone packed guns. Sheepherders were even more apt to go armed, for wild animals do more harm to their flocks than to steers. The revolvers, however, were seldom suspended from well-laden cartridge belts. Though picturesque, such accouterments hamper work, and the pistols were generally put out of sight in a chaps pocket whose bottom had been cut away and refitted to accommodate the barrel. Or a brush-scarred rifle might be lugged along in a saddle scabbard. Under these conditions a gun could not be brought into play with great speed, and that of itself indicates how little consideration the possessor gave to his weapon as a means either of defense or of attack on another man.

Still, temper and temptation are unpredictable things. Once in a while a man would decide to use a gun as a persuader. This phenomenon is by no means confined to the West, but in sparsely settled ranch districts the inhabitants know the participants and, indeed, are often dragged willy-nilly into the uproar. Hence the situation takes on a sharper drama than, say, an anonymous gang killing in Chicago.

One day a strange, meek little man named Cotter trudged on foot into the summer camp. He spent the night, and the next morning repaired to the ditch that supplied us with water, where he bathed and washed his underwear. Then away he went, still walking and carrying his damp underwear over his shoulder.

John, who had watched the ablutions in some amazement, asked, "What do you suppose he did that for?"

"Why," Mike said, "he's goin' over to Dove Creek to be married."

"My God!" said John. "It's forty miles to Dove Creek! Don't he reckon to get dusty again?"

"It'll be fresh dust," Mike said reasonably.

In due time Cotter reached Dove Creek, was married, and retired to a homestead deep in the piñons. Near him lived Ned Hilton, a surly wild-horse trapper. They quarreled several times over a certain spring, and one day Cotter vanished. It is possible he walked out of married life just as he walked into it—he and his domineering bride never got along—but local gossip inclined to the unprovable opinion that Hilton had killed him and hidden the body.

Hilton was capable of murder. Not long after Cotter's disappearance the wild-horse trapper engaged in an altercation with another neighbor. The pair met inside a tiny log cabin and proceeded to empty their six-shooters at each other. Even granting that a man in a gun duel is apt to be nervous and of poor aim, the results were extraordinary. Hilton was slightly wounded in one hand. His opponent was creased across the small of his back.

How a man could receive such an injury while shooting at an enemy in a cramped cabin caused endless speculation.

Their guns empty, the two opponents went their separate ways. Hilton's trap began to catch horses that were not wild; also, he branched out into cattle. Numbered among them were Pitchfork stock, and a delegation of cowboys rode to his homestead to remonstrate. They were deterred by the sight of Hilton's common-law wife aiming a .30-.40 at their heads from behind a boulder on the hillside. The sheriff—his election had been a matter of political expediency—likewise found it advisable not to meddle. Disgusted, my stepfather offered, under county auspices, a reward for Hilton's capture.

Four men laid siege to the rustler's cabin. Hilton fought back while his wife reloaded his guns. One of the bounty hunters, un-nerved by a bullet that took away a slice of his shirt, crawled off through the brush, reached his horse, and fled to the nearest telephone. He called the sheriff at Telluride to "come quick." The sheriff said it was impossible. He was half a day's ride away; besides, he was erecting a new stovepipe in the jail and could not leave.

Meanwhile, Hilton succeeded in shooting one of the attackers through the stomach. The wounded man rolled out of the brush onto a patch of bare ground, groaning and bleeding profusely. The sight dampened the ardor of his companions and they departed. Hilton bound the now-unconscious man's hurts, drove him to Norwood in a wagon, and turned him over to a doctor.

Upset by the incident, my stepfather revoked the reward before it caused more bloodshed. Hilton continued his rustling unmolested, but the sheriff, in a burst of bravery, did arrest the wife as she was alone in the forest collecting firewood. Hilton thereupon telephoned her in jail, plotted her escape over the wire, and charged the call to the county. With the aid of a little dynamite he effected a spectacular delivery, and the pair started for more kindly climes. They were arrested in an auto camp by an officer who, unaware of Hilton's fearsome reputation, simply walked up to him and laid a hand on his shoulder.

Hilton was sentenced to the penitentiary. He blamed my stepfather for his downfall and threatened that as soon as he was out he would slay the entire family. Years passed and we forgot the matter. Then one day while my stepfather was in Norwood and the rest of us were out riding an ancient car rattled up the road and debouched a seedy-looking individual. He asked Mother, who was alone at the house, where the owner was.

"In Norwood."

The visitor scowled. "You don't know me, do you?"

"No."

"I'm Ned Hilton."

"Oh."

"I've come to kill your husband." Whereupon he climbed in his car, drove off the road to a place of concealment, and halted, leaving Mother in considerable trepidation.

In due time my stepfather appeared, left the car in its shed, and walked to the house. As Mother was warning him Hilton darted into the barn. My stepfather, who certainly bore none of the physical attributes of a brave man, being very short in stature and wearing a neat, clipped gray mustache that reflected his methodical nature, bit off a chew of tobacco and walked down the path. The barn's open chinks made it a perfect ambush, and Mother screwed her eyes shut, waiting the shot that would announce her widowhood.

No sound came. Hilton emerged from the barn and drove away. My stepfather returned to the house, looking somewhat abstract, as though pondering the ways of mankind.

"What happened?" said Mother when she could speak.

"Nothing."

"What did he want?"

"Hilton? Oh, he wanted to borrow twenty-five dollars."

"What did you do?"

"I lent it to him." And that is all my stepfather, an inordinately taciturn man at best, would say.

Another event developed less happily. Shortly after Martha reached the ranch she and I were driving along the narrow dirt road that threads the deep, lovely, V-shaped, red-soiled canyon of the upper San Miguel. We rounded a bend, and there before us several armed men crouched behind boulders.

We were stopped by the rifle of a wild-eyed individual who declared, "We've got 'em!" He didn't seem very pleased about it, however. He kept plucking at his lower lip with thumb and fore-finger and darting frightened glances up the slope beyond the river.

"Got who?"

"The killers!"

"What killers?"

By asking questions as fast as we could—by now Martha was convinced she had indeed reached the woolly West—we patched together the following clarification:

Two youths had murdered a man in a county to the south and been arrested in the north. The southern sheriff and his deputy were fetching them back for trial. With colossal stupidity the deputy opened the glove compartment of the car for a pack of cigarettes, thus revealing a pistol to the manacled pair in the rear seat. They bided their time. Then, as the car was rolling through San Miguel Canyon and the sheriff's attention was cen-tered on the cliff-girt road, the captives larruped the deputy over the head with their handcuffs, stunned him, reached into the compartment, and obtained the gun. All the sheriff could safely do on that dangerous road was stop the car. He did, was shot dead, and tumbled out into the middle of the highway. Through some quirk the groggy deputy was spared and allowed to go staggering away toward the closest town, Placerville, in great fright. The murderers, meanwhile, found that management of the car while handcuffed took more co-operation than they possessed. They drove it over the embankment and rushed off afoot, concealing their tracks by wading in the brush-lined river.

Summoned by the deputy, Placerville's braver souls seized arms and rushed down the canyon where they quickly, so our informant said, cornered the killers in a dead-end gully high on the opposite slope.

"Drive to town and get us reinforcements!" he gasped, plucking again at his lip.

Visible in the field were at least twenty men armed to the teeth. Opposing them were two manacled youths short on ammunition. A cynic might have been permitted a small snort, but of course there was the matter of justice to consider.

"Sure!" I said and drove away pell-mell in a fever of excitement.

The rest was dismal. My only grain of personal comfort is that I functioned as an unarmed spectator—albeit a willing one. Jostling, shoving, and sweating, the reinforced cordon crossed the gray, mill-fouled river. As individuals, many of the posse had performed and would perform deeds of quiet heroism—battling fires and outlaw horses, helping comrades trapped by snowslides, or stampeding cattle, enduring pain, ill fortune, and monotony. But now the evil alchemy of a mob gripped them. The social aspect of the situation, the attack which the murderers had made on the underpinnings of society, was in no one's mind. Nine out of ten of that gang were lured by the prospects of the greatest hunt of all—a man hunt, a legal opportunity to kill forbidden game. Blood lust rode them like a physical sickness. And cowardice, that abject cowardice which makes a person go ahead lest he be called yellow for retreating. Blind hate engendered by fear that the prey might strike back. Anger, because killing needs the backbone of anger . . . That gully was raked by lead until a mouse couldn't have survived. A charge at a prostrate form dimly visible through the brush. Lo, we have bagged—a stump!

The details of the next few days only add to the miserable

picture. Hundreds of men swarmed in to taste the drama. An airplane scouted the mesas. Posses galloped far and wide, shooting first and questioning later. A Mexican sheepherder, who knew nothing about the affair, was walking across a lonely glade intent on his business. When half-a-dozen armed riders swarmed into sight and shouted for him to halt he naturally took to his heels and was drilled through the shoulder. Bloodhounds, amateur sleuths, and sensationmongers turned up one false trail after another. The murderers were reported in a dozen different places, including the Cone. A self-appointed deputy, seeing two cowboys cooking dinner at a spring near the summer camp, leaped from his pickup truck and investigated them with brandished revolvers. Satisfied, he started backing into the truck. Lying on the seat was a loaded shotgun. It went off, an angling discharge that none-theless removed the seat of our hero's trousers and kept him sleeping on his stomach for some time to come.

The murderers? They had simply walked away. Discovering a half-witted goatherd, they forced him to cut off their handcuffs with his blacksmithing tools. He, simple soul, believing their threat to kill him if he opened his mouth, said not a word to the deputies who passed his camp a dozen times. The criminals dropped down to the highway and thumbed a ride with a motorist who gave them a detailed account of their doings. Crossing the mountains to the central part of the state, they got a job on a hay farm. The farmer recognized them from newspaper pictures and took them into custody with a pitchfork. San Miguel County hung its head, perhaps reflecting that although a man will fight for any number of causes, he does a poor job of it unless the need somehow touches the secret springs of his heart.

Even the conversation afforded by these affairs was limited, and for daily sport we had to rely on the materials at hand: breaking colts and roping wild cattle. In earlier days a horse was seldom touched until it was three or four years old. Then a young rider would decide to take the kinks out of it. In a swirl of dust, squeals, and flashing hoofs the colt would be roped, thrown, blindfolded, and saddled. While one man "eared the critter down"—twisted its ears to make it stand still—the rider would mount, reach forward, and slip off the blindfold. Now the horse could see where it jumped, and jump it did, exploding as far and as high as it could go.

Cowboys who had reached the weary age of thirty regarded this procedure with jaundiced eyes. There you sit, beaten mercilessly between the hard cantle and the hard pommel of the saddle. If you are pitched off the ground is waiting like a club. Or perhaps the horse falls on top of you, snapping a leg or collarbone. Even if you become adept at sticking, your innards simply cannot stand that pounding many times; as the cowboys say, "It makes an old man out of a young one right quick."

It doesn't do a horse much good either, often leaving the animal sullen, wind-broken, or treacherous. When ranches had more horses than they could use a spoiled colt wasn't so much of a loss. But now that cattlemen have to utilize fully each acre of grass the horseherds have diminished in size. Every animal must be productive, and more care is shown in their breaking. They are eased through their training and cajoled not to buck, instead of the other way around—all of which suits the older hands right to the ground.

Still, a great deal of excitement attends the whoop "Let 'er buck!" and mere roughness never yet deterred a youngster feeling his oats. Until their bodies begin to revolt, the ranch boys cannot resist the fine, salty taste of having it out with a fractious colt. Sometimes they have to repair to an isolated corral where the boss won't catch them at their sport, and as they gain proficiency their ambitions turn toward organized rodeos.

In the last quarter of a century rodeos have become a major American show business. The war has cut into them severely, but before the war they were almost numberless, ranging from a score or so famous ones offering fat cash prizes on down to side attractions at county fairs, where the rewards are mostly applause. Young hopefuls started at these fairs and seldom got beyond them. Entry fees at the major shows, travel, and food expenses for self and horse were too high for cowboy wages. And the competition lured by big money was terrific; professional rodeo stars need superlative skill to win even bread and butter. Only a talented, grimly determined, play-for-keeps rider could rise far. The rest—the ordinary, amiable, workaday boys—bled the fever from their systems with a fling or two, came home with a wry smile, and settled down.

Fame did strike one of our neighbors a fleeting blow. He was Dick Milner, enormously strong and theoretically old enough to know his limitations. Intending to be only a spectator, he visited the Sky-Hi Stampede at Monte Vista, Colorado, a show of good proportions. He looked into a bottle, came up with a vision, and entered the bulldogging. Only alcohol can account for the inspiration. Bulldogging—leaping from a galloping horse onto the head of a running steer and twisting it to the ground— is strictly a rodeo stunt. Non-utilitarian in the extreme, the feat is almost never seen during normal ranch procedure, and except for moments of horsing around Dick had had no experience with it.

The gods that care for bibulous amateurs were with him that day. He not only won first prize but came within a tenth of a second of tying the world's record. He returned home with a hang-over, an expanded chest, and a medal pinned to his shirt. Irked by skeptical remarks, he offered to show how the deed had been done. We took a milk cow up a gentle hill, where she could get a down-slope run, and away they went. Just as Dick left the saddle the cow turned one way, the horse the other. Dick lit flat on his face in the middle. The cheers echoed for months.

There is one effort, however, at which I believe well-practiced cowboys can outshine professional performers. This is roping.

In rodeos the animal to be thrown is locked in a flat arena from which it cannot escape, and its capture is reduced to a race against a timekeeper's watch. But let the calf grow to half a ton of wild weight in a thick forest of oak brush and cedars liberally sprinkled with rimrock. Subduing it then with forty feet of hard twist and a good horse takes more than showmanship. And here neither age nor judgment seems to exercise restraint. There are some cowboys who would "ruther rope a calf than eat"—which is saying plenty—and when the calf becomes a wild steer all else, hell and high water included, pales into insignificance.

Inveterate roper was Old Man Barnard. He must have been close to seventy. He wore long white hair and a flowing mustache, and he rode a tall, fleet, sad-faced black mare named Maud. Barnard never said "I did so and so," but rather, "Me and my mare Maud." He was a tiresome old windjammer. His favorite monologue, spun out in a welter of redundant detail, was hunting wolves in Oklahoma Territory. "Now, young man," he would begin, "when I was a boy in Oklahoma . . ." Whereupon everyone in earshot groaned, sunk chin in collar, and prepared for the torture.

Barnard always went with us on our greasy-sack rides to Hamilton Mesa, a humpbacked tableland whose northern slopes dropped into a tangle of piñons and dry washes. On its sides scrub oaks grew thick as the hair on a dog's back. "It's so dark in them brush jungles that owls hoot all day," said John. In that country the gentlest cattle grow mean and sneaky. They were hard to find, hard to head when spotted, and hard to drive when gathered. First we would round up what we could and hold them as decoys in an opening. While one man stood guard on the gather the others wormed their way back into the brush and tried to drive any near-by animals into the central pool. It had to be done with care; the least sign of trouble would boo the whole kit into flight. Often we would thrash about for three or four days and come out with little more than a cow apiece.

Toward the close of one strenuous afternoon we succeeded wonderfully in rounding up twenty-five or thirty head. While I stood watch the others radiated out for a final circle. Soon a racket rose on the slope above. Pops and crackles, a howl, a drum of hoofs. Someone had spotted a renegade, an outlaw steer or cow that had eluded us for years.

My cattle threw up their heads. Out of the wall of brush burst a high-horned, brockle-faced cow. I knew her—Old Spot. Every cowboy on the range had at one time or another futilely chased her. I fumbled at my rope, but I was too slow. She slammed into the middle of the decoy herd and right on through into the brush on the far side of the clearing. Hard on her heels came Old Man Barnard and "My mare Maud." He had taken off his hat and stuffed it inside his shirt so he would not lose it. His white hair streamed; leaves and twigs hung all over him. If he had pulled up I might have held my alarmed cattle together. But I don't believe he saw them. He glimpsed Spot's disappearing tail, gave one piercing shriek, and whammed straight through the herd in pursuit.

Those laboriously gathered cattle scattered in every direction. There was no use trying to stop them. I took after Barnard, but his momentum was too vast. He split the brush asunder and roared on, leaving me tangled in a labyrinth of branches.

We had long since finished supper when old Lochinvar returned to camp. "My mare Maud" was limping on all four feet. Her ankles were a mass of rock bruises; dried blood caked the long scratches on her flanks. Torn and cut, Barnard was in no better shape. We were furious with him for his destruction of our herd, but we could not censure him. There was a light not of this world on his brush-gouged face as he stood before the fire and dreamed aloud.

"Me and my mare Maud caught her goin' down through the rimrock. When she hit the end of the slack I thought she'd jerk us over the moon. But we busted her proper. . . ."

We listened, green with envy and troubled by premonitions.
The wolves of Oklahoma were forgotten. Old Man Barnard had
a new saga which he would carry with him to the grave.

At that, those Hamilton Mesa cattle were tame compared with
the renegades that foraged on Al Scorup's range in southeastern
Utah. Herefords, they were, and, old-timers insist, less "snorty"
than longhorns, but few traces of domesticity clung to them. The
Scorup riders had to stalk them as you would a deer, slipping
down dizzy trails to secret water holes, probing hidden bed
grounds in windy canyons. No cattle (or, for that matter, few
wild animals of any kind) are as smart as some accounts lead one
to believe, but they do learn what hurts them and how to avoid it.
Man is the renegade steers' greatest enemy, and when they scent
him they sneak into the brush with the adroitness of a cottontail
rabbit. There they freeze motionless while the pursuer gallops by,
and then before the subterfuge is detected they double back and
are gone.

It takes alert ambushing to bring one to bay—and then it bolts.
When the desperate race begins you have no time to wonder
what your life expectancy will be if your horse falls. The chase
is right up a good cow pony's alley, and he grows as reckless as
the steer. He swoops full tilt down rocky ledges, over boulders and
gullies, through thorny undergrowth. Heavy leather chaps,
leather wristlets, and stirrup tapaderas—stiff hoods that shield
boot toes—help protect your body from the raking brush. Duck-
ing and dodging, grunting with the pain of a cudgeling piñon
branch, you attempt to maneuver the quarry into an opening
large enough for you to use your rope. Often you are outdistanced.
There is not much give in these animals. I recall one Colorado
heifer who ran until she dropped dead in her tracks, literally
bursting her heart in her fury to escape. And the Utah cowboys
tell of an occasional steer jumping off high rims, preferring suicide
to capture.

At this headlong speed and on this rough ground you have no opportunity to aim your rope for the renegade's feet and trip it. Horns or neck have to do. You cast and with your heart in your mouth frantically take your dallies around the saddle horn. The shock of the steer hitting the end of the lariat staggers your horse for half-a-dozen convulsive steps. Sometimes he goes over. . . .

If you have caught the animal by the horns you dart for the handiest tree, snub the steer up short, and tie it there. But if you lassoed it by the neck you must transfer the rope before the animal chokes itself to death. At this point it is handy to have help along. As soon as the steer realizes it is trapped it will do its best to murder either you or your horse, and its sharp horns make formidable weapons. While you dodge the maverick's charges your companion lassos its hind feet. You stretch it out between you, dismount, and bind its legs together. As further precaution you saw off the ends of its horns with the little hacksaw that is often carried on wild-cattle gathers. Lacking a saw, you simply hope you are more nimble than the outlaw.

A good steer buster can accomplish the feat alone. He forces the running maverick into hitting the rope so hard that it—and, he trusts, not his horse—is "busted," or slammed to the ground. When it gets up he busts it again. If the rope holds the creature will eventually have the wind knocked from it and will lie gasping long enough for the rider to jump from his pony and tie the wild one down.

Sometimes leaving it tied flat on the ground for a day or two will take the fight out of it. A surer way is to lash it by the horns to a tree. After it has fought the rope for twenty-four hours or so the roots of its horns grow sore. The rider then snubs the rope to his saddle and lets the renegade get in front of him. This gives it the notion it is escaping and it bolts. A few yanks on the rope tied to its sore horns may overcome the habit. Meanwhile, of course, it lunges at its captor from time to time. He beats it away with boots or quirt as best he can. If rider and horse are not exhausted

—if, indeed, they are not maimed—they have a fair chance of getting the renegade to camp.

The question arises: Why? Surely one lean, tough steer is not worth all that time and trouble? No, not if you consider only the butcher-shop value of its gristly meat. But a renegade can cause endless grief. A herd of cattle is as mean as its meanest member. One or two outlaws can stampede a whole bunch; they can turn a trail drive into a swirl of confusion. They lure away gentle cattle and turn them wild. Contemptuous of fences, they break into stackyards and cornfields. They devour quantities of grass better devoted to more profitable animals. The quickest way to dispose of them would be to hunt them down with high-powered rifles, and in days when renegades were more numerous than they are now this was sometimes done. But many cowboys prefer the rushing excitement and hot triumph of the chase. Some owners, like Al Scorup, add incentive by offering a bonus for every wild one brought in alive. After a little fattening the creature can be sold to an unsuspecting buyer for enough to repay at least part of its grazing bill.

Often distance and other factors make it impossible for a man to lead his captive home at the end of a rope. And since an outlaw won't willingly join a gentle herd and be driven, many devices have been developed for keeping it in check. One way is to lash a stout stick horizontally across the beast's horns (if these have not been sawed off). When the steer rushes into the brush the stick catches on branches, retarding it. Another method is to "sideline" the animal; that is, to tie a rope from one hind leg to its neck in such fashion that it cannot take more than a short step without falling.

Two wild ones may be yoked together, head to tail or neck to neck. They will bolt, but trouble begins when they get different ideas of direction, or when one rushes past the left side of a tree while its companion chooses the right. After a few such interruptions they settle to a walk. Perhaps the best method is to neck-yoke a big, heavy, gentle cow to the wild one. The tame animal soon wearies of the other's fits and starts and drags it where it ought to go. In the mesquite thickets of Texas the "brush poppers," as wild-cow hunters are known, have trained lead oxen to return home like carrier pigeons. When a wild animal is caught it is tied to a lead ox, and the pair are left to settle matters between them. In a day or so the patient ox shows up at the ranch with its bedraggled captive.

There may even be a mòral to the tale. The lead ox knows what it wants: the grain and warm stall, the rewards of effort waiting at home. The wild steer aims simply on whooshing off willy-nilly. In the end the fixed purpose is triumphant.

XIV   BUNCH GRASS

AS THE SUMMER SUN WARMED UP
there emerged from Paradox, like a grizzled bear from unhappy
hibernation, the lord and master of Beaver Park, old Ben Carson.
He was as timeless as the hills. The years tried to mark him,
turning his mustache gray and thinning his hair and teeth, but
when they met his tough hide they gave up. His face stayed apple-
shiny and brick-red, laced with little crimson veins. Across his
forehead was a sharp line where his hat had rested for three
quarters of a century. The unsunned portion of his head was
white, giving him an oddly variegated appearance whenever the
presence of women inside the house forced him to remove his neat
tan Stetson.

Ben lived so long we expected him to live forever. Indeed, he
did not merely die. He was killed not long after his eighty-second
birthday when his horse fell on him. We found him lying in the
brush, his handsome yellow-and-white dog crouched by his side,
so savage with heartbreak that we had to muzzle it and drag it
away before we could touch the old man's body.

During winter Ben lived in a state of near dormancy at one or
another of the West Paradox hay farms. Some people, seeing him
only when he was humped and stiff with cold, scorned him as
"another of them Pitchfork pensioners." My stepfather did nurse

along many crippled old wrecks. He manufactured small chores for them, found cabins they could batch in, and on occasion hid a sack of groceries or a pint of whisky under their beds while they thoughtfully stepped outside and pretended not to see him do it. But Ben Carson was not included in their numbers. Summer thawed him marvelously, and he supervised the fattening herds in Beaver Park with complete efficiency.

He was a walking refutation of all health theories. He used to say that when he first came to Colorado—he had run away from his Michigan home at the age of thirteen and drifted West with the frontier—he tried to keep the rest of the population sober by consuming all liquor as fast as it was made. "The state grew too big," he mourned, "and I couldn't quite keep up."

When he was seventy or so he decided to stop. He had gone to Placerville to load a shipment of steers on the train. With the rest of the cowboys he spent the night in the hamlet's creaky, yellow frame hotel. Bright and early in the morning he came downstairs for his usual eye opener. The cook was in the kitchen starting breakfast, and he asked her to join him.

What was an eye opener to Ben thoroughly floored the cook. "When I left her, her long hair had tumbled down, and she was stirrin' it up in the bread dough. The boys didn't get no breakfast and had to ride home hungry. I felt bad about it. I didn't want to starve anybody else, so I told myself to get on the wagon and stay there."

Stay he did, though I doubt if lack of breakfast had much to do with the decision. He was carrying two pint bottles of whisky in his saddle pockets. He pulled them out all of a sudden, cracked them together, threw the bottle necks away, and rode on, a complete teetotaler. He did not abandon tobacco, however. When his fingers grew too stiff for him to roll smokes he switched to "tailor-mades," consuming at least two packs a day.

He would not touch a fresh vegetable. An occasional can of tomatoes or peaches fortified him against scurvy, but what preserved the lining of his stomach I do not know. A pot of fiery Mexican chile con carne simmered always on his stove, his main course at breakfast, lunch, and dinner. Once a week he baked a huge batch of potatoes. These he left lying cold in his pantry, surrounded by mousetraps and quickly available for slicing and frying in inch-deep grease. He ate quantities of pancakes and bacon and, when it was obtainable, fresh beef. He liked his meat rare—"just stunned a little," he would say. He was particular about his coffee too. He brewed it by adding fresh grounds to the stale leftovers of the previous meal. This went on until the pot was chock-full; then he threw out the accumulated debris and started again. Once Mother, in all innocence, boiled out the vessel with lye, made Ben her most fragrant concoction, and waited for his delight. He took a sip, jerked back his head, spat, and bawled, "Who in hell washed the coffeepot?"

At last the day came when the rangers let us move the cattle to the forest. As the cool glow of an early-summer dawn limned the hills we pointed the first bunch of steers around the north side of the Cone toward Beaver Park. We could not take more than four or five hundred animals at a time. The rough, timber-bordered wagon road was steep and narrow. Where it pitched into the shadowy crossing over Beaver Canyon we had to split the herd into segments, each man working a portion of it along the dugway. The crowding cattle advanced as though they expected devastation around the next corner. They would leave the trail for the precipitous slopes where a horse could not follow. We scrambled after them afoot, falling, swearing, throwing rocks, and dancing in fits of rage. Before we were across our tempers were razor-thin. But not Ben's. He stayed serene as a snowbank, knowing well that man must suffer on his way to paradise.

Toward midafternoon we reached the pole gate opening onto our part of Montezuma National Forest. Sometimes a ranger would be there to count the animals in, sometimes not. Ben could be trusted to keep the tally the government wanted. He sat his horse by the gate as the steers streamed by, his finger pointing out each one, his lips registering it. When he reached a hundred he tied a knot in his bridle reins and began again. "One, two, three —hold it!" The animals were coming too fast. He spurred his horse into the flow, checked it. "Four, five, six . . ." Now the herd was through. We closed the gate while Ben penciled the total in a little black notebook. The rest of us turned back to the summer camp for another drive. Not Ben. His cabin, six or seven miles away in the heart of the park, had already been stocked by truck. He would stay there and meet us somewhere along the way as we brought up the next herd. He waved his lumpy old hand to us and jogged off through the knee-deep grass, singing to himself.

Strange to say, cattlemen for many years ignored the high-altitude grazing grounds of the Colorado mountains. The curly buffalo and grama grass on the plains east of the Rockies was limitless—or so it seemed. But by 1883 nearly five million head of longhorns had been driven north from Texas into Colorado alone. Sheep were coming; settlers were advancing with fences and plows. Suddenly the plains were no longer limitless, and the grim evil of overgrazing turned tens of thousands of acres into dusty desert.

To oversimplify a diffuse and haphazard process this is what happened:

Slowly the cattlemen were forced into the foothills. They tried to protect themselves as they went. The favorite stunt was to assert ownership over a strip of land along both banks of a stream and, by controlling the water, to hold an iron grip on the adjacent range. Forgetting their own overgrazing, they turned their rancor full flood on the overgrazing of sheep.

When held together in tight bands sheep do eat grass right down to the roots. What they don't eat they tramp out, and on flat land a poorly managed flock can do enormous damage. But, also, they will devour weeds and flowers a cow won't touch. On steep hillsides, where feed is sparse and cattle cannot forage well, sheep will thrive—provided the herder is active enough to keep stragglers from wandering away.

The herders had to be active. The cattlemen saw to that. They hated sheep anyhow: their habits, their smell, their stupidity. And since the cattlemen were established first in wealth and power, they were able to make their prejudices stick. The poor sheepherder, despised and rejected by men, was elbowed deep into the mountains.

He didn't suffer. He discovered those high grass pastures and brought back to market skin-bursting, fancy-priced herds of lambs. But what evidence is a "dirty, brainless, goddamn sheep" to cowmen? They continued to ignore the mountains. To be sure, there were some who penetrated the open valleys, and stock raising on a small scale was early introduced to the more accessible parks. But the majority of the cattle raisers wanted none of it. The growing season in the mountains was too short, they said. Steers wouldn't get over the effects of the long drive in before winter ran them out again. There were high-altitude diseases. Larkspur and other poisonous plants would kill off the animals like flies.

"It can't be done." Nothing can—until it has to be. Soon the squatter-crowded cattlemen were wild for cheap land too steep for damaging plows. And by now narrow-gauge railroads, built for the mining towns, enabled them to ship their steers to market without a long trail drive shrinking weight. Gradually they followed the sheepman back into the hills, hunting summer pasture.

And there they got a large surprise. They could no longer have things their own way.

After centuries of flagrant waste America had at last discovered the word conservation. The Federal government took over as national forests the timberlands, together with their grass and water. Henceforth these resources were to be used with tomorrow's needs and not today's quick profits in mind. To graze stock on the forests both sheep and cattle ranchers had to pay a fee and abide by many regulations concerning the quality and handling of their animals. They could put no greater numbers on the land than the rangers felt it would carry—and no fewer, for in theory the Federal policy demands use while preventing abuse. A lessee also had to have holdings outside the forest, to prove he was an established rancher and not some fly-by-night speculator hoping to get rich on a summer's gulp of government grass.

At first there were howls of indignation. Western politicians beat the drum of state's rights, insisting Washington had gone too far. Back home there were lawsuits, name callings, defiance, and letters to the editor. But gradually, as the beneficial results of the program became manifest, opposition simmered down. In the main even sufferers admit that the forest policy is correct in principle, despite some errors in application, and it provided invaluable groundwork for the more recent spread of government control to the entire public domain. The day of the "free" or "open" range is forever gone, and in spite of occasional bunk-house fumings over bits of local injustice, there is not a rancher who would willingly return to the former catch-as-catch-can ways of obtaining grass.

The minute our cattle reached Beaver Park they were turned loose and left alone. They were there for one purpose only: to stuff themselves roly-poly fat. The less they were disturbed, the better, and now a lone man could keep a lazy eye on herds it had taken half a dozen of us to gather.

It made a perfect job for old Ben Carson. He knew every foot of the park—so called because the center of it was a great, open meadow and all such natural clearings in the West are known as parks. He had come there the day the first of my stepfather's cattle were turned through the forestry gate, and every spring he led each new drive back to that gate. On the darkest night he could go to any rocky spire, any spring, any treacherous mudhole he chose to visit. He spotted the favorite haunt of almost every steer and knew where to find it when the fall roundup got under way. Whatever notion we might have developed about his being a pensioner was dispelled the day he was killed, and we had to ferret out for ourselves the thousand and one little things about the park that he had long ago stored in his memory.

He was truly happy nowhere else. He had a two-room log cabin built on the loveliest site any cabin ever occupied. From the front door he looked out on the steep, rusty-colored, snow-wrinkled face of the Dolores peaks, 13,600 feet high. Back of him was the Cone, only its snout visible above the timbered ridges. East, Main, and West Beaver creeks branch from Beaver Canyon toward these upthrusts like the ribs of a fan. Between their gentle valleys are countless brooklets, hillocks, and glades, rising from an elevation of some nine thousand feet to above timber line. High on the slopes are dusky forests of spruce and fir. Lower down are endless islands of slim, silvery-barked quaking aspens—"quakers," the cowboys call them. Their foliage is flat-stemmed, and the tiniest breath of air will twist the light-colored undersides of the leaves about until the whole tree seems to dance and twinkle.

The Utes have a legend about these delicious groves. In olden days, they say, the aspens were the proudest of trees. When the Great Spirit visited the earth and all other things shivered with anticipation the aspens remained stiff and unbending. The Spirit cursed them and ordered that henceforth they should tremble whenever eye was turned upon them.

You rarely see a lone aspen, for the male and female flowers are on separate trees. There are few females, and as a result young aspens seldom grow from seeds but sprout in dense stands from the underground roots of established parents. Slowly they crowd each other to death until only the strongest are left, and there is room between their cool, pungent-smelling trunks for lush growths of fern and grass. Dew-bright openings dot the groves, and the long swells of land along the creeks are often entirely bare of trees. Here the bunch grass grows, not in smooth carpets, but in myriad tall clumps, and when the wind hums down from the peaks the great, green swales billow and stir, catching the sunlight until the whole expanse seems to roll like water.

Ben's cabin stood at the edge of such a grove, overlooking such a meadow. He had a dark little kitchen where he could fry his vile food to his heart's content and a high-ceilinged bedroom large enough to hold the six or eight riders who descended on him for the fall roundup. Whenever Mother or my wife visited the park he hung a blanket across the room and in the mornings politely lay abed long past his usual 5:00 A.M. rising time, smoking countless cigarettes and stifling his thunderous belches. No one would have blamed him for hurrying outside when the light first came, however. The flaming sunrises that leaped over the misty peaks were indescribable.

Surrounding the cabin was a square-mile holding pasture, where we let the cattle gorge for a week or two before shipping them to market in the fall. Otherwise the meadow was little used. Mountain flowers seeded and reseeded. Armies of mariposa lilies swayed on their slender stems. Solid banks of blue columbine, red slashes of honeysuckle, yellow asters, pale phlox, bluebells, harebells, and a hundred more strutted in an almost shameless rampage of color. Quietly munching them at the end of his picket rope stood an old twisted-face sorrel horse with a white nose. His name, because of his facial deformity, was Crook. Ben rode him to the horse pasture each morning to gather the cavy. Crook stayed alone so much that he became a hermit, and even when turned loose he fed by himself, disdaining the company of his kind.

He always knew how to find the other horses, however. One of the remuda was belled, but in the mornings this sly old beast and his fellow conspirators stayed perfectly still in the trees for fear they would be caught and ridden. Ringing bells or no, they could not fool Crook. He struck through the dewy grass at a keen trot, following their tracks with his nose to the ground like a dog, in a fever to round them up and get back to his perpetual eating. When the horses were discovered Ben bellowed at them with the most powerful vocal cords, activated by the most powerful lungs, ever heard by human ear. He sounded as if he meant to slay each one the moment he reached it, and on still mornings his horrible profanity was audible a full mile away—a fact which never entered his mind when women were about. He seemed to think that once he was out of sight behind a bush he was also out of hearing.

It was all bluster. Ben's instincts were kindly, and, like old Cy Orr, he never in his life abused a living creature. When stinging horseflies and deer flies were at their worst Ben rigged up suits of gunny sacks for his horses, cutting out eye holes and draping the unhandsome garments over their heads, chests, and withers. Gaudy-striped chipmunks ran all over his cabin and at mealtime snatched morsels of soggy bread from his fingers. Ben was even well disposed toward people. Once he saw Mother trying to wash some clothes in his tin hand basin. He eyed her thoughtfully, and the next time she visited the park he presented her with a washtub and an ironing board. "Ma'am," he said, "I bought these for your comfort."

Beaver Park was divided into two sections. The upper, much the larger, was kept empty until midsummer, for the forestry service wanted the slowly maturing high-altitude grass to become well established before cattle began tramping on it. While our herds marked time in the lower section we did our chores, and in this Ben needed help.

First there was drift fence to fix, log-built miles of it running along the topmost ridges that marked the boundaries of our range. Winter played havoc with them. Falling limbs and falling trees each season smashed several panels flat. Now fence repair is any cowboy's pet peeve. We gave it only a lick and a promise, heaping branches and brush into the holes, creating a meretricious camouflage that looked far more effective than it was. A contented steer wasn't likely to force the issue, and we got away with the patchwork until the fence dwindled to a string of bramble piles, and the entire barrier had to be rebuilt.

Also, there were lumps of rock salt to haul out, either in a wagon or on Crook's resentful back, to spots carefully designated by the ranger. During the heat of the day, when flies were bad, the animals swarmed by hundreds to these licks for a taste of salt. Then, unfortunately, they stayed there, switching their tails in gregarious solemnity until evening's coolness drove away the stinging insects and the animals straggled back to their grazing.

This bunching of cattle to fight flies is one drawback to high-altitude grazing. Ben, with a pantheistic sort of philosophy that saw good in all natural things, said the pests were necessary to suck "bad blood" out of the cattle. This is nonsense, and even if it were true both the steers and the ranchers would have accepted a little more "bad blood" in return for fewer flies. Luckily the cold rains and nights of early fall killed off the insects, and during their last weeks in the mountains the cattle could feed undisturbed.

Another trouble was "poison," the hated name applied to larkspur, a beautiful blue-flowered plant that grows, in some sections of the park, as tall as a cow's back. The whole plant, roots in particular, will kill cattle (but not grown sheep), and it is especially virulent when the leaves are wet from dew or rain. Its evil propensities diminish after the blossoms form, and much of its danger can be avoided by turning the animals onto the range after the flowers appear, deep blue jewels in the damp hollows.

The active ingredient in larkspur is delphinin, paralytic to heart and respiration. The afflicted animal starts to stagger and slobber. It pitches onto its nose; convulsions seize it. There are pharmaceutical antidotes, but cowboys seldom have the necessary drugs and hypodermic needles in their pockets. The best you can do is turn the animal's head uphill, so it can breathe more easily, and puncture its belly with your pocketknife if it is badly bloated.

In most cases, of course, you don't see the poisoning occur. Your first intimation is a ripe, sickening smell wafted to your nostrils as you ride along the trail. Following the odor to its source, you find a putrefying corpse. You had hoped it was a wild animal, but generally it is domestic. Sadly you note its brand, sex, and age in your record book and ride on.

Keenest corpse smeller between the Cone and Placerville was Slim Hawley, government trapper. He always rode with his long nose pointed toward the wind, and he could detect the faintest stench of death through forty acres of flowers. Predatory animals visit carrion, and a dead cow made a fine location for Slim's traps. He was a superb woodsman, soft and deliberate of speech. When he hunkered on his heels with his battered old hat pushed back on his thick shock of graying hair he looked like an embodiment of all wisdom and goodness. But he was an anatomical lie. His skills were with things rather than with thoughts, and beneath his admirable exterior he had the cruelest nature I have ever known.

His business was killing. Several bears and many coyotes roamed about the Cone and the Dolores peaks. They were hated with unreasoning prejudice. Their movements coincided somewhat with those of domestic flocks; they did kill a few sheep and an occasional weak cow. These facts, plus man's native antipathy toward all large carnivores, turned every rancher's hand against them.

A coyote's appearance adds to its disfavor. In summer its coat is apt to look mangy, and when detected it slinks off into the brush with its tail between its legs. The hangdog mannerisms have given coyotes a reputation for cowardice, though they are no more abject than any wild creature yielding the field to an all-powerful enemy.

Rabbits, prairie dogs, ground squirrels, grasshoppers, beetles, and other small prey are their normal food. And coyotes are one of few animals who have learned the art of co-operation. One will lie in ambush while his partner runs a rabbit toward him. He seizes the bunny as it rushes past, and they share the feast together. In winter a hungry pack will once in a great while trap a young steer floundering in deep snow and cut it down. They will attack straggling sheep; and a rare coyote, like a rare collie dog, will on occasion develop a blood lust, killing several lambs in a single night for sheer sport. Such individuals must, of course, be eliminated, but I believe the grass which the average coyotes save by putting a check on foraging rodents and insects far outweighs the value of the stock they harm. It is whistling in the wind to say so, however. Most ranchers remain adamant in their determination to exterminate "every one of the danged varmints that walks." When they kill one they often hang its body to a fence as "warnin' to the others"!

Bears, despite their greater size, do less damage than coyotes. They feed principally on berries, insects, roots, and small rodents they dig out of dead logs and rock piles. They vastly prefer carrion to fresh meat and so cause trouble for themselves. They leave plain tracks as they gobble up a dead animal, and stockmen jump to the conclusion that bears did the killing. To be sure, a bear now and then develops a taste for mutton, but this can in part be blamed on herders who have let some sick old ewe wander off to die, easy prey for any predator. The ewe is killed; the herder forgets it would have died anyhow and sends out a frantic call for the government trapper. Admittedly there are grounds for fear. Sharp in every sheepman's mind are stories, usually exaggerated, about a berserk bear charging into a flock, killing fifteen or twenty animals and stampeding the rest all over the countryside.

Out come rifles, dogs, and traps. During a single month sixteen bears were killed near the summer camp in vengeance for seven or eight sheep. The Mexican herders enjoyed the fruits of the chase. They love bear steak and had a field day rendering out lard, which they use for many purposes—cooking, as salve for rheumatic joints, boot grease, and for hairdressing. Still, the damage to the sheep was demonstrably the work of a single individual, and there is a Nazi-like sound in the statement that since the real culprit would be hard (but not impossible) to find, *all* bears should be executed.

Slim Hawley was our executioner, legally hired. He was supposed to exercise restraint in his activities, but since sheep surrounded Beaver Park on all sides, he had no trouble manufacturing excuses for himself. He did his work well. He knew that coyotes, like dogs, go to posts and bushes and leave their calling cards. Accordingly, he would capture a live coyote, keep it in a tin kennel, collect its urine and droppings, add extracts from the genital organs of a female dog in heat, stir in secret compounds of his own invention, and thus create a ghastly potion that would batter down the caution of every coyote in sniffing distance. He would sprinkle a few drops of this on a bush and ride on. That night a socially inclined coyote would come to investigate. A cunningly placed trap under the bush did the rest.

But coyotes were small game. Slim's ambition ran to bears. Whenever he found a "bear tree" he stood in rapt contemplation, reading all sorts of things into it. Bears have an odd habit of picking out a particular tree, rearing on their hind legs, and clawing its trunk as high as they can reach. Slim insisted that the biggest bear in the neighborhood used the bark as a threatening letter, warning all others to gauge his size by his reach and to decamp. This ignored the obvious fact that little and medium-sized bears regularly clawed the same tree, either in foolish defiance or perhaps just to stretch their muscles. So far as I know, this ursine custom has never been satisfactorily explained.

Slim told many a tale about the animals. He claimed that when one wanted to descend a hill in a hurry it put its head between its forelegs and somersaulted down like a hoop, gaining more speed this way than through its ordinary lumbering methods of locomotion. Slim's adventures were equally remarkable. Late one spring he wriggled into a bears' den despite the fact that tracks outside indicated the hibernation period was ending. There he found an old she-bear and two yearlings in restless sleep and dispatched them with a hatchet. On another occasion he roped a full-grown male, casting the lariat over the limb of a tree. The bear charged; Slim wheeled his horse and raced away. The tree limb acted as a gallows frame. Suddenly the bear was hoisted into the air and hung by the neck until dead.

It is possible that these exploits are true. Slim had the strength, nimbleness, and courage to do them. He was indeed a bully, and bullies are supposed to be cowards, but there was not one grain of timidity in Slim Hawley's make-up.

He used poison at times, impregnating carrion and bait with strychnine. This killed not only bears and coyotes but also large numbers of small animals and birds. And it did not suit Slim's vicious need for direct action. He wanted his animals in a trap, alive and fighting. When he caught one he cut a long willow switch and, whooping with delight, whipped the animal until it lunged at him in snarling fury. The trap was not staked down hard and fast but chained to a heavy log toggle. The bear or coyote could drag the toggle about enough "to make things sporting." And so the game went on until the victim was reduced to whimpering impotence or Slim grew weary and finished matters with his revolver.

Slim Hawley was not typical. Most trappers are honest men, doing what trapping has to be done for pelts or stock protection as humanely as they can. Slim was an aberration, a sadist to the soles of his boots. I wish I could report that some animal caught up with him during one of his playful moods, but none did. He

enjoyed considerable success, and when he was removed as
government trapper he opened a very efficient packing service,
carrying on his hunting as a mere diversion.

Other visitors more cheerful than Slim occasionally stopped
at the Beaver Park cabin: fishermen, campers, and picnickers.
And there were two neighbors. The ranger station was three miles
away, but the supervisor's territory stretched far beyond the park,
and he was frequently gone. Nearer at hand and always ready for
one of the rummy games Ben dearly loved was the husky-voiced
ditch rider who looked after the long canal that tapped the
park's icy streams and whisked their water to Norwood, thirty
miles away.

These diversions paling, Ben rode fifteen miles over Fish Creek
Divide and dropped down into the thick forests and alpine
meadows along the headwaters of the Dolores River. Here stood
the dead mining town of Dunton. Once four or five hundred
people had lived there, but with the dearth of the mines the
population dwindled until less than a dozen persons remained.
Among them was a family of Italians who owned the local hot
springs and "hotel," a decrepit frame building equipped with a
few thin mattresses and sagging iron bedsteads full of piercing
shrieks.

Originally the hot springs fed a cement tank about eight feet
square and chest deep, roofed over by a windowless cabin of
logs. Later the owners built a crude little outdoor swimming
pool, but Ben disdained the improvement. He always went to the
cabined tank and stripped naked in the cramped closet that
served as dressing room. The mineral springs smelled like rotten
eggs; steam curled up from the dark water. Grunting and
snorting, the old man descended inch by inch into the blistering
depths, steadying himself by a rope hanging from the low ceiling.
There he sweat and stewed for hours on end. When he emerged
he was boiled to staggering, groggy incoherence. But the next

morning he would prance about "fresh as a yearlin' rooster. Yes sir, there's nothin' like that place for fryin' the pizens out of a man."

There also lived in Dunton a blind youth seventeen or eighteen years old who, during winter, attended school in Colorado Springs and there learned music. Now and then we prevailed on him to play the piano for us. The only instrument available stood in the abandoned, dusty, dilapidated Miner's Hall. The boy kept the instrument tuned, and local residents used it for their infrequent dances. As evening darkened we would go into the vast, empty old shell of a building and sit on the creaky chairs lining its storm-stained walls. The boy would come in with his mother or sister, ignoring their arms and tapping his way with the assurance of familiarity to the scarred upright piano.

I have no idea how good his technique was. But as he waked the yellowed keys, his audience two cowboys and three or four relics of a dead mining town, with a kerosene lamp flickering in one corner of that bare vault where long ago so many feet had danced and voices laughed, he achieved a poignancy that melted all self-consciousness and carried us—I don't know where. He always finished with the "Moonlight Sonata." Ben didn't know the name of the piece, who had written it, or what it was about. Yet somewhere in the eighty years that lay behind him it found and struck a terrible chord, and the old man sobbed as though nis heart would break.

I never heard the blind boy play in Dunton without remembering another piano episode that occurred when the first homesteaders were pushing into Dove Creek. A man and a woman, obviously foreign to local ways, got off the narrow-gauge railroad at the town of Dolores and hired a wagon to take them to the creek. They seldom spoke, and all anyone learned of them was that they had acquired, sight unseen, a cabin and a piece of land. Their luggage consisted of a small trunk, a suitcase, a box or two —and a baby grand piano. The wagon driver and his helpers

—he told us all this years later—had to remove the instrument's legs and struggle mightily to load it, while the couple hovered anxiously about to see that the satiny finish was not marred.

The three of them then climbed on the wagon seat. All one raw spring day they rode. Melting snow had turned the adobe earth to a quagmire. The horses played out, and they were still far from their destination. Sullen clouds banked the sky, and the feel of rain was in the air.

"We'll have to stop," the driver said.

The couple looked blankly about at the sage and the mud and the piñons. "How will we shelter the piano?"

"There's a cowboy line cabin up the draw yonder. 'Tain't used this time o' year, but the door is open an' it's got food. We'll leave the piany there until the roads dry. Horses can't pull it through this mud."

Reluctantly the couple agreed. After great effort the three of them tugged the legless piano into the flimsy plank shack, where it was set up on four wooden boxes. Without words they went to bed on the straw-tick mattresses in the double-decker bunks and without words departed the next morning.

It must have been that evening that Mike and Long Tom stopped by the cabin. Long Tom was a taciturn rider who a year or so before had drifted into Paradox from no one knew where. Cold and wet and hungry, Mike and he put their mounts in the barn and walked to the cabin. In the door Long Tom froze dead. So did Mike. Finding a grand piano in a one-room shanty miles from other habitation is a surprise at any time; in a country where the only musical instruments were cheap fiddles and mouth organs the jolt had double impact.

But something more than surprise was working on Long Tom's face. He stood so still, so pale, that Mike thought he was sick. Suddenly he lifted his hands and seemed bewildered to find buckskin gloves on them. He pulled them off and rubbed his fingers.

"God in heaven!" he whispered. "A piano!"

He went to it, pulled up a box, and sat down. For a long time he just looked. Then slowly, "like he was scared," Mike said, he began to play. He never noticed Mike cook dinner, never answered when called to the table. Until long past midnight he played and at last tumbled exhausted into one of the bunks. When Mike awoke the next morning Long Tom had saddled up and gone, riding off through the rainy dawn into a future as trackless as his past. We never saw him again.

Summer slipped by. With an abrupt flash fall hit the hills. By mid-September the aspen forests were glinting masses of gold. Stray tongues of them ran like yellow threads through the somber verdure of the evergreens. Snow dusted the peaks, and in the morning cellophane-thin panes of ice shone on every puddle. The sleek yearlings drifted down from the higher meadows, gorging on the cured grass until "their pants sure stretched tight."

By November the snow has reached into the park itself. Out into the forest with the brittle dawn goes the roundup crew, shivering under heavy Mackinaws. It is the hour of fulfillment. The few cows, calves, and poorer steers that are not to be shipped are strung out in a thin little line and headed down-country, back over the long trail to the winter range. The others are pointed toward the loading pens at Placerville.

Oh, so slowly, so gently now! They are not overheated, not run a step that might shrink weight. Two days they spend on a trip which, with pushing, they could make in one. At the Placerville corrals the slat-sided, narrow-gauge stockcars are waiting, chutes ready. Confused, bewildered, the yearlings are driven aboard. Here is where the title "cowpuncher" originated—a yard employee who prodded cattle through the chutes with a pole. Range workers were dignified as "riders" or "cowboys," and even after years of magazine stories and movies they are reluctant to accept the degrading name "puncher."

It is midnight before the loading is finished. The headlight of the lead locomotive cuts a yellow swath through the snowy night. Steam hisses; couplings bang. The three diminutive engines, roaring with a noise befitting monsters twice their size, creep up the winding canyon, lifting their twenty or thirty little cars over the backbone of the Rockies on the long haul to the cattle marts in Denver. The weary workers, stamping their feet and blowing on their fingers, stumble to the thick beefsteaks waiting in the hotel, to the raw whisky in the bars. There will be headaches tomorrow on the ride back to Beaver Park for another shipment, and another. And then, icily sober again, down the road to the rimrock, to the low country.

Winter has come.

XV   CRAZY AS A SHEEPHERDER

SHEEP CANNOT BE AVOIDED ON THE
Western ranges. They are more numerous today in Colorado than
cattle. Sooner or later every cowboy comes up against them, no
longer as enemies, necessarily, but often as creatures he must be
able to handle. All of us on different occasions spent many a night
in sheep camps between Paradox and the high country, and
there we learned that this trade, too, has its fine, rich moments
and its black disappointments.

On its face, however, sheepherding is plain misery:

Wintertime. Out on the bleak Wyoming prairie a canvas-
covered wagon, looking like the old Conestoga schooners of
pioneer fame, hunches on a snow-cased hill, its chimney smoke
streaking across a cold yellow sunset. A dirty gray mass of sheep
huddles near by, blatting hungrily. A man walks around them,
headed for the only home he knows, his sheepskin collar turned
against the wind. He climbs into the wagon. The door bangs shut
behind him. An empty sound in an empty world.

"Good God," a person thinks, "only a half-wit would live
like that!"

Such is the common assumption. A standard simile throughout
the stock-raising West is, "crazy as a sheepherder"—never shep-
herd; that word apparently has too idyllic a connotation. Every-

where the same old yarns are told about them. One perennial favorite says that three herders happened into town at the same time. They sat on the steps of the store, munching apples and talking earnestly. But not to each other, not even to the apples. To themselves. And then there's the tale about the poor fellow who died of exhaustion while trying to make his bed—he couldn't figure out the long way of a square blanket.

If the impact of environment is enough to drive a man insane, then those stories would seem to be well founded. For the impact of sheepherding is terrific. You can never, not for an instant throughout the year, escape it. From the minute—— But let's go back to that lonely wagon on the prairie and take a look.

The quarters are not as unbearable as they appear. The bed is off the ground; the canvas reflects the heat of the roaring sheet-iron stove. The wagon sides contain built-in cupboards for food, dishes, clothes, and books—except for the Mexicans, many herders do a surprising amount of reading. When the camp mover takes the equipment to new grazing grounds, as he does every few days, he simply hitches a team to the wagon and goes, while the herder follows with the sheep, unworried about packing up— until the wagon tips over in an arroyo, which always happens sooner or later.

Things are more complicated if the herder lives in a tent, as he must in the mesa lands of Colorado and Utah, or wherever the terrain is too rough for wagons. Every four or five days his entire household is put on muleback and relocated. He can't accumulate any little comforts; traveling light is too important. He sleeps on the frozen earth. Heaps of dirt banked around the edges of the canvas are the only means of keeping drafts out and heat in.

Whether his home is wagon or tent, the herder spends little time in it. The sheep are up at dawn, hungry and on the move for the thin feed—the cured rice grass, shad scale, even the bitter sagebrush tips—of the winter range. Their guardian must make sure they move together, where he can keep an eye on them. For a sheep is the most helpless of animals. Its only teeth are grinders far back in its upper jaw, useless for fighting. It does not have fleetness enough to run from attack, or sufficient size and endurance to buck a storm or flooded gully. Whatever chance at life it has, the herder gives it.

At nights, especially when the moon shines and you think you can see frost dancing in the air, the coyotes are bold. Their yap-yapping trembles over the hills—a sort of sarcastic laugh, it sounds—but you don't worry so long as they are noisy. Then they fall silent. Your wise, shaggy dog, lying by the tent entrance, lifts his head and growls. A frightened bleat runs through the bedded herd. You grab a rifle and .pile out into the cold. You shoot to frighten the marauders away. Sometimes you set off firecrackers. The echoes fade, and it grows terribly still. You listen until you are shivering too hard to hear and go back to bed.

The utmost vigilance isn't always enough. One morning you find several carcasses near the bed ground. This is the work of a killer coyote. He has cut a bunch of ewes from the main herd, struck one down, eaten her warm liver, and raced after the others, killing for the sheer lust of it. A furious desire to hunt him down rises in your throat, but you cannot leave the herd. When the camp mover comes you send for the government trapper.

The man is apt to use more poison than traps. All the carrion he finds he shoots full of strychnine, working on a canvas spread from horseback before he dismounts and wearing canvas gloves so as to leave no warning scent. The coyotes are wily, but they are hungry too; the poison gets a lot of them.

You keep an eye on your dog, but one afternoon he wanders off and does not come back for supper. You stay up until midnight, whistling and calling. The next morning he is outside the tent, dead, frozen hard. You can see where he has dragged himself through the snow, trying to get back on the job. You dig a grave, roll him in, and go on after the herd. A few days later the camp mover brings you another pup, full of ambition and mischief.

Training him lightens the monotony. But you don't forget; you don't think any better of poisoning, even when the trapper boasts that he got six coyotes last week and the killer visits you no more.

Always you watch the horizon, smell the wind, study the way birds fly, drawing on every bit of lore and superstition you have gleaned for predicting storms. When dawn comes with that still, steel-gray look you keep the sheep in the trees or behind a protecting ridge. A blizzard catching you in the open can be catastrophic. No sheep will face wind-driven snow. They turn and drift before it, knowing only fear and the need to escape this thing they cannot fight. They pile blindly into arroyos, one on top the other, until there is a bridge of dead for the living to cross. They jam into dead-end pockets, crushing each other, smothering each other.

You drift with them, cursing them, fighting them, hating them, doing your best to save them. Finally you get them stopped in a sheltered basin, build a fire with numbed fingers, and hunker down to wait out the storm. Your belly is hollow; you are cold and lonely. You know the boss will say plenty, not about the animals you have saved, but about the ones you lost. . . . At last the wind feathers out. You start working the listless herd back toward the bed ground. There are drifts to buck now, worries about the feed buried deep under this new fall. The nights seem longer. Your thoughts turn in on yourself, and that is not so good. . . .

But it ends. Spring is on the way. You can smell it in the thawing earth, hear it in the soft whistle of bluebirds, come suddenly from you don't know where. You feel it in the new resiliency of willow shoots, see it in the swelling abdomens of the ewes. Even the camp mover softens into a smile now and then. You begin to step livelier. You need to; the hardest, dirtiest part of your work lies ahead.

Shearing comes first. Here the machine age has intruded. Smaller outfits own or hire ancient automobiles which can move from camp to camp, where their engines furnish power for mechanical clippers not unlike, except in size, the ones used by a town barber. Larger operators have a regular shearing "factory": a long frame shed roofed with corrugated iron and surrounded by a maze of corrals. From it rises a whir like a hundred egg beaters working at once. Toward it a dozen herds creep, traveling on schedules timed to the hour, though some have come half a hundred miles, three or four miles a day.

You ease your bunch along in turn. Through the trees you can see other sheep in the pens around the shed. Shorn of their mattress of wool, they appear different animals entirely. Their heads seem too big for their gaunt, ungainly bodies. Their hides have a bluish tinge, spotted here and there with blood where the hurrying shears have nipped too close.

You shiver in the raw wind, thinking how you would like to be turned out naked to the unpredictable mercies of the weather. For months the strange tyranny of man's economics has let you alone, and now it has found you out again. There is nothing you can do about it. You walk on, kicking at stones, angry without really understanding why. Protecting your sheep for the shearer and the butcher is part of your job, isn't it? The justification of all you've done and will keep on doing.

Generally the shearing is contracted to professionals who move from ranch to ranch. Piece payment, averaging twenty-five cents for a ewe, half a dollar for a big, husky ram. Their job folds on them with the season, and so they have developed astonishing skill. A good man can make twenty dollars a day.

Inside the shed a gasoline motor drives an overhead shaft, powering a line of a dozen or so clippers, one man to a clipper. Behind each worker is a small pen, kept filled with sheep. He reaches into it, seizes an animal by the hind leg, drags it out, wrestles it into a sitting position, and kneels by its left side, using his left hand to hold its underjaw.

The sheep lies helpless on the round of its rump, dumb terror in its yellow eyes. *Snip-snip-snip*. Along the neck and side from back to belly travel the shears. Sweat pours from the operator. This is work, holding a ninety-pound mutton with one hand while the other races against time. *Snip-snip-snip.* The fleece comes off in one unbroken greasy mass. The shearer—his hands are always debutante-soft from the lanolin in the wool—folds it with the clean hair inside and tosses it onto a conveyor belt running overhead. He pushes the shorn animal through a door in the outside wall, reaches back for another.

The conveyor belt dumps the fleece in a huge burlap bag taller than a man. A Mexican boy is in the bag, tramping the wool tight. When the sack is full it is removed for another. Its open end is laced and it is piled with a score more on a loading dock, waiting for the snorting trucks that will take it to the railroad, to the busy textile mills of New England. Great business, sheep raising. The rancher gets two cracks at the market, where other stock raisers get only one. Foolproof—on paper.

Next come the lambs. Your stomach begins to tighten as you think of all the things that can happen. Not enough feed on the lambing grounds. Not enough water. Or too much water: a cold rain, a late snow. Coyotes. Bears. Stampedes. One or all these things, striking when the newborn lambs are utterly helpless, can break an outfit overnight.

Breeding is controlled so that the lambs all arrive in the spring. When this mass motherhood is due you hurry to a protected spot. You split the herd up (you have helpers now), letting each bunch graze slowly along. Each day's and night's drop is left behind. As mother and child get acquainted (by smell first, by voice later) you put them with others until at last the herd is reassembled, double its former size—on paper again.

Actually it is an appalling event. You've had to drive nineteen hours a day to reach the lambing grounds. You marshal your forces and decide you'll have time for one good night's sleep before things start. Unutterably weary, you crawl into bed. An hour later you are up. The stork (two thousand storks for the average herd) never waits—and he's brought an icy fog with him.

You light your lantern and stumble off through the mist. You are a midwife now: straightening twisted heads, changing positions in case of breached presentations, delivering the stillborn. The drizzle is chilling the live lambs to death. The mother won't —can't—do anything to help. You take the feeblest to the tents, give them a warm bath, dry them, wrap them in sheets, feed them canned milk from a small-necked bottle with a rag tied over the mouth. You dare not keep one too long, for the ewe will forget its smell and refuse to own it. You hustle it back, though it still seems pitifully weak. You stand it up by a ewe. But you have made a mistake; she's not the mother. She butts the lamb flat. You try another. The same thing happens. You want to kill them all. They are butting back to death this frail little life you've struggled so to save. At last you find the right one. She snuffs the lamb over with maddening suspicion, then accepts it.

Sometimes a mother will refuse her child for no apparent reason. You resort to subterfuges to wake the maternal instinct: rub the lamb's head with the ewe's own milk, or drag its tail through her mouth. Sometimes you have to build a pen and lock them up together before she will decide this really is Junior after all.

Your opinion of a sheep's character sinks to the nadir. A ewe now and then doesn't even seem to know whether her lamb is born or not. Often she will get up before the event transpires and start looking around for what is not yet there. Old ewes or weak ewes with no milk will walk off and leave their young. Apologists say this is smartness; the ewe knows she can't raise her offspring and isn't going to wear herself out to no gain. But somehow you think she ought at least to try.

You'd think, too, that a ewe whose lamb is born dead would be willing to adopt one which has been orphaned. But no, she has to be tricked into it. You slip her dead lamb onto a canvas and, by a rope attached to the canvas, drag it off. The ewe associates this movement with the lamb and not with you, since you aren't touching it. She thinks it must be alive. She calls for it to come back. When it doesn't she runs after it, bleating and stamping the ground in anxious bewilderment.

You get the dead lamb out of sight, skin it quickly, and fasten the hide over an orphan. You take the orphan, thus disguised, back to the ewe. Now she is in a quandary. She snuffs the little thing over inch by inch while you watch and hold your breath. She walks away, the lamb tottering after her and blatting hungrily. She looks back. This does not seem to be her child. And yet—the smell is there. She emits a tentative rumbling noise, and you breathe again. (It is a strange noise, this sound of affection between sheep: a sort of deep grumble made well down in the throat without opening the mouth. It must be affection. Ewes talk so to their lambs; bucks to the ewes at mating time.)

The enforced parent is likely to remain doubtful for several days. But gradually the odors—particularly the tail odors—of the dead lamb and the live one intermingle until she can't detect one from the other. By the time the disguise has lost its potency and you take it away she is convinced.

When you reassemble the herd to move on each ewe has learned the voice of its lamb, and the lamb its mother's. It is their salvation. In the evening the sheep mill on the bed ground in indescribable confusion. The lambs gang up in companies along the edge of the herd, race back and forth, and suddenly spring high into the air in their glee at being alive. Gradually they grow hungry and begin to hunt their mothers. The din is terrific: thousands of throats, each calling for one particular object. It seems impossible they can mate. Yet out of the bedlam a lamb or ewe will pick the proper call. It starts running. Hundreds of others are also running every which way. Suddenly there is a quiet island in the turmoil. Lamb and ewe have joined. Down on his front knees goes the lamb, sucking greedily, his tail bobbing in ecstatic jerks.

Late spring blizzards are tragic now. The tiny lambs are helpless; the shorn ewes have no resistance to cold. Fortunately,
though dust-lashing winds are usual, there is little snow. But
sometimes it comes. One May a three-day storm howled down
from the San Juans, catching the herds moving toward the
forests near Mount Sneffels and Telluride. Half a thousand
blinded sheep, stampeding before it, piled into the water reser-
voir above the railway junction of Ridgeway and drowned. Other
herds were trapped on the main automobile highway between
Placerville and the top of Dallas Divide. When clear weather at
last came the tight-lipped herders threw corpses out of the road
into piles higher than a man's head, soaked them in kerosene, and
set them afire. . . .

On you go. The sheep must be dipped: prodded one by one
through a vat of foul creosote mixture which rids them of
parasites. The lambs must have their tails docked (cut off) and
be castrated. Brands must be painted on. And always feed and
water be found. Days and nights merge into a blur of sheep, dust,
smell, and noise.

Many sheep are ranged in one section throughout the year.
But more are moved tremendous distances with each shift of the
seasons—to the comparatively snow-free desert in winter; to the
high country, the fringes of timber line and above, in summer.
Every mountain is a focal point; Colorado, because of its
abundance of hills, draws hundreds and hundreds of thousands.
How many sheep are on the trail throughout the Western United
States each spring is hard to say. Government estimates indicate
close to twenty million head.

That many sheep eat a lot of grass. They are bound to encroach
on range claimed by someone else. In the old days of swift
expansion quarrels inevitably passed from violent words to violent
deeds, occasionally to open warfare that swept whole counties.

Here again the fights have been exaggerated in countless fiction
stories. Trouble was there, however. Even after Colorado became

a state in 1876 little attempt was made to extend the supervision of courts and law officers to the grazing lands. The country was thinly settled and deemed valueless except for pasturage. Here the range users ruled supreme; if controversy arose they settled it between themselves and to the devil with legal procedure.

The first move toward organization had come in 1872, when the proprietor of the Bull's Head Corral in Denver called a meeting of all agriculturists "to protect the interests alike of stockmen, ranchers, and farmers, and to harmonize whatever might be conflicting." The dice were loaded from the start. Cattlemen controlled the organization, and the farmers did not bother to show up and watch them pass resolutions for their own benefit. An attempt was actually made by the Colorado association and others to have Congress set aside as pasture land a thousand-mile stretch of continent between the one hundredth meridian, which passes through Kansas, and the Sierra Nevada Mountains of California! Farming was to be forbidden on these hundreds of millions of acres, and vast tracts were to be leased or sold to stockmen at a nominal sum. President Hayes himself told Congress that such a sweeping act would "be a source of profit to the United States, while at the same time *legalizing* the business of cattle raising." (The italics are mine.)

For a few years sheepmen were admitted as members of the Colorado Stock Growers Association, but antagonism between the groups soon flared hot, and the sheep raisers withdrew. Public sentiment favored cattle, and violence against sheep was blandly shrugged aside. Rewards were offered for the perpetrators, but there is not a single record of a man being arrested for molesting sheep. And molested they were. Near Pueblo, Colorado, eight hundred of a flock of sixteen hundred were killed with poisoned bran; other hundreds were clubbed to death or had their throats cut. A reward of three thousand dollars for information leading to the arrest of those responsible went begging. Goat Creek, near Beaver Park, received its name when several masked cowboys charged into a mixed herd of sheep and goats and stampeded several hundred animals to death over a high cliff.

Naturally the sheepmen fought back, often with success, for there was money to be made in the business, and its followers were by no means without influence or ability. On many occasions there was bloodshed and even death. After such a fracas both the cattle and sheep associations passed pious resolutions of "deep regret," but that did not solve the problem. Indeed, it was never solved until the "free" range was brought under outside control and the so-called "rights" of the competing factions were established by official supervision, first through the national forests and, more recently, over the rest of the public domain through the Taylor Grazing Act.

One of the first decrees of the grazing boards set up stock driveways for the herds of migrant sheep. The width of these driveways varies from many miles to as little, in places, as a few hundred yards, depending on the terrain and the lay of adjoining deeded land. Each herder naturally tries to reach his particular driveway ahead of other outfits. The early flocks grub out the grass; the laggards are often hard put to escape starvation. Some men (not you, of course) have been known to resort to such skulduggery as stealing supplies, destroying bridges, etc., to delay their rivals.

Sooner or later you stray onto some cattleman's range. You may do it innocently enough, but the cattleman never believes it. Up he rides, purple with rage. He no longer dares shoot you, but, nonetheless, he makes you squirm in spite of yourself. There is something of the old feudal lord-serf setup inherent in facing afoot an angry man on horseback; you can't help feeling you ought to doff your hat.

The cattleman roars at you to get those blankety-blank sheep out of there pronto, and a lot he cares that you have neither feed nor water to take them to. Your maddening sense of inferiority makes you sore. You've read enough magazines to know you should invite him down for a punch in the nose. Indeed, you consider it. But you don't act. If you do he'll sue your boss. Probably he will sue him anyhow. Since there are four or five court actions coming out of this trip at best, you swallow your pride and spend half the night fighting your herd off all that good grass to a bare dobe flat. It's things like this, rather than lambing troubles or blizzards, that make you resolve never to look at another sheep.

But you keep on and at last you reach the mountains. Tough herding now: thick brush, down timber, raging streams. A forest ranger generally shows you where you may establish bed grounds. You grumble only as a matter of principle, for you realize that a bed ground, with thousands of sheep jammed on it every night for a week, takes a terrible beating, and public policy demands restraint in its location. In the main the ranger is considerate. He may not give you that flat, lush meadow you've been eying by the trout stream, but if possible he will pick a spot that's not too steep, that has some open ground with firewood and water near by and a few tall, straight aspens you can cut down and hollow out for troughs to hold the salt crystals you feed the sheep.

Tourists—you meet a lot of them during the summer: fishermen, mountain climbers, campers—wonder how you can be sure you haven't lost some of your sheep in the tumbled hills. You can't count them all each day to check, of course. But you know, anyhow, and it is not so mysterious as it seems. Sheep are clannish. As a herd feeds it breaks up into subherds, each with a leader. Goats make good leaders, so you use a few of them. Also, you bell the aggressive wethers. (You soon get to know the sound of these bells and can tell with surprising accuracy whether your sheep are feeding or resting or growing nervous and where, though to all outward appearances you are snoozing under a bush.) In addition you spot markers in each clan: black or spotted sheep. You can count these animals—the goats, the bell-wethers, the markers—as you drive the herd to the bed ground at night. If one of them is gone it is a cinch that others have strayed with it, and you set out to track them down.

Higher and higher you go, onto range too rough and too near the peak tops for even cattle to follow. Now you are in the wide green basins above timber line. Splintered, snow-creased peaks rear on every hand. It is the climax of your year. Soon trouble will start again: shoving back down the mountain, separating the terrified lambs from their mothers, driving them to the loading pens at the railroad, and betraying them with Judas goats into the cars that will take them to the slaughterhouses. Then winter again. But you don't think about that now. The nights are crisp, star-hung, the days an indolent delight. Everything is open, everything clear. From yonder pinnacle you can see your whole fattening flock without stirring. You lie on a warm grass bank, chewing a flower stem and dreaming with the clouds.

In such moments you are apt to kid yourself. You like to think that the freedom of these clouds and these mountains is your freedom too. Actually, of course, you are shackled to your job as no other wage earner is to his. Some states even have laws making it a penitentiary offense for a herder to leave his band without notice. You can't so much as set your own pace in moving from spot to spot. You've got to be at the next bed ground when the camp mover and his pack train arrive or you will go hungry and shelterless.

Yet there is something to the craft. The strange assortment of men in it indicates that. College graduates, unlettered Mexicans, engineers, writers, farmers' sons, paroled convicts, merchants—it seems no sheepherder ever started life as one. Perhaps they chose the profession as an escape from the spirit-bruising facts of the modern world. It is not a complete flight, however. The job takes too much courage and resourcefulness, too much faith and responsibility. No one makes decisions for you when trouble strikes; no one fights your fights. Come what may, it is squarely in your own two hands.

Maybe that is the freedom of it. You have been the slave of this flock, but you have been its god too. You have made the weak strong, have led the timid and the faltering. Only sheep, to be sure, but part of creation. Your creation. And you have done it alone. Aloneness is your habit and your reliance.

Are you crazy? You really don't know. Nor do you care. Because whatever else you may or may not be, you're still a damn good sheepherder.

XVI CANYON CAMP

DEEP IN THE LOWER SAN MIGUEL
Canyon, four miles above its junction with the Dolores River, was
the headquarters camp of the cow-and-calf range. The establishment was called the Club Ranch, not because it was a chummy
gathering place but because the founder's brand had been an ace
of clubs. It was ten miles from the nearest neighbor's, twenty-two
from an electric light, more than a hundred from a competent
doctor. Nonetheless, housekeeping facilities for a woman with a
baby not yet old enough to walk were more extensive there than
in Paradox. Consoled by the purchase of a battery-powered radio,
Martha loaded the car with a first-aid kit and several books on
"what to do until the doctor comes." Away we went.

Our post office was in the "town" of Naturita. Once it had
been a brawny camp abustle with radium miners and ore wagons,
but after the mines closed fire, vandalism, and decay left little
to admire. We picked up the mail from a postmistress who looked
as ruined as the town and drove on down the canyon, careening
along more than twenty miles of narrow dirt road that nowhere
contained a straight stretch a hundred yards long. It twisted
around mammoth boulders, stood on its nose to drop into dry
gulches, looped crazily out of them. Here it overhung the river;
there it retreated far back into the rocks to avoid impassable cliffs.
A good-weather trip to Naturita took almost two hours, and

during storms travel was impossible. Martha got a fresh grip on her first-aid kit and endeavored to find solace in the scenery.

That, too, was austere. The San Miguel River, born so beautifully in the mountains near Telluride, had become a miserable thing, gray with tailings from the gold mills and charged with alkali by the desert barrancas emptying into it. On one side the land rose swiftly to the aspen-crowned skull of Uncompahgre Plateau. On the other side was the piñon-covered, harshly eroded sandstone hogback that separates the canyon from Paradox Valley. These upthrusts can be rarely glimpsed from the road, however. Engulfed in the canyon, we saw only the twisting river and the steep tan hillsides, littered with dun-colored boulders and grubby juniper trees.

Once the land had not been empty. The river, rising in the auriferous San Juans, for untold centuries washed a burden of fine-grained gold toward the sea. Part of the metal lodged in crevices in the stream bed; then, as the water changed course and dug deeper, the old channel was left high and dry on gravelly, tierlike benches. Placer miners soon discovered these "high bars" and went eagerly to work, scraping off the accumulation of detritus from the gold-bearing sands and transporting worthy gravel by wagons, chutes, and wheelbarrows to the river edge, where it could be washed in a variety of placer machines.

One high bench held forth seductive promise. It was too extensive to be covered by hand operations, but engineers swore that hydraulic mining would uncover a fortune. This involved difficulties. The giant nozzle of a hydraulic hose requires tremendous water pressure, and the only source of water, the river, was four or five hundred feet below the bench, locked between perpendicular walls of dusky red sandstone. Pumps could not supply sufficient volume. A ditch carrying sixty or seventy miner's feet of water was the only solution, but there was no flat land in which the canal could be dug. "Never mind," said the engineers. "We'll hang a wooden flume along the cliff face!"

It was a staggering piece of hopefulness. Surveyors laying the gradient went eight or nine miles upstream, past the Club Ranch to a point where the cliffs fell away and the river could be reached by blasting a tunnel through an obstructing ridge of rock. From this tunnel workers dug more than a mile of ditch toward the bench. And then they hit the cliffs. There they started constructing a flume box something more than three feet wide and two feet deep.

Suitable lumber was not available in the warped cedar forests and groves of soft cottonwoods lining the canyon. Breakneck roads had to be gouged through the rims to stands of yellow pine in the mountains. Several wagons and horses were smashed to bits and one or two slow-jumping drivers killed when freight vehicles broke out of control and plunged over the grades. But lumber was a minor problem compared with hanging that flume in mid-air. Workers had to be lowered as much as two hundred feet down the cliff on movable scaffolds. Lines of heavy braces, numerous as porcupine quills, were set into the rock and mile after mile of flume box laid on them. In places the cliffs bulged over the river. One old-timer deemed trustworthy by the neighborhood told me with straight face that he had fallen a hundred and fifty feet from his scaffold, landed in a growth of young willows on the side of the river opposite the flume—and suffered no worse hurt than a broken wrist! I am inclined to doubt him myself, but certainly the labor that went into stringing that wooden monstrosity across seven miles of vertical precipice makes it one of the herculean, man-killing—and completely forgotten—feats of Colorado history.

It was a total failure. Why, I do not know. The two or three local residents remaining who saw the conduit built are vague in their accounts. They claim the job cost more than a million dollars, and the mere sight of the flume lends credence to the figure. Water was run through it just once. The thing worked, but some miscalculation occurred at the receiving end, and the entire project went glimmering. It is said that the head engineer promptly blew out his brains.

One tiny bit of fruit the effort bore. We used the abandoned ditch at its upper end to bring water to the Club Ranch's hayfields. Wood for our barn and outbuildings and furniture, including the desk on which I write these words, was taken from the edges of the structure. But only birds have touched its central portion; no man has felt inclined to shinny down two hundred feet of rope to salvage a two-by-four, and enough rotted lumber to have built an entire city hangs uselessly there in space.

This and other failures dampened the ardor of would-be investors. The canyon gold was too dispersed and fine to be recovered in commercial quantities, and organized placer mining faded from the picture. Still, gold has a charm no other thing possesses. A handful of prospectors kept grubbing away at the high gravel bars. They drifted downstream each winter when snow drove them out of the mountains and took up residence in unused shacks or riverbank caves, weather-stripping the cave entrances with patchwork walls of discarded plank and canvas. Most of the prospectors were wild, shy hermits, avoiding human contact and needing only the meagerest returns from their labor to exist.

Other mining activities were more profitable. All around the ranch were crumbling mementos of the boom days ushered in by the discovery of carnotite ore bearing uranium. Surely one of those collapsing old mines should have a memorial tablet in its walls, for from somewhere in this district came ores on which Pierre and Marie Curie experimented while isolating radium. Also, from this gaunt countryside came the gram of radium that the women of America presented to Mme. Curie in token of the world's appreciation, and for many years western Montrose County was the world's principal source of the magic mineral.

At first the mining was carried on in haphazard fashion by scattered groups of dusty men. Then along came Joe and Mike Flannery, cherub-faced Pittsburghers from a family of undertakers. Environment must have molded them more than heredity. Starting with donkey trains and later building breathless roads to such spots as could be reached by road at all, they helped link the widespread efforts together, built central reduction works, and in general laid foundations on which big business could stand with efficiency. Then in the 1920s cheaper foreign sources knocked out the underpinnings of Colorado ore. Directly across from the Club Ranch's upper alfalfa field a shattered red hulk leaned against the canyon wall, its stinking acid baths and roasting furnaces apparently petrified forever.

But the giant was sleeping, not dead. Hitler's armies started to march in Europe, and the clank of hard steel reached into the desert. Vanadium hardens steel. It gives strong fiber to alloys for boiler plates, gun shields, and heavy forgings; it increases the red-hardness on the cutting edges of machine tools working at high speed. And vanadium as well as uranium can be extracted from carnotite. Desperate men raced back to the ruins. New monsters belch fire and smoke. Today the city of Uravan, housing a thousand workers, their families, and their suppliers, stands on part of the Club Ranch fields. Overnight almost it sprouted, and the incomprehensibility of it will not leave me, for Martha and I learned to live there in the dead period between two eras. Then no spot could have seemed farther removed from the turmoil of industry or the hot fingers of war. Evening after evening, not long ago, we climbed high on the rims where we could look for miles both ways along the canyon, seeing not a sign of life, hearing not a sound but the river and the wind.

Partly because of the desolation of its surroundings, the ranch looked warm and "lived-in." As the canyon deepened the drab, tawny cliffs took on richer hues of orange and red. We came rocking past the hayfield bordering the river, and abruptly the neat pattern of the buildings appeared before us. A lane shaded by cottonwood and mulberry trees, bright gold with frost, separated the ranch in halves. To one side were the low red barn, machine shop, grain bins, miscellaneous outbuildings, and the cowboys' yellow bunkhouse. On the other side of the lane was the apple, pear, cherry, and peach orchard, the white, steep-roofed farmhouse, and the four-room bungalow Martha and I would occupy. The altitude was exactly five thousand feet; a government bench mark in the lane solemnly said so with bronze letters.

Plumbing was non-existent. River water for all the houses was stored in a huge underground cistern, and we watched the stream with calculating eyes. Now and then heavy rains in the mountains would raise its level. The high crest would, we hoped, sweep away assorted substances accumulated between Telluride and the low country. As the flood receded the water cleared for a few days. Hurriedly we threw open the ditches and captured half a year's supply in the cistern. It was hard as nails and bitter with alkali. Soap never lathered in it but merely scummed. The men growled when they shaved, and women approached washday with grim resignation.

The pump on the cistern lifted an endless chain of leaky dippers, and a person had to twist the handle like mad to produce more than a trickle from the iron spout. There was a broken tooth in one of the cogwheels. Every so often it slipped; the jar shook the apparatus like an earthquake and all but broke the operator's arm. Why we endured such a heinous mechanism I do not know. Temperamentalism was never tolerated in barn or machine shop. The watering system for horses and cows was much handier than for humans, but of course the animals were the reason for the ranch's existence, and after tending to them all day we had little ambition left to waste on ourselves. The women found this hard to understand, especially after staggering through the snow with a tub of dirty water and dumping it over the fence into the cow pasture. Many a dexterous skirmish was waged over catalogue pictures of sinks, but somehow no such luxurious contrivance ever found its way into the canyon.

Each building was heated by two or three round-bellied stoves liberally decorated with nickel scrollwork. These multitudinous Molochs consumed quantities of a peculiar kind of soft coal, called peacock lump because of iridescent hues of purple, red, and green glinting on its shiny surface. We paid only $1.80 a ton for this fuel but had to haul it ourselves in a wretched old truck from a mine near Naturita. The wheezing vehicle once betrayed us monstrously. A disgruntled cowboy and I were creeping along with our eighth or ninth load of coal. The road veered at right angles away from the river, pitched up a steep grade. Just short of the crest the truck stalled. While I jabbed frantically this way and that at the recalcitrant gear the weary brakes relaxed their hold and the truck rolled backward. An inexplicable immobility gripped our limbs, and we sat glassy-eyed in the seat. Over the embankment we went, crashed through the scum of ice on the river, sank gurgling, and came to rest with decks awash.

There was nothing to do but lighten the load and try to extricate ourselves. Lump by peacock lump we clutched the coal to our bosoms, waded with it through the hip-deep water, and piled it neatly beside the road. We walked five miles to the ranch, secured extra man and motor power, pulleys, crowbars, jacks, boards, and horses. After many hours of chill, wet labor we succeeded in building a sort of ramp underneath the truck and hauling it ashore. In high hope we dried out the engine and filled the tank with undampened gas. To no avail. The motor started without a stutter. Lump by lump we dourly reloaded the coal, and up the hill we went with a lovely purr. Thus are dreams shattered. Had the villainous vehicle smashed itself we would have had excuse for requisitioning a new one. But no. When at last it expired it did so undramatically in the ranch garage, refusing to waken one morning when no one cared whether it happened to start or not.

In all things that could be grown at home the ranch wrought with bounty. Because of transportation difficulties the outfit had to be as nearly self-sufficient as possible. By late fall the corncribs bulged and fat haystacks dotted the alfalfa fields. Stone-lined underground cellars were stuffed with apples, pumpkins, squash, turnips, carrots, and tons upon tons of potatoes. Shelves groaned under the weight of nearly eight hundred quart jars of peaches, pears, cherries, tomatoes, beans, applesauce, pickles, preserves, and jellies. There were hams and sides of bacon. The hen house produced eggs and fryers, the milk cows a golden stream of thick, glubby cream and butter and cheese. All a cook had to do was shut her eyes and reach.

The advent of freezing weather enabled us to add fresh meat to the stores. When taste so moved us we shot a deer, often without stepping from the porch. The animals drifted with winter from the mountains and congregated around the hayfields, lunching freely. In the main the few ranchers living along the hundred-mile stretch of canyon killed only what they could use and deemed it fair trade. We fed a lot of deer; why shouldn't a deer or two feed us, game laws notwithstanding? The game wardens secretly agreed and did no snooping unless they had reason to believe the ranchers were permitting outsiders to hunt out of season or that the meat was being sold instead of eaten—events that sometimes occurred.

Venison is all very well, but it takes beef to suit a cowboy's appetite. We would keep our eyes peeled for a short yearling steer that was still sucking its mother. We would put the pair in a feed lot and stuff them with feed for three or four weeks. Then we would take that roly-poly, milk-fed baby beef to the corral, shoot him through the forehead with a .45, and go to work. First we cut his throat to bleed him, then skinned and disemboweled him, rolling the big, bluish ball of guts on a flat sled and dragging it off with the team. By pulley blocks on the hay derrick we hoisted the carcass off the ground, so we could keep it clean while we quartered it, our labors lightened by the thought of the two-inch steaks and juicy roasts on which we would soon be feasting.

The cowboys had notions that the liver, heart, tongue, and sweetbreads weren't worth eating. Martha disagreed, but to prevent these delicacies from being thrown to the glutted dogs she had to be on hand to claim them when they appeared. She would wrinkle her nose, swallow her feminine revulsion at the sight of gore, take up a pan, and resolutely pick her way through the muddy snow of the lane to our outdoor slaughter yard. We were amateur butchers, of course, smeared with blood from head to foot. I guess we did look pretty unsavory as we grunted and swore with bared knives around the heavy carcass, and Martha was generally three shades paler than the snow when she seized her tidbits and hurried away.

The population of the ranch was unstable. A good boss farmer to take charge of the fields, the irrigators, and seasonal hay crews was hard to find. Competent men were self-employed either as share croppers or possessors of their own farms, and when we did secure one his wife soon began picking at him to leave. The work the women did in feeding the crews didn't seem to bother them, but they hated the terrible loneliness of the place, the lack of Saturday nights in town, of stores and afternoon sewing circles, of churches, and, above all, of schools for their children. We "dang near wore the road out" hauling families in and hauling them back again.

The ranch's two cowboys had to pinch hit in the fields between farmers, and it almost slayed them. They fawned over each new "sodbuster" and his wife, trying to make the canyon appear like heaven on earth, but never was affability more false. Behind it lurked the horrid vision of milk cows, hay rakes, and irrigating ditches.

This pair of riders, George Salton and Roy Barnes, were thick as thieves. I can't imagine why. Roy was agreeable in all things. George was the contrariest man that ever drew breath, even in his appearance. Though the incisive lines of his mouth and chin gave him a certain handsomeness, he looked more fitted to a

bookkeeper's stool than to a saddle. He was short and stocky; he
wore steel-rimmed spectacles, and by the time he was thirty his
hairline had retreated to the top of his pink head. If he felt like
it he would drop a job in the middle and ride to town on a drunk,
during which his fondness for other men's wives kept him in continual hot water. My stepfather fired him many times, but it made
no difference. When he got ready George returned to the ranch
with neither apology nor defiance and picked up where he had
left off. Pretty soon my stepfather, in baffled exasperation, hired
him back again. Beyond doubt George was the best all-around
cowboy between the mountains and the Utah border, but the
sometimes amazing prodigies he performed were spun out with
a curious lack of interest, as though the doing bored him unendurably.

His partner, Roy Barnes, had enough enthusiasm for a dozen
men. Much heavier and taller than George, Roy wore a perpetual
grin on his homely face. His mouth was full of gold teeth and,
except when women were about and shyness overcame him, those
teeth glinted and gleamed without cease. He told stories, asked
questions, chuckled with delight, grew gape-mouthed with astonishment. He was no mean cow hand himself, but he made his
efforts seem as difficult as George made his seem easy, leaping
on the tasks with a violent boil of voice and muscle. His dearest
amusement was one George never considered—chasing wild
burros.

During the flush days of the uranium mines numbers of
donkeys were used to pack ore down the difficult trails from the
mesas to the mills. After the mines closed the donkeys were turned
loose. They retreated into the hills bordering Paradox and the
San Miguel Canyon, multiplied, and became an amazing form
of local fauna. They liked to assemble on some knoll at evening
and hold tumultuous congresses, fighting, breeding, and making
loud speeches. Far worse than their hideous hee-hawing were the
depredations they made on the range. At last the ranchers banded

together and hunted them down with rifles, slaughtering such numbers that for weeks the countryside smelled like a charnel house. For two or three years after that my stepfather hired an old man as full-time burro stalker, and by the time the campaign was over the few surviving donkeys were wilder than deer. They traveled separately now, living on the roughest of the mesas. The hunters were called off, but security did not return. Roy Barnes took up the chase with rope instead of rifle.

He spied out their secret water holes and feeding grounds; he followed their tracks like a hungry Indian. Spotting one, he abandoned all else and took after it with a cry of glee. It was a more headlong race than any wild-steer run and rarely successful. Not only were the burros nimble of foot, skimming over rocky pitfalls where a cow or horse was apt to break its neck; they were also cunning. Even those born in the wilderness seemed instinctively schooled by their ancestors' long service to men. They understood ropes. They did not run blindly as a steer does, but with their ridiculous ears at full alert and their heads twisting from side to side as they watched their pursuer. When the rope was cast, they bobbed like a marsh coot, and nine times out of ten the noose whizzed harmlessly by.

One fine big jack lived defiantly on the mesa back of the Club Ranch. Because of his soft gray color Roy named him Mouse and hunted him at every opportunity. The pursuit went on intermittently for two years and cost Roy a crippled horse, two or three bloody tumbles, and at least a month's salary in brush-ruined clothes. But at last he caught Mouse and dragged him home in triumph. Because the donkey was young and strong we decided to break him for packing and turned him in a corral full of weaner calves, so he could feed with them on cotton cake, hay, and grain while waiting his training. There Mouse stayed. Somehow we never got around to tutoring him.

He stayed so long he forgot there was any other life. He quarreled with the calves, lay with them in the shade, tried to teach them the donkey trick of mutual massage, wherein two animals stand side by side, face to tail, and scratch each other's back with their teeth. When the time came to move the weaners we cut Mouse back and left him alone in the corral. He was heart-broken. Again and again he hurled himself at the fence, trying to follow. Failing, he grieved in great, lugubrious brays that kept us awake for nights. At last we turned him loose. Instead of break-ing for the hills he galloped wildly to another weaning corral full of heifer calves, peered through the fence rails, and talked to them in hoarse mutters, to their evident amazement. Touched, we let him in and he was happy again. When the calves were driven onto the range the next summer Mouse trailed along, convinced by now that he, too, was a heifer. He stayed with them for several weeks. Then one night he disappeared. Perhaps the scent of a lady burro reminded him of his true identity; anyhow, we never saw him again.

Cold crept down the canyon, and by the end of November the river gurgled sluggishly between irregular stringers of rumpled ice. The sun was laggard. It rose late over the canyon walls, shone palely for a few hours, and disappeared again. Long before the stars faded we were eating by lamplight the breakfast that would have to fortify us for the entire day's riding—bowls of canned fruit and oatmeal, beefsteak, fried potatoes, coffee, and syrupy towers constructed from alternate layers of pancakes and fried eggs.

This inner fuel left us logy but unwarmed. A man on horse-back can't depend on exercise to keep him from congealing, and we attempted to combat the frosty immobility of our saddles with mounds of clothing. First we donned "long-handled underwear" (union suits), then woolen trousers covered by blue jeans, a flan-nel shirt, a sweater, and a thick canvas coat lined with sheepskin. We topped the load with hairy Angora chaps and under our hats tied bandannas to cover our ears. On our feet we wore two pairs of socks, heavy shoes, and canvas overshoes—not rubber, for that would be like riding with your toes in an icebox. Iron stirrups, too, were chill, so we used wooden ones, or else wrapped the metal in strips of cowhide. Metal saddle horns were likewise covered with leather, the favorite source being a bull calf's scrotum, which fitted the horn like a glove.

Up to the corral we waddled. The farmer was already harnessing the work team to the hayrick so he could scatter feed to the cattle in the lots. The horses' breath floated whitely in the lantern glow; the wagon wheels squealed as they crunched over the frozen snow. We picked up our bridles, warming the bits before putting them in the ponies' mouths. (Did you ever try touching your tongue to cold iron? It will peel the hide right off.) Then in the first faint glimmer of dawn we rode off, heading for one of the tributary gulches that would let us onto the mesas bordering the canyon.

Slowly the sky brightened overhead, but shadows still lay thick under the cliffs. When our feet began to ache unendurably we found a dead cedar tree, dismounted, and set it afire. Any winter range is dotted with these charred stumps left by frigid cowboys and sheepherders. "Unnumbed," as Roy said, we went on. Now the first rays of the sun gilded the high rims. We eyed them wistfully, thinking how nice it would be there by the warming rocks. The contrast seemed to make the gulch bottom colder than ever. Maybe it was colder. It certainly felt as if the icy air on the mesas fled from the sun and came pouring down the canyons in invisible waves. Withered by it, we dismounted again and trotted clumsily along the trail, leading the horses while we restored circulation by exercise.

From the San Miguel the land rose in a series of steplike benches, each rimmed by a battlement of cliffs. Above the topmost benches were flat mesas reaching like fingers back to the steep, brushy slope of the Uncompahgre Plateau. Whiskery with dark forest of piñon and runt cedars and split by parallel gulches

knifing from the plateau to the river, these mesas could be reached
only by rocky trails coiling up through the rims. Wagon roads
were non-existent, and supplies had to be packed in on horseback.

The bunch-grass and aspen-crowned plateau sloped southwest
toward the spring sun, forming what was called a natural drift.
Distances were not great; there were no native barriers. The cows
started themselves upcountry in the spring and came piling off
the hump with the first snow of fall. Often we had more trouble
holding them back than in shoving them forward. To prevent
their jamming up in the river canyon we strung a few yards of
fence across the mouths of the tributary gulches. Cliffs fenced the
rest of the land, and scores of square miles could be blocked off
by a log.

As the animals began edging down from the plateau to the
mesas we rode out from the Club Ranch each morning and
picked them off the innumerable benches and swales they penetrated in their search for food. So long as they had to stay near
water in seeps in the gulch bottoms, they were not hard to find.
But snow brought trouble. The cattle could lick it for moisture.
They scattered far and wide, three or four on one rocky hill, half
a dozen on another. At times it seemed they chose their grazing
grounds with deliberate malice. "Imagine a cow gettin' up on a
bench like that!" Roy would grumble a score of times every
winter. "If you wanted them there you couldn't drive them with
a hundred men."

Part of our difficulty lay with the sun. During the middle of
the day the scuff of snow on the warmer slopes melted. At night
the mud froze and the cattle could clamber over it. But by the
time we came pushing up from the canyon the ground was thawing again. Not deeply. Just a scum of slippery grease above the
brick-hard soil. On steep hills this made travel insecure. We
equipped some of our mounts with never-slip shoes—horseshoes
into which sharp calks were screwed. This helped the animals
obtain firmer grip, but it was a mixed blessing. Horses sometimes

had difficulty adjusting themselves to the protruding calks; now and then they misjudged the clearance of a step. At high speeds the failure could produce uncomfortable results.

When riding through the ice-smeared rims, with a long drop to the gulch bottom hanging under his boot toe, a man sooner or later finds himself faced with an exact appraisal of the amount of iron in his soul. It takes a certain fortitude to trust your neck to outside agencies, and it is small comfort to reflect that your horse is no more anxious to fall over the cliff than you are. About the time he slips a little and your breath wads up in your belly you begin to wish you were walking on your own legs. This is fear and you are ashamed of it—so much so that you force yourself to stay in the saddle longer when in the company of witnesses than when alone. No one was completely immune, however. Not even George Salton, whose indifference to all things extended to his own hide. Eventually he, too, would dismount and lead his horse; the rest of us would heave sighs of relief and scramble to the ground after him like sheep.

The decision was harder when rounding up cattle. Frosty weather, long rambles to find food, and the beckoning opportunities of escape offered by the rough country bred rebellion into the gentlest of them. The appearance of a rider was an immediate challenge. Away they bolted.

It wasn't like a wild-steer chase. Once the animals were headed off they would in all probability settle down and tend to business —once they were headed. The horses enjoyed trying. The nippy air made them feel good, and they had been trained during the months of solid footing never to let a fleeing animal get out of sight. Off they lunged in pursuit, headlong over boulders, slashing between trees. Sometimes we got around the cattle. Sometimes we pulled up, shamefaced, and let them go until another day. And often as we relaxed we were surprised to find that our backs actually ached, so tight had our muscles been strained against a tumble.

At that, there was a kind of lure to the races, a rich sense of pride and achievement in winning one. And as soon as we had pushed the cattle off the mesas into the cliff-girt, escapeproof gullies leading to the river our troubles were over until tomorrow. Once in a while, to be sure, a foolish yearling would run out on a patch of ice and fall flat. He couldn't get up; the smooth surface gave his smooth hoofs no purchase. We would dismount in a body, seize his tail and legs, and haul him, bellowing in panic, back to the bank. Then on again, the white faces of the little cavalcade bobbing rhythmically and the warm cow smell drifting back from their winter-woolly coats. Generally we reached the ranch by four o'clock in the afternoon, and the rest of the evening was ours to loaf out around the chuckling stoves, reading and listening to the bright magic of the radio.

At the ranch the calves, big and fat now, were cut away from the cows and put in weaning corrals. For the first few days they made a ceaseless racket, bawling for their mothers, but before the week was out they grew used to the separation and lunched happily at the feed racks. We grew enough provender to carry the weaners through the winter, but not the cows. The youngest and strongest of the she-stuff was turned on the mesas across the river. The others were driven in several small bunches to the hay farms of West Paradox, over twelve miles of single-file trail which, in bad weather, required two days to negotiate.

The first step was the river crossing a mile below the ranch house. The ford was half frozen—rims of ice along both banks and a black channel of cold-looking water in the middle. The cows objected. After screeching, crowding, whipping, and finally butting the leaders ahead by hurling our horses against them we forced a few head on the shelf of ice. *Cra-a-ack!*—it split and they fell through. The water was only four feet or so deep, for the mountain sources of the river were frozen, and the cows didn't quite have to swim. Snorting and grunting as they milled and floundered over the boulders in the stream bed, they scared the animals behind them, and the rest of the herd would not follow. So after riding into the river with our legs doubled back to keep them dry while we forced the leaders to crack out a path through the ice on the opposite shore we had to return, butt another little bunch into the water, and another.

Just below the crossing the San Miguel funneled between dusky red cliffs of sandstone. Between two tiers of cliffs was a ribbon-like trail, following a narrow bench rough with trees and boulders that ran parallel to the river but some four or five hundred abrupt feet above it. This mustache of a path clung to the lip of the slope for about three miles. Then it reached the point where the crimson-canyoned Dolores River tore through the walls of Para-dox Valley and absorbed the San Miguel.

The junction took place far below the trail, in the bottom of a great, round red well. Incongruously a tiny cabin sat in this pit. A placer miner had once lived in it, getting to and from his abode by a series of ladders and dizzy handholds hewn in the rock. Came one of those rainstorms that freeze as they touch earth. From various bits of evidence it was deduced that the miner fell from his ladder and broke his leg. He must have been unconscious for a time, because his tightly buttoned slicker froze to the ground. When he recovered he was too weak to free himself, though scuff marks showed he tried. He was lying on the slicker buttons; he could not loosen them and wriggle out of the imprisoning gar-ment. How long he was there no one knows. When found he was as hard as iron and perfectly preserved.

High above the cabin the bench trail opened on a shelf eighty or ninety acres in size. Here we left the slow-moving cows late in the afternoon and rode back to the ranch. They could not escape; two sets of bars five feet wide fenced off the only two exits. The next morning we returned and started the animals down a trail that dived through a break in the cliffs to the edge of the Dolores River. It was Satan's own job to make the cows take that descent, especially one shoot-the-chutes near the bottom. The first animals down churned the muddy, snowy slope into a liquid slide. The next one's legs suddenly shot out from under it. It sat down hard on its rump, front feet braced and mouth open on a protesting cry. Down it whizzed like a Walt Disney cartoon.

Necks craning, the others watched without applause. They had no desire to duplicate the performance. They broke back and scattered over the precipitous hillside. Cursing and howling, we rounded them up again and crowded them together so hard that sheer lack of room forced a few more into the chute. Slowly, with no small risk of a dazzling slide ourselves, we belabored them into the canyon bottom. Here another trail wound between the base of the cliffs and the river, and here we relaxed. The rest of the way through the deep, lovely gorge, with its absolutely perpendicular walls of smooth sandstone, was open. By afternoon we had reached the hayfields of Paradox and turned the cattle over to the boys who were riding there.

XVII CHRISTMAS IN THE RIMROCK

THE MAIN PART OF THE CLUB RANCH winter range lay on a craggy, rectangular mesa thrusting up between Paradox, the Dolores, and the San Miguel. Grama, rice, and other grasses grew in lonesome pockets on its broad cracked summit. Unlike soft Eastern and mountain grasses, these desert growths contain little moisture and do not wilt under severest cold. Indeed, their nutritive value seems higher when they look dry and dead than when they are green. But the mesa across the river from the Club was waterless. We could not use its forage until enough snow fell to provide the stock with moisture.

It was cold and dry the year Martha first came to the Club. Scuds of snow swirled down now and then, but not until late December did it storm in earnest. Then on the morning before Christmas we woke to find a foot of fluffy white on the ground. We got busy. We were running short of hay and had to move the huskiest cows out of the feed lots onto the range as soon as we could.

At dawn we crossed the river on the bridge above the ranch and turned the herd up a crooked old mine trail. It was slow traveling, and the afternoon was running out when we let the cows go in Saucer Basin, a shallow declivity spiked with sandstone monoliths lying far above the junction of the rivers. We

had to ride clear across the basin to the Dolores rim to shut the
gate that blocked an exit on that side. We were cold and hungry.
Snow slanted in long streaks on the wind, powdering the green-
black cedars and giving a queer, ghostly look to the looming
rocks. Half a mile away was shelter: an abandoned mine building
crouched by the circular rim of orange-colored sandstone that
lent aptness to the basin's name. We sometimes used the shack
when working the mesa and had equipped it with bedding, a
stove, and food.

But none of us suggested staying there. For now it was Christmas Eve.

Down in the rimrock there are, as far as the cowboys are concerned, two unbreakable holidays each year, Christmas and the
Fourth of July, with Election Day thrown in every other November for good measure. These festive dates you can celebrate as
your mood dictates. Generally the program consists in doing nothing whatsoever. Until evening. Then the countryside bestirs. By
automobile, wagon and horse the tide flows to the nearest town,
where invariably a dance is scheduled.

Roy hauled out his dollar watch, shook it as always when he
discovered it had again stopped running an hour after winding,
and put it back in his pocket. We didn't need a watch, though.
The sky showed plainly that we could not reach home if we rode
back across the basin and followed the roundabout trail we had
ascended.

Common sense pointed right to the shack. But if we slept there
we would miss one of Christmas' most singular privileges. We
would have to get up the next morning and ride home. We would
not be able to yawn in the face of the alarm clock and then bur-
row back into our blankets with the luxurious knowledge that for
once we did not have to rise in darkness and set the teakettle on
the stove to thaw while we made ready for another day's work.

"I reckon it's got to be Shamrock," George said. The Shamrock
trail (heaven knows why it was dignified by that sound Irish

name) is a short cut which falls down the red wall of the mesa to the bench above the river junction. Traveling it is bad in summer; in winter, when snow and ice make footing slippery above the five-hundred-foot drops, it is plain folly.

But this was Christmas Eve, and that bench way down below opened the way home. Down Shamrock we went with just the tips of our boots in the stirrups, ready to leap clear if the horses fell. We were too scared to talk, too hurried to get off and walk. The only sound was the crunch of snow under the ponies' feet, the scrape of a piñon branch across our sheepskin coats.

And then we came to the ford over the river. When I saw the shape it was in I thought, "My God, if we had stayed in the Saucer we would at least be full of supper now."

Rolling ice stretched across the stream from bank to bank. It didn't look very solid. But it was too late now to follow the tumbled canyon to the bridge. Gingerly we urged the horses on the ice. Sure enough, it split open beneath us. Somehow the animals kept their feet as we dropped through into the belly-deep water. But now the ice which had been too weak to support them proved too strong for the horses to push through with their chests. They had to rear on their hind legs and by striking and lunging with their front hoofs break out a channel. I don't know why they didn't upset with us. Christmas luck, I guess.

At the ranch we rubbed down our horses and grained them. I got an ax and called Martha. The sky had cleared a little, and the last glimmer of a lemon-yellow sunset lay on the cliffs. We climbed the rise back of the barn, hunting a Christmas tree for the baby. There were no spruce such as you buy in cities, but we found a fragrant piñon pine that was almost straight. While I cut it Martha broke off an armload of cedar boughs. Laden with blue-gray berries, they would make handsome garlands.

As soon as the baby was asleep we set up the tree in the living room of the cabin we occupied across the lane from the cowboys' bunkhouse. Then we brought out the ornaments we had made:

shiny stars hacked from coffee-can lids and black walnuts wrapped in lead foil we had been filching from the farmer's chewing tobacco since early fall. Extra foil we cut into "icicles." Colored yarn made festoons; snips of paper did for snow.

Hanging the decorations, we forgot that it was ten miles to the nearest neighbor's, twenty-two to the post office. And after we had gone to bed with our three cats curled up at our feet we lay awake for hours, whispering in the dark like a couple of kids who know that Santa Claus is on the way.

The farmer left at the crack of dawn. He said he would come back in a day or two, but after one look at his wife's face we knew he wouldn't. Well, we weren't going to worry about that yet. We had our presents, a yearling baby and preparations for a fitting feast to keep us busy. The cowboys, however, were bored stiff with their long-anticipated leisure. They fired the bunkhouse stove to unbearable heat and stubbornly lolled around it, rereading the month-old county paper, yawning, and paring their fingernails to the quick. They were waiting on their toes like sprinters when I rang the dinner gong.

We were just sitting down when a timid knock sounded on the door. I opened it to a furtive-eyed man, horribly hunchbacked. His odorous black hair fell in snarls below his shoulders. It was Ike (his last name we never knew), a hermit placer miner who had holed up for the winter in a cave down by the riverbank.

He said nothing, and for a moment I could not imagine why he was there. Generally Ike ran for cover when anyone approached him. Then I realized that even hermits can be lonely on Christmas. I invited him in. Martha brought out another plate, but we couldn't get him to sit down. He stood there in the center of the room, shuffling his feet and darting glances over his shoulder at the door, like a stray dog in an unfamiliar place. Finally Roy whispered, "Pay him no heed." We commenced eating as if he weren't around. Finding himself no longer the center of attention, Ike sidled by degrees into the vacant chair and with a grin of agonized embarrassment passed his plate.

After dinner—venison soup and roast turkey, mashed potatoes, squash, carrots, and stewed onions from the root cellar; golden sourdough rolls and strawberry jam; apple pie and ice cream frozen with ice chopped from the river—we pushed our old automobile out of its shed. But not even a radiator full of hot water was blandishment enough to soften the engine's stony heart. So we hitched a team of horses to the car. Up and down the lane we dragged it. At last the oil loosened a bit. The motor coughed, died. Up and down again. Another furious spin with the crank. This time success.

Ike slipped back through the leafless willows to his cave. The rest of us piled in the car and, passing the baby from lap to lap, slued and slithered up the snowy road. We went right through Naturita and up a long grade to a broad mesa where stands the once socialistic colony of Nucla. The founders of the town had decided that lawyers, churches, and saloons were equal evils and had banned them all. Everything was to be run on a share-all, co-operative basis. The first problem had been an irrigating ditch. A considerable job it was, too, seventeen miles long, including a mammoth log trestle supporting a flume. Each colonist received for his labor on it credit at the commissary for food and supplies, plus water credits toward the purchase of ditch rights. The canal succeeded, and several prosperous farms sprang up. But the beautiful mist of socialism had soon faded under the hot sun of private ownership. Except in one or two minor respects Nucla today is like any other remote farming town. Even the lawyers, churches, and saloons came creeping back.

It was dark when we reached the settlement this Christmas Day. We went first to old Jeff Grable's to leave the baby. Three or four other cars were already there. Jeff never went to the dances, and it was his self-imposed duty to, as he said, "ride herd on the young'uns while their folks kicked up their heels."

His bedroom was bedlam. Rolling delightedly about on his bowed legs was old Jeff. His fingers have been warped by frost-bite, and his pointed white brows stick out like owls' tufts above his pale blue eyes. He shooed each mother out of the house as soon as her child was tucked into one of the impromptu beds. It was his claim that parents are a distraction and that he could quiet the children better without them. Apparently he was right. Within an hour the house was as still as a prairie dawn. Heaven knows how he managed.

Next we went to Rial Payne's general store. It was open—too much business in town for Rial to lock up, holiday or no. The women gathered around the dry-goods counter in front. The men drifted to the rear. There, throned on a barrel under the horse collars, Buck Murphy was holding court.

He was a huge man, Buck was, with great pouches under his eyes. He looked flabby, but in the hayfields or at the branding fire he could work any two men to exhaustion. The biggest cattle owner in the district, he directed the roundups when we all got together and gathered the animals that had strayed off their home ranges—it was all public-domain land, of course, but what with permits, custom, the lay of the terrain, and so on, each rancher had what he called "his" section. The winter ride always started the morning after Christmas, and we were seeking Buck out for instructions. In a voice astonishingly small for the amount of flesh behind it he told us where tomorrow's gather would be held on Tabeguache Mesa and the country each of us should cover.

At eight-thirty the dance got under way in the town hall. Despite the crowd that packed the raftered room, it smelled musty and unused. The huge round stove by the stage could not drive the chill from the corners. Nonetheless, most of the women were in flimsy gowns, selected from mail-order catalogues and almost as new as Fifth Avenue in style.

The men were less fashionable. Those who wore neckties were outnumbered by those who did not. There was a generous sprinkling of crinkly new overalls. "Dress-up pants" are expensive and the opportunities to wear them limited.

Benches line the wall. These are for the women. You don't waste time with your partner during intermissions. She selects a seat on one of the benches, to which she returns after each number. When a new piece starts there is a stampede for partners. The system has its advantages. You know where to find the girl with whom you want to dance. All you have to do is reach her first.

Not all the women dance. Those who can't just watch and gossip. "Puncture ladies," the cowboys call them, because their tongues are ever ready to prick some reputation.

Nor do all the men dance. Some group in the corners and talk crops and livestock. Others, the more tipsy, hang around outside the door. This is the place where all the fights start; where, if you are in the mood, you pick one of your own. Many riders are visiting town for the first time in months. A pint of whisky and a rousing battle are the best release for high spirits. After the necessary amount of wordage the opponents, followed by a gang of spectators, step around behind the building. It is all in fun. When the combatants see each other at the roundup tomorrow they will most likely be as friendly as ever. And a black eye or split lip is a mark of distinction.

Inside, the dance goes on unrestrained. Even Amy Luce is down from Lost Park. This is the first time in ten months that she has seen another woman. Mrs. Williams, who has twelve children, is outstepping everyone.

The orchestra is a four-piece affair—piano, fiddle, banjo, and saxophone. It is very bad. But it can keep time, and that is enough. There are fox trots and waltzes for the younger folk, but many of the pieces are quadrilles, square dances, and Virginia reels. Pete Hubbard does the calling. He stands on a table, his shirt sleeves rolled to his elbows, the sweat pouring down his round, wrinkled face. By midnight his stentorian bellow has sunk to a croak.

About one o'clock the arrival of old Jeff Grable causes a flurry. One of his charges is howling and will not be comforted. Jeff can't tell whose baby it is. So the mothers all rush down to his house, which the single malefactor has by now roused to a nerve-shattering uproar. What goes on inside, no mere male will ever know. But soon all is well and the women come trooping back.

At one-thirty there is a pie-and-coffee supper, served by the ladies of the Farmers' Co-op. The orchestra had been hired to play only until the supper, but a hat is passed and the weary musicians agree to continue.

Enthusiasm is waning, however. Most of the people have a long way to go to reach home. By three o'clock the last automobile has pulled away from the hall, and the town is a patchwork of black shadows in the frosty moonlight.

When we reached the ranch clouds had obscured the sky. Snow swirled in the yellow beams of the headlights. We were groggy with weariness as we put the car in the shed, drained the radiator, and carried the sleeping baby to the house. And in another hour we would have to be moving again, getting ready for the bitter ride to Tabeguache, for the long, long wait until summer.

But somehow we forgot all that as I lighted the lamp and the lead-foil ornaments gave back the flickering light. We stood there a moment looking at it. Then Martha said, "Let's keep it a little longer."

So I built a fire and we sat there, watching the tin stars twinkle on the branches.

Then pretty soon Martha said, "You'd better put the teakettle on the stove."

And I said, "Yes, Christmas is over."

XVIII URANIUM

ANOTHER SANTA CLAUS, TO USE A
stale trope, came to the canyon with World War II. Change
piled on change—still piles, for that matter—and out of the
welter emerged a new economy, new goals, new questionings,
not only for the San Miguel but for all the hundred thousand
tumultuously torn square miles of the Colorado Plateau.

As suggested earlier, the change began with a search for
vanadium, prime alloy for hardening steel. At first the effort
was modest enough. A handful of carpenters began shoring up
the old red mill across the river from the upper end of our hayfield. A couple of their wives actually moved into the boardinghouse, where we went to look at them just for the amazement
of the thing. Equally amazing, because the labor seemed dispro-
portionate merely to obtain a drink of clear water, a crew under
Pete Campbell, one-time foreman at the Club Ranch, began
laying a pipe line down to the mill from Tabeguache Creek.
Martha envied the women at the boardinghouse their having
another source than river scum out of a cistern for washing
diapers, but we did not imagine the spasm would amount to
much. In those days we still thought of Hitler as a joke with a
vaudeville mustache and a forelock.

That concept did not last, of course, beyond the Nazi march into Poland. With equal suddenness new mill buildings marched up the side of the canyon; a new housing development named Uravan usurped part of our fields by the river. Even more miraculous, to me, was the twisty little road that snorting machines bulldozed down the bottom of the canyon, under the sagging frame of the old placer flume, to the deep-walled junction of the San Miguel with the Dolores. From the junction the road wound calmly up the Dolores to salt evaporating tanks in Paradox, for salt was necessary in the reduction of vanadium, and Paradox is at least full of salt. Within a matter of weeks our hanging trail on the side of the bluffs was so complete an anachronism that not a dozen of the new immigrants suspected its existence, though perhaps a hundred thousand head of cattle had been hazed over its dizzy hairpinnings during the preceding half century.

Any mushroom growth has, I suppose, its own forms of violence. So it was with this one. Jack Andress, with whom I had herded sheep in Beaver Park, slid one morning down a rope into the ore bins at the Uravan mill. His purpose was to kick loose some clinging ore on the sides. Generally the stuff crumbled away in small chunks. This time, however, the whole mass let go with a rumbling thunder, caught Jack's legs, jerked him from the rope, and tumbled him to the bottom of the bin, to be smothered under tons of soft tan sandstone. The turn of the cards, to be sure. If Jack had stayed working with livestock, he might have had a horse fall on him or lightning strike. We would have understood that, however much we regretted it. But somehow this death left us vaguely upset, vaguely troubled. Or so we thought, remembering it later. And still the town spread along the strip of hayfield; still the hungry mill climbed higher up the canyon's tawny slope.

The pipe line from Tabeguache finished, Pete Campbell was transferred to a coal mine that the vanadium company was now operating near Nucla. One day his pick struck into a missed charge—an intact stick of dynamite. The resultant explosion blew off his right sleeve, draped it neatly over his pick handle. Later his wife, in Pete's words, "picked a quart jar of little rocks out of my face and shoulders." But she could do nothing for his eyes. They were gone.

One cannot prove with statistics that spirit, like an electric shock, is communicable. Still, there had been a day when the town of Nucla had been content to sit on its hands, waiting. Why bother? What would tomorrow bring that was worth going out to meet? In those days, I think, Pete too would have sat in darkness, waiting. But now a new stir was abroad, busy-fingered. It touched him and "one morning," he says, dismissing the private agonies when he had tried to find the meanings behind all this, "I decided to go to Denver and learn to make brooms."

Along the way he learned much more. When he returned to Nucla some years later to open, in a tiny cubbyhole, a candy and tobacco store, his neighbors measured his new depth and sent him to the state legislature. The governor put him on the board of the Colorado Industries for the Blind. He represents his district at various conferences. All he knows of the alterations tormenting this land where once he had ridden as a cowboy comes from what he is told by others. Yet he sees more clearly than some of the others on the Plateau, for the only way many of them will look is backward.

By Pearl Harbor Day the vanadium company owned the entire Club Ranch headquarters camp in the canyon, and one of the officials conceived the bright idea of building (no pun intended) a club for visiting brass. Our old white farmhouse was chosen as the proper starting place. (For reasons needing no elaboration here, Martha and I had left before the shooting started.) Workmen fell on the building with wrecking bars, destroyed its lines, and then, for reasons unknown to me, left the gaping shell unfinished. Only one new item was completed—a fireplace of sandstone erected in layers to correspond with the geologic structure of the region. It starts with a foundation of Jurassic rock and rises through various bands with jawbreaking names to a capstone of Dakota. Key segment is a block hewn from the Morrison formation. Embedded in this, with geologic reality, are samples of carnotite ore ranging in color from canary yellow through green to a dirty gray.

Whether the symbolism is conscious or not, that fireplace is an accurate portrayal of the new order—a great block of sandstone dominating the wreckage of a ranch. No longer is the stockman king. The miner is—he and the promoter who gets financing for the mines—and although the minerals for which they search may occur in a hundred or more ores, the main one, so far as the Uravan mineral belt is concerned, is carnotite.

During the early years of World War II the nation's chief concern with carnotite was its vanadium derivative, or "red cake," as the soft red substance is called. Everything else, uranium included, was thrown out on the tailing dumps or washed away down the San Miguel River—except for a trifling bit that Blair Burwell, superintendent of the Uravan mill, decided to recapture, partly out of curiosity.

Today on the Colorado Plateau, Blair Burwell is, in many people's regard, Mr. Uranium himself. He knew of course about the part uranium oxide had played in the days of the radium boom. He knew that uranium is radioactive and hence theoretically fissionable. And of course he had heard of Albert Einstein, though perhaps not, in those days, of Enrico Fermi. These names, however, were associated with the thin, high ozone of theory. Meanwhile, down in the canyon bottom, the only market for uranium oxide, called "yellow cake" by the millmen, was as a coloring agent for pottery and glassware. It was not a big market. But it did furnish an excuse of sorts for setting up a little pilot plant to see what could be done about improving the known methods of extracting the oxide from the refractory wastes left over from milling vanadium. Call it accident. Call it hunch.

Anyhow, Burwell's pilot plant was chugging along, practically ignored even in Uravan, when Albert Einstein wrote his famous letter to President Roosevelt.

Almost overnight guards were thrown double deep around the mill. Such yellow cake as Burwell had produced was rushed to refining plants in Niagara, and under the stadium at the University of Chicago Enrico Fermi set up his laboratory. To get more of the all at once priceless oxide, carefully screened men began reworking the old dumps. Local residents, unable to guess what the tension was about, shrugged it off as more mumbo-jumbo by the bureaucrats. Until Hiroshima, that is. Then everyone knew.

The end of the war also brought a pause to the excitement. Peace forever—no more need for vanadium armor plate or for uranium bombs. The Russians were our allies, weren't they? The Uravan mill shut down. Only a watchman remained to keep an eye on the rows of buildings along the river, and when Martha and I came back to show the ranch to our son, just then entering his teens, we found that a farmer had moved some cows onto the feed lots behind the half-dismantled house. It was even possible to close our eyes, smell the alfalfa, hear the locusts in the mulberry trees, and believe for a moment that the old ways might return.

That was in 1947. At about the same time, for reasons well enough known today, the AEC—the Atomic Energy Commission—decided that national safety demanded immediate stimulation of the United States' almost nonexistent uranium production. Glittering inducements were held forth. In the days when carnotite had been mined for radium, ore could not be profitably handled unless it contained at least two per cent uranium. Now the AEC agreed to buy rock assaying as little as one tenth of one per cent. Fat bonuses were given for new claims brought into production. Because transportation has always been the region's severest problem, the AEC helped finance access roads and granted haulage allowances for distances up to a hundred miles.

Promises of big money led engineers to look at the Colorado Plateau with an entirely new regard. Once miners had searched for carnotite primarily in the form of "logs." The word is literal. In the remoteness of geologic time, when this land had been moist and tropical, vast trees had collapsed into slimy sediments that eventually petrified into sandstone. Somehow uranium salts, which are soluble in water, displaced the cells of the trees; indeed, most uranium occurs in carboniferous areas. Crumbly yellow fragments of these high-grade mineralized trees were what the early Indians had used in smearing bold, slashing stripes across their skins. Similar fragments had baffled the first white settlers in Paradox; since the ore was golden-colored, obviously it should contain gold, and on this theory it was fruitlessly assayed again and again.[1] French scientists seem to have been the ones who pin-pointed its nature. Certainly its name is French (for A. Carnot, inspector of mines, according to Webster, and not, as is often

[1] Who discovered carnotite in Colorado is uncertain. Some evidence points to J. L. Wade, a thirteen-year-old boy who, while hunting in 1888, picked up greenish samples where Disappointment Creek empties into the Dolores. Through his father, a mining engineer, young Wade's samples eventually reached the hands of a French geologist named Louis Giroux. It seems that even before this, however, the Talbert brothers of Paradox had found samples across the ridge from the valley on Roc Creek. (Roc Creek fights a losing typographical battle. True, it is lined with rocks. But it is also tributary to a collapsed salt dome whose fantastic formation led the discoverer to remember *The Arabian Nights,* name the basin Sinbad and the creek—printers please note—Roc.) Before the turn of the century, the Rajah Mine on Roc Creek shipped several tons of ore to the School of Mines in Paris, some of which, along with more potent pitchblende ores, was used by Mme. Curie in her experiments.

Mme. Curie, incidentally, never visited the Colorado Plateau, though some promoters will show you the very chair she sat in. Other Frenchmen did work in Paradox, however. Recently two valley ranchers decided to prowl around the old Cashin copper mine nearby. The needle on their radiation counter suddenly "pegging off," they dug down and discovered an ancient vat where, local surmise says, two Frenchmen conducted early experiments attempting to locate the uranium that kept bobbing up in the Cashin's copper ore.

said, for others of the versatile Carnot family, including a one-time president of the Republic). The French, too, by isolating radium in 1898, are the ones who first made carnotite commercially desirable—so desirable that at one point a pair of miners built a hair-raising suspension footbridge above the Dolores River, a few miles down from the Club Ranch, so that they could stagger out to the roadway with sacks of ore on their backs. Eastern financiers actually considered building a railroad into Paradox Valley, no less; and over in Central Utah farmers living near the gaudy escarpments of Capitol Reef found unexpected profits in breaking up and hauling away the petrified trees that littered their land.

Throughout our winter range the more accessible of these log deposits had long ago been found and their rich cores worked out. The vanadium quest of the early 1940s, during which period Colorado produced 75 per cent of the world's vanadium, resulted in a reworking of the peripheries. With the start of carnotite's incredible third boom, another scrabbling commenced, for each log is surrounded by a sort of halo of decreasing values, untouchable once but commercially feasible under the AEC's current buying scale. The two big companies of the district promptly went to work again. Some mining they did on their own. Mostly, however, they leased their claims to individual contractors or else bought ore for their mills at Naturita and Uravan from scores of independent producers digging away at small claims hung breathlessly to nearly every rim in the neighborhood, a situation that still prevails today.

The AEC was not primarily interested in revitalizing old holes, however. It wanted new deposits—and, by paying enough, it got them.

The story of this leapfrogging new rush—said by local chambers of commerce to be the greatest mining rush in the history of the West—is still too chaotic to appraise accurately. Part of it is hardheaded mining economics. Part is rampant speculation, chicanery, and humbug. And part is pure romance, an unbelievable offspring of the hell-may-care spirit of the frontier commingling with a wide-eyed faith in the magic wand of modern science.

The miracle aspects of the search are the ones that have caught popular fancy. Uranium in its inexorable disintegration emits beta and gamma rays. These rays can be detected by Geiger counters with their tubes or by more sensitive and more expensive scintillation units with their sodium iodide crystals. So presto!— and away with the old-time prospector's blister-making pick and shovel. You simply buy a machine and walk around or drive in a jeep, counting clicks, reading a dial. Pretty soon a buzzing starts, the needle jumps. A hot spot. That's the word now, "hot." Ore is "hot," a drill hole is "hot," even stock certificates are "hot," although actually the hottest thing around is probably the prospector's own imagination—"uranium on the cranium," as they say locally.

In 1954 alone a hundred different manufacturing companies peddled, at a cost of hundreds of dollars per machine, more than 30,000 Geiger counters to the Plateau's sudden influx of so-called "Sunday prospectors." Stories about greenhorns are legion. There's one about the tenderfoot who went into ecstasies over a high reading picked up from dust blown off a passing ore carrier, and still another about the man who filed claim to a highway because his counter showed him where a truck bogged in the mud had dumped its load of pay dirt to get free. So it goes, though these same Sunday hopefuls have bought more than 266,000 copies of a sober government pamphlet entitled *Prospecting for Uranium*. In this pamphlet they are warned that all radiation does not come from uranium, that sometimes uranium does not stir reaction on a dial, that deep ore bodies cannot be detected save by drilling. Yet still they come—a bunch of clucks counting clicks, in one man's words. In 1955 the AEC's Grand Junction office answered the questions of more than 40,000 hopeful visitors—a figure that leaves out of account more thousands who took to the field without bothering to find out anything.

All this is not to gainsay the value of the various radiation measurers. As adjuncts and not as primary tools they are invaluable. Attached to the end of long probes, they yield revealing data about rock penetrated by deep drills. Mounted in small, low-flying airplanes, they have enabled the reckless rim-flying pilots of the desert to make in a few hours' time preliminary investigations of a convulsed land that by other methods could not be examined in years. Just to keep the fairy stories alive, they have even, in a few fabulous instances, done what the Sunday prospector thinks they will always do and have uncovered profitable ore bodies all by themselves.

More useful than a Geiger counter is a knowledge of geology —a somewhat glib remark, since uranium geology still isn't fully understood. In the early days in Colorado, uranium ores were supposed to occur only in the Salt Wash sandstones of the Morrison formation. Since then, and often by sheer accident, ores have been found in a number of other formations—the Chinle and Shinarump, to name two of the more notable. Yet, though patterns are beginning to emerge from thousands of explorations, an element of doubt remains. Not long ago I was talking with a drill operator south of Moab, Utah. A gossipy visitor stopped by to see what was going on and to offer gratuitous advice that "you won't hit anything here." When the driller passed him off with banter, the visitor grew piqued. Sourly he watched the churning rig, then climbed into his pickup. His parting shot: "It's damn fools like you that find ore." He was half right, too. Not many miles distant one of the region's multimillion-dollar bonanzas had been struck three years before by a man who was aiming his drill at an entirely different formation from the one that actually contained the mineral.

The basic geology of the region is comparatively easy to read. The same forces of erosion that created the canyons, the spires, and the rainbow cliffs have also laid bare the ribs of the land.

Some naked ore outcrops could be seen from miles away and as a result were long ago staked out. Johnny-come-latelies have perforce had to move back from the exposed rims onto the mesas. Since they can no longer see the ore with their eyes, they must feel for it with mechanical fingers. The result is a vehicle more common to the country today than once was the pack mule of the cowboy or the chuck wagon of the sheepherder. It is the mobile drill rig. Jeep-borne or truck-mounted, it presents a multitude of variations, but nearly all are marked by a spindly steel tower that supports the pipe on whose restless end is a deep-probing bit.

The drilling technique is borrowed, in part, from the oil industry. In fact, though it seems lost in the shuffle, considerable oil exploration is going on concurrently with drilling for uranium. The men on either kind of rig look, in their colored plastic helmets, much the same. Many of their problems are also similar, not the least being the providing of water whenever "wet" drilling is resorted to, as sooner or later it generally is. Fat tank trucks snort over the sagebrush, wind among the piñon trees, dive with a shrill of brakes down to canyoned water holes that are often a score or more miles away from the rig they are servicing. As you watch them out of sight, each smothered in its own cocoon of dust, it occurs to you that the reckless effort which built the hanging flume for carrying water to the placer bars in the Dolores was not very different from the spirit being poured into today's drill holes.

Money also is being poured. A fence of holes spaced five hundred feet apart is about the minimum necessary to detect favorable ground. If an ore body is struck, at least four more holes are necessary to suggest its extent—an outlay, say, of $5,000 just for exploratory drilling. If the mineral lies a hundred feet deep, dropping a shaft to it will cost another $33,000. And of course the ore may lie much deeper, perhaps a thousand feet and half a million dollars away. That is why unromantic, week-around mining men on the Plateau say that a prospector has one chance in a hundred of clearing expenses in a deep mine. And yet . . . the ore is there. At least fifteen bodies 100,000 tons or more in extent have been uncovered—blocks massive beyond the credence of the former miner for logs.

This sort of situation is made to order for the wistful and for the jackal. Hundreds of square miles of desolate mesaland have been staked solidly in hope that some big company will find ore nearby and purchase the adjacent claims. Each move of the region's major operators is watched like a hawk. It is said that an airplane survey crew dares not circle around for another look at a hot spot; for if they do, watchers with binoculars will note the attracting area, rush over, and stake out the ground before the plane is back at its airport.

Until recently, obsolete mining laws added to the chaos. Colorado, for example, demanded that a discovery "cut" ten feet deep be dug into the mineralized area, a manifest impossibility if the uranium lies hundreds of feet under the caprock. Other laws predicated mineral titles on the actual discovery of an ore body; if the original prospector did not produce ore, an adverse claimant might move in, open the vein, and establish certain rights of his own. Further clouding came from land closed to entry because of ancient and forgotten oil leases, power-site reservations, and what not. When finally new laws were passed ironing out some of the inequities, Preston Walker, editor of the Grand Junction newspaper, deemed the news of sufficient moment to load an airplane with copies of the story, fly over every isolated prospector's camp he could find, and literally bomb the region with the joyful news.

Lack of proper surveys also tangles matters. Much of the area remains known only as a cowboy or a coyote might know it— intimately but not scientifically. Many range and township lines have never been delineated; even the exact physical location of part of the Colorado-Utah state boundary is said to be undetermined. Obviously, many claim lines stepped off by amateurs and described in haphazard terms are equally hazy. Because of this, claim jumpers will sometimes record overlapping entries with the deliberate intent of forcing a survey. The survey, they hope, will, by readjusting boundary lines, leave gaps of a few feet between claims. Into these slivers crawls the adverse claimant, and if the locale is heavily mineralized he can perhaps sell off his nuisance value at a good figure. At times, of course, double filings are the result of honest mistakes. Either way, there is trouble. As one disgusted prospector said of a popular locale, "This place is filed in so many layers that all the uranium between here and hell won't pay the lawyer bills that are coming."

Because of the nutcracker squeeze of litigation, tax problems, development and operational expenses, the speculator finds fertile fields to plow. Though many stock issues, land leases, and claim amalgamations are legitimate, others are as shaky, in local parlance, as a burlesque queen's hips. In Utah alone nearly a billion shares of stock were sold between 1951 and the end of 1955. Profit taking isn't the only motive behind the huge turnover. Partly it's the gambling fever. And partly it's a desire to share in this unexpected return of the rosy romance that was supposed to have disappeared with the frontier.

Against such a background one would anticipate more lawlessness than has occurred. True, you hear tales of high-grade ore being stolen from loading platforms. A few drill holes may have been salted for the tenderfoot's probe by lowering the ash of gasoline lamp mantles, which are composed of radioactive thorium alloys, into a drill hole and then blowing the ash into the walls of the hole with a half-pound charge of black powder.

Even in town the saloon of hallowed memory, with its batwing doors and mustachioed bartender, no longer exists. Though Moab's consumption of bottled goods did double in a year when liquor sales elsewhere in Utah were declining, the increase was more than matched by an increase in population. The people themselves have made the choice. Early in the boom Moab's new residents gathered together in a vigilante meeting and publicly expressed their determination to keep violence at a distance. Outlaws, if any, took the hint. Similar spirit prevails throughout the Plateau. To be sure, over on Grand Junction's promoters' row, as a certain lodging district is known, raucous calls are said sometimes to be heard at moonrise and pretty secretaries are reputed on occasion not to finish their typing until dawn. But these matters, so insist the civic boosters, are not necessarily reserved to uranium booms.

The country likewise has been gentler than one might expect. It is a harsh land, full of potential traps: heart-stopping cliffs, quicksand bogs, trackless miles of juniper forest; scorpions and rattlesnakes; heat and thirst. Yet mostly you hear only of embarrassing contretemps. A dignified broker is physicked by alkali water; a greenhorn's sedan is mired by a flash flood and he has to sleep hungry in a cave; a young M.I.T. graduate flees from a boulder that in the dusk looks like a mountain lion. One person only seems to have been fatally lost, down in a weird place of spires and hollows called Silent City, south of Greenriver, Utah. By contrast, another prospector lost near Moab was spotted by an airplane, which then landed on a roadway in front of an ore truck and told the driver where to go to pick up the missing man.

The area is so enormous and so convulsed, however, that in spite of airplanes and trucks you sometimes feel that it has swallowed the rush without trace. At times you will drive mile after lonely mile without seeing a soul, without hearing a manmade sound other than your own. Yet contradiction for the feeling lies in the very word "drive." Not a decade ago thousands of square miles of this country were entirely roadless. Such tours as could be made were adventures in nervous survival. Once Joe Weston, who has been in these hills almost as long as the uranium, was driving a female cook toward Gateway on the throat-jamming shelf "road" below the Club Ranch. The woman grew so terrified that she would not ride, yet was afraid to get

out and walk. Finally Joe had to blindfold her like a balky mule
to get her across. In the summer of 1955, however, the big
machines moved in and now the roller coaster has been tamed,
like the one from Uravan to Naturita, where the two-hour maul-
ing we used to endure on the way to town has been reduced to
a twenty-minute commuters' run.

These refurbished old roads are but a scratch beside the net-
work of new ones. Each day, it seems, another one appears.
Once a spot of dust out in the heat-misty distance meant a whirlwind. Now, if you put your binoculars on it, you will probably
see a yellow bulldozer heaving out boulders, uprooting trees.
The bawl of Diesel motors reverberates through the gorges. Far
up on the side of the toppling landscape you'll see a tractor
lurch around some colored corner at an unbelievable thirty-five-
degree angle, snarling meanwhile at the protesting rocks. The
wildest teamsters of last century's storied frontier would not—
could not—have taken wagons into some of the places where
now those khaki-shirted, dirt-caked cat skinners push their metal
horses.

They have opened up a world of scenery. From Al Scorup's
ranch on Indian Creek you can drive now to the rock jungles
of the Needles, where not so long ago Cy Thornell told Martha
no other white woman had ever been. Or you can bounce south
out of Cottonwood Canyon, skirt the red-and-white layer-cake
formations of Salt Creek, climb dizzily past the deep loveliness of
Dark Canyon, and so reach White Canyon.

As you drive down White Canyon toward the Colorado River,
the encircling battlements grow taller, wilder. Suddenly the gorge
mouth opens onto the silty river, and there between the red
teeth is a straggle of bright green cottonwood trees sheltering a
jerry-built town of wooden shacks and trailer houses. This is
Dandy Crossing, where once the Scorup brothers dragged bulls
across the river behind a rowboat. Now, half a mile below the
"town," is a different conveyance, a groaning wooden ferry just

large enough for a single truck. A Model-A engine, mounted in its original cab and attached to the lower side of the ferry, drags the ramshackle contraption forward by means of sagging cables. Bulls, horses, Indians, prospectors, trucks, limousines—the whole varied traveling public of southern Utah—crosses dry-shod over this sole highway link between Moab and Lee's Ferry, Arizona.

Many of the desert roads, it should be noted, are insults even to the jeeps for which they were constructed. Drive, for example, over a relatively good highway onto the mesa that lies between the junction of the Colorado and Green rivers. Some of the vistas you'll see will rival anything else in the United States—notably the burst of color and canyon, depth and distance that over-whelms you from Dead Horse Point. Equally breath-catching is the sight of the wheel tracks diving over rims a thousand feet high to reach mines perched precariously on the edge of nothing. Other roads are merely rough, with high centers to disembowel a care-lessly handled car or with prodigious "thank-you-ma'ams" that with one bounce can break an ordinary tire in half. Still others are merely steep, so steep they'll boil a motor into immobility three times over before the top is reached. In short, carry extra water.

Wheels—the jeep, the pickup, the trailer—have altered the setup of the range. Instead of building shacks or sleeping in caves as the old-timers did, the newcomers, turtle-like, park their mobile shells under whatever tree or beside whatever water hole suits their needs. This tends to interfere with established routines of stock grazing by frightening cattle from their normal runways. More serious, a few of the invaders have not been above butcher-ing a yearling or two, cutting fences, moving into handy line cabins. Ranch labor, meanwhile, has become difficult to get.

These are the annoyances about which the ranchers growl when discussing the boom. The real trouble goes deeper, how-ever. They have been elbowed aside and left bewildered by the abrupt shift in values, the hurry, the speculative frenzy. Some of them, not really knowing what they were doing, leased out their holdings to the first soft-voiced tempter. Others have held back, refusing glittering opportunities to make fat sums of money by letting their lands and names be used as the foundation for stock promotion schemes. But all of them have felt themselves supplanted in influence and prestige, and they do not like it.

Still, they have found some of the new conveniences welcome. Too old now to ride a horse, Al Scorup has himself driven around his range in a jeep, although some of the hills are so steep the vehicle has to crank itself up by a winch attached to the front end. He is just as indomitable as ever. Recently, aged eighty-three, he broke his foot but refused to go immediately to a doctor because he wanted to supervise the cutting of a herd of cattle. Out to the bunch ground he went—in a jeep—and there, surrounded by the bawling steers, he sat as solidly as once he had sat his old white horse until every animal had been turned the way he wanted it turned.

The small airplane is useful for other things than surveying. Even Paradox has a landing strip now, on Andy Riddle's farm; when the local women want to shop, they telephone Grand Junction for a taxi and within half an hour are walking down city streets once so difficult to reach that the effort was resorted to only once or twice a year. There's the matter of communication also. Last spring Al Scorup's grandson—Harve Williams' stepson—was getting married. A last-minute change of plans occurred. The boy and his mother wanted to get hold of Harve, who was off somewhere in the jumbled wastes south of White Canyon. A few years ago riders could not have dug him out in weeks. Young Merrill, though, knew the range. He also had a friend who was a pilot. After some breathless rim-jumping they located Harve near one of his cave camps and dropped a note wrapped around a rock attached to a flour-sack parachute. Some delay occurred because the note landed in the only tree in the vicinity and Harve had to shinny up the trunk to retrieve it. Even so, he was able to drive his jeep to a nearby landing strip, be picked up by the boys, and flown out to Provo before dark.

Whether or not convenience is also progress is another thing. The old-timers aren't entirely sure. Their pasts have made them self-reliant, thorny individualists, and they look askance at the fact that this is the only mining rush in United States history initiated and wholly maintained by the government. Ore prices, financed ultimately by every taxpayer, have been guaranteed until 1962 by the AEC, the sole purchaser. After that . . . who knows? Uranium men insist that when the government moves out, private industry will move in, for uranium is destined to be the number-one fuel of the atomic age. But will the price hold? Supplies are enormous now as new deposits continue to be opened up not only on the Colorado Plateau but throughout the western states. And suppose, skeptics whisper, thorium or solar energy proves to be still cheaper.

The little towns of the Plateau, engrossed in their growing pains, refuse to listen. Population-wise, they remain comparatively small. Percentage-wise, however, they have doubled, even trebled, in size. Schools, water and sewage systems, utilities, and city government itself founder under the load. If you want to communicate between Moab and Grand Junction, it is often quicker to drive the 116 miles than to try to put a telephone call through the jammed switchboards. But at least there is housing of sorts. Trailers stand on every vacant lot, in nearly every back yard. Acres of them surround the false-fronted, startled-looking buildings that once formed the heart of each village.

Back at Uravan the jumble of mill buildings has climbed out of the canyon bottom clear to the top of the first mesa. The rows of neat houses and new shade trees stretch farther and farther along the river. There are stores, gas stations, a theater, a hospital. It has a pattern; everything supposedly has a pattern if you can find it. In an effort to detect this one, we climbed, not long ago, to the top of the workings.

The mill rumbled and shook and smoked. Huge trucks were dumping tons of gray ore into the crusher bins at our backs. Far down below, at the bottom of the spidery ladderways, the finished product was being wheeled out onto the loading platform: black steel drums packed with yellow oxide. A complex chemistry, no doubt, full of leaching vats and fiery roasters. But what I kept looking at, off in the center of the town, was a swimming pool. Mountain-blue . . .

"River water?" I asked, for Pete Campbell's pipe line wasn't large enough to account for it.

"What else?"

I remembered the cistern at the ranch, the washday scum. Chemistry indeed!

We picked our way down through the dust. "Last one in is a monkey!" my son yelled. He did not remember any cisterns. Besides, it was too hot for nostalgia.

A blond girl in a yellow suit was rubbing sun-tan lotion over her legs. Two freckled boys raced by, grabbed their noses, and sailed far out, one after the other, into tremendous splashes. Under our curled toes the edge of the pool felt cool and slippery.

"Who's a monkey?" And the shock of the water sliced through thought like a silver knife.